FAMILY CAREGIVERS

Disability, Illness and Ageing

edited by
Hilary Schofield

with Sidney Bloch, Helen Herrman, Barbara Murphy,
Julie Nankervis and Bruce Singh

ALLEN & UNWIN
in association with the
Victorian Health Promotion Foundation

VicHealth
Promoting a state of health.

'This comprehensive book presents the human face of caregiving and shows why it has emerged as a major area of social policy—central to aged care, disability and gender inequalities. Schofield and her colleagues have provided a "must read" book for researchers and policymakers—and more than a few caregivers themselves.'

PROFESSOR HAL KENDIG,
DEAN OF HEALTH SCIENCES,
UNIVERSITY OF SYDNEY

First published in 1998 by
Allen & Unwin
9 Atchison Street
St Leonards 2065
Australia
Phone: (61 2) 9901 4088
Fax: (61 2) 9906 2218
E-mail: frontdesk@allen-unwin.com.au
Web: http://www.allen-unwin.com.au

HV
1451
F35

National Library of Australia
Cataloguing-in-Publication entry:

Schofield, Hilary, 1941– .
    Family caregivers: disability, illness and ageing.

    Bibliography.
    Includes index.
    ISBN 1 86448 707 0.

    1. Caregivers. 2. Chronically ill—Home care. 3. Aged—Home care. I. Victorian Health Promotion Foundation. II. Title.

362.1

Set in 11/13pt Goudy by DOCUPRO, Sydney

Printed by SRM Production Services Sdn Bhd, Malaysia

10 9 8 7 6 5 4 3 2 1

CONTENTS

FIGURES

PREFACE

The idea for a research and intervention study focusing on family carers was born during a meeting of VicHealth's Mental Health Working Group in 1989. Bruce Singh and Helen Herrman employed Virginia Lewis to review the literature and prepare, in consultation with them, a research proposal. Thus in recognition of the vital support for people with disabilities provided by families and other carers in the home, VicHealth funded the proposed five-year research and health promotion program under the direction of Professors Helen Herrman and Bruce Singh (chief investigators), and Professors Richard Scotton and Robin Eastwood and Dr George Szmukler (associate investigators), later joined by Associate Professors Sidney Bloch and Anna Howe. The Project Team was developed with my appointment in August 1991 to run the project on a day-to-day basis. A collaborative and lively relationship between the Team and investigators was important throughout the life of the project. We acknowledge with gratitude VicHealth's generous support, their understanding of the need for a degree of flexibility in allowing the project to *evolve*—for example devising interventions on the basis of our early findings—and their prescience in recognising the project's likely importance in terms of future policy directions.

Indeed, since the project's inception a vast change in community awareness of carers and their needs has taken place. Both Federal and Victorian State Governments have recently launched carer strategies which demonstrated a new commitment to carers. We are confident that our findings will contribute to the development of policy. This was made possible by a thousand carers—representing *all* Victorian carers—who were willing to share their pains and joys, to tell us their experiences and needs, thereby enabling us to represent their views to the decision-makers. We thank them for their time and commitment. We thank also the numerous support organisations who helped us get in touch with carers for our qualitative work early in the project.

With her consummate understanding of policy and the bureaucratic process, in mid-1995 Anna Howe suggested consultations to explore the implications of our findings. The first involved senior representatives from the Commonwealth Departments of Human Services and Health (Office of Disability; HACC), Social Security and the Australian Bureau of Statistics; from the State Department of Health and Community Services (Aged Care Division and Disability Services); from peak bodies including the Carers Association, the Council of the Ageing and VCOSS; from research bodies such as the Australian Institute of Family Studies and the Australian Institute of Health and Welfare. In the second, carers who had participated in the research were invited to hear what we found and tell us whether this reflected their own experience. We thank them for their interest and attendance.

It would be difficult to overestimate the importance to the success of the project of the support from staff at the Australian Institute of Family Studies—particularly Helen Glezer, Eva Mills and Andrew Prolisko—in terms of technical expertise, understanding of the issues, refining the questionnaire for computer-assisted telephone interviewing, and coordinating the data collection. We pay tribute to the team of interviewers—and Sue Kelman their supervisor—who were able to get reliable and quantifiable data while maintaining a sensitive rapport with participants, so much so that 99% were happy to be reinterviewed. In some ways we regard our first interview with carers as our most successful 'intervention': being asked, possibly for the first time, about their experiences and needs perhaps raised their own awareness and enabled them to talk more openly with family and friends.

This book reports the findings of the Victorian Carers Program and their policy implications. In Part I we acknowledge the contribution of Suzanne Bozic to Chapter 1; Barbara Murphy made a substantial contribution to Chapters 1 and 3; and Julie Nankervis had the major role in Chapter 4. Barbara and Julie took the main responsibility for Chapter 8 and for Part III, which among other things briefly describes our three interventions. In evaluating the Federal Government's Carer Support Kit we acknowledge the co-operation of the then Department of Health, Housing and Community Services and the Carers Association of Victoria. In examining the role of general practitioners and pharmacists in linking carers with local services, our gratitude goes to the GPs and pharmacists in the Western region of Melbourne who participated despite their busy schedules. We appreciate the endorsement of the Western and Westgate Divisions of General Practice and the Pharmacists Society of Australia (Victorian Branch), which undoubtedly contributed to the high participation rate. In assessing the value of a non-crisis home assessment to carers and care-recipients, we express gratitude to the aged care assessment teams in the Northern and Eastern metropolitan regions and the Western rural region for their willingness to participate, and their time and expertise which ensured the success of the intervention. We also thank Ngaire Kerse, Lynette Kramer and Carol Hogg who assisted the research team in doing the assessments. Part III also presents findings from the survey of counselling services—largely the work of Julie and Sidney, whose idea it was. We thank the counsellors and service managers who took time to reflect on their experiences and respond to our survey, and to participate in our counselling workshop. The policy implications in Part IV, which also summarises the key findings, were largely drafted by Julie.

Our thanks go to Simon Freidin, our computer whizz and trouble-shooter, who set up our computer network, managing the large, complex data sets and doing most of the computing with speed and accuracy.

Throughout the project various part-time research staff have each contributed to the success of the project. In the formative period Suzanne Bozic contributed her knowledge of service provision and policy; and Elizabeth Dickens, with her warmth and sensitivity, was the right person to liaise with support organisations and assist with exploratory, in-depth work with carers. Our thanks go to Robert Pedlow, Greg Macaskill, Caroline Coffey and, more recently, Michael McLaughlin for computing assistance at various times; in particular we acknowledge Michael's contribution to analysing the effects of caregiving over time. We thank two work experience students: Eli Finkel for drafting a review of counselling literature, and Mike D'Onofrio for coding the counselling survey responses. We also express our warm appreciation for the administrative and secretarial support provided successively by Dawn Balson, Viola McMahon, Laraine Kirwin and, for a short time, Rhonda Bateman and Belinda Singe.

We thank the University of Melbourne's Department of Psychiatry (and in the first two years Monash University's Department of Psychological Medicine) for administering the project, and St Vincent's Hospital (and earlier the Victorian Health Department's Psychiatric Epidemiology and Services Evaluation Unit) for providing comfortable accommodation for the project.

Finally, we acknowledge our publisher, John Iremonger, for his persistent faith that there was a book lurking in our research. And Venetia Somerset, our editor, did an outstanding job in transforming a somewhat ungainly and highly technical manuscript into a well-structured and readable book—we had no idea just how much statistical, psychological and bureaucratic jargon we had used. We salute her intellect, energy and commitment.

Dr Hilary Schofield is a psychologist who, as a Senior Research Fellow in the Department of Psychology at the University of Melbourne, directed the Victorian Carers Program.

Associate Professor Sidney Bloch is Reader in Psychology at the University of Melbourne, consultant psychologist at St Vincent's Hospital and the author of many books, including (with Bruce Singh) *Understanding Troubled Minds*.

Professor Helen Herrman is Director of Psychiatry at St Vincent's Hospital and the Community Psychiatric Service, and Professor of Psychiatry at the University of Melbourne.

Barbara Murphy, a psychologist, has many year's research experience in health-related fields.

Julie Nankervis, a social worker and psychologist, is a policy maker at the Carers Association, Victoria.

Professor Bruce Singh is Chairman of the University of Melbourne's Department of Psychiatry and Director of Psychiatric Services at the North Western Mental Health Program.

GLOSSARY

carer/caregiver: a person looking after the daily needs of someone who is ill, disabled, or frail

care-recipient: the person being cared for

care-dyad: the pair of carer and care-recipient

co-resident: (of the carer) living with the care-recipient

high-intensity caregiving: caregiving that involves many hours a week and a lot of personal care

instrumental activities of daily living: social activities, communicating, organising appointments, medication use, managing finances, etc.

longitudinal study: one carried out at different stages so that a comparison of data over time can be made

mental disability: intellectual, communication and/or psychiatric/emotional problems

non-resident: not co-resident

(physical) activities of daily living: dressing, bathing, eating, toileting, getting in and out of bed/chair, etc.

physical disability: physical/mobility, coordination, sensory and/or long-term health problems

primary carer: the person with the main responsibility for caregiving

secondary carer: someone, usually a family member, who assists the primary carer

stressor: a factor which causes stress

ABBREVIATIONS

ACAT	aged care assessment team
Action	Action Group for Disabled Children Inc.
ADLs	activities of daily living
AGPS	Australian Government Publishing Service
AIFS	Australian Institute of Family Studies
ANOVA	analysis of variance
BIPR	Bureau of Immigration and Policy Research
CATI	computer-assisted telephone interviewing
CAV	Carers Association of Victoria
CDA	Child Disability Allowance
ci	confidence interval
CNS	Community Nursing Service
CP	Carers' Pension
DNCB	Domiciliary Nursing Care Benefit
HACC	Home and Community Care
H&CS	Health and Community Services
IADLs	instrumental activities of daily living
na	not applicable
NES(B)	non-English-speaking (background)
N	number of total sample
n	number of sub-sample
ns	not significant
VCP	Victorian Carers Program

INTRODUCTION

No doubt many readers have their own experience of caregiving, as we do. In a sense each story is unique, each with its pain and joy, its desperate and funny moments. What we have aimed to do in our research is to capture the full spectrum of caregiving roles and experiences: a young mother caring for her small son with Down's Syndrome, with each developmental milestone reliving the loss of the child she expected to have; a daughter caring for her mother with dementia, adjusting to the loss of the person who once cared for her, balancing this role with her other roles as mother, wife and part-time worker; a mother in her early seventies whose caregiving started 43 years ago with the birth of her son, severely disabled both physically and mentally with cerebral palsy; an elderly husband caring for his frail wife who has recently moved into a nursing home after 50 years of being together, and whom he visits every day.

WHAT PROMPTED OUR RESEARCH?

With an ageing population, increasing rates of disability and a shift in emphasis from institutional to home-based care, in Australia as in other developed countries there is a growing expectation that it is families who will care for people with chronic illness and disability. It is not surprising, therefore, that caregiving within the family has become a major focus of research interest overseas and, more recently, in Australia. It is also not surprising that informal carers have been gaining increasing recognition in government policy. Our knowledge of the prevalence of caregiving, the socio-demographic characteristics of caregivers, the impact of caregiving on their health and well-being, and their needs for various supporting services has nevertheless remained fragmented and inadequate.[1]

AT THE POLICY AND SERVICE DELIVERY LEVEL

Factors which may account for the recent recognition of community care as a priority policy issue include:

- demographic trends, such as the ageing of the population, with a concomitant concern about the increasing burden on the health and welfare system in a climate of monetary constraint and the principle of 'user pays'
- changes in family structure (fragmentation and blending of families)
- decline in the fertility rate
- increased female participation in the workforce, with concerns about a diminishing pool of informal carers
- changes in the attitudes of professionals about the treatment and accommodation of people with disabilities.

At the same time there are serious impediments to the development of effective policies and services. There is a need for comprehensive documentation of the prevalence of caregiving, the socio-demographic characteristics of carers and their requirements for services. More coordination is needed between different levels of government and voluntary organisations in the funding, administration and provision of services. We also need to clarify what counts as a service for carers so that the existing range of services and patterns of use can be adequately documented. Finally, there is a need for a comprehensive and integrated approach to the evaluation of services to ensure closer links between policy and practice.[2]

AT THE RESEARCH LEVEL

Little is known about the risk of health problems among carers compared with others in the community who are not caring for someone with special needs ('non-carers') or about changes in caregivers' health or feelings of well-being over time. Past research has for the most part been based on small samples drawn from support organisations or service providers which preclude generalisation of findings beyond the study sample.[3] Likewise the interpretation of findings has been problematic because of limitations in research design.

Past research has also largely focused on carers in a particular disability group, for example dementia, schizophrenia, intellectual disability. But factors other than the nature of the disability might contribute to the impact of caregiving on the physical and emotional well-being of the caregiver, for example life-stage, sex, relationship to the person cared for, and so on. The experiences are likely to vary within and between various disabling conditions and illnesses. In past research, then, it has not been possible to explore the diversity of caregiving roles and the variety of responses.[4]

THE VICTORIAN CARERS PROGRAM

The Victorian Carers Program (VCP) was a large-scale, population-based longitudinal research study and a series of interventions for promoting health. Based on the assumption that the impact of caregiving varies significantly with relationship, sex, stage in the life-cycle, residential status and many other factors, the study aimed to identify the broad spectrum of carers in the community and investigate the experience of caregiving across the full range of disabilities, age-groups, relationship groups, geographic locations and so on.

Our project was unique in its blend of research and health promotion, its strong design and its innovative method, which enabled the identification of a large, representative sample of carers. These features make it particularly useful for future planning and policy development. It is *generic* in focus, including in its purview the whole range of caregiving in the community, and it is based on a clear analysis of the concept of caregiving. Through the issues of responsibility and dependency we distinguish caring for a relative or friend with a disability (the 'care-recipient') from other caring roles such as those of professional caregiver, volunteer and parent/spouse.

The project consisted of a *longitudinal research component*, which enabled us to look at the effects of caregiving over time, and a *health promotion component*. These two proceeded in parallel and interacted with each other, so that information progressively available from the research could be used in the development of interventions which were implemented and evaluated with subgroups of our representative sample in the context of the longitudinal research.

Figure 0.1 represents a timeline of the main components of the project. To the left of the first vertical line are the three stages in the longitudinal survey. To the right are the health promotion strategies.

Figure 0.1   The Victorian Carers Program

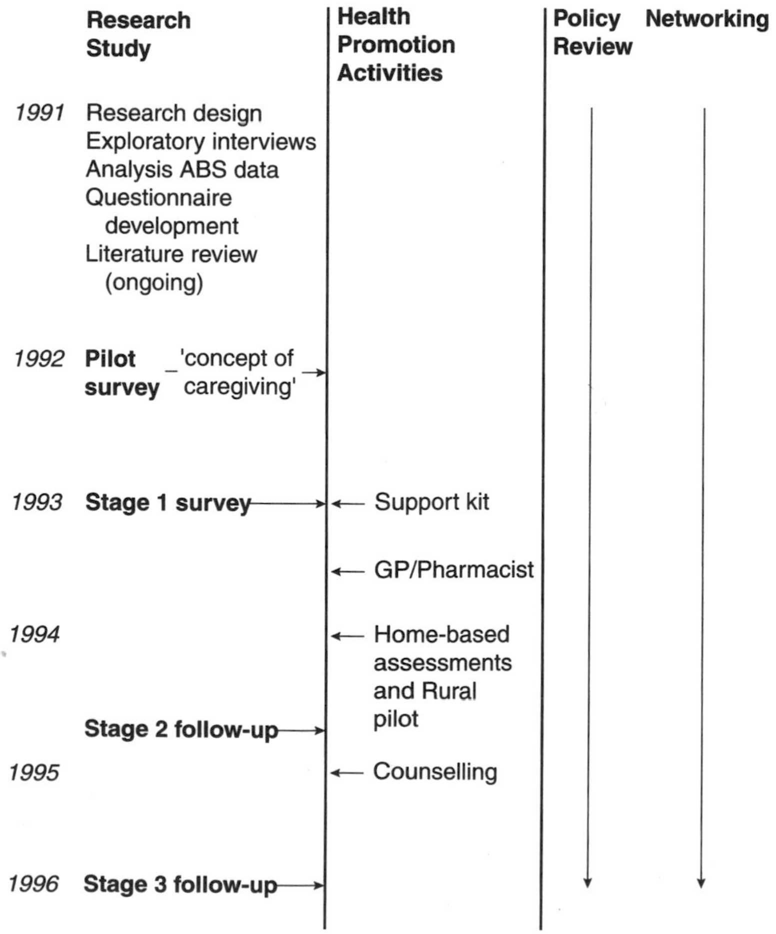

Research Study	**Health Promotion Activities**	**Policy Review Networking**

1991 Research design
Exploratory interviews
Analysis ABS data
Questionnaire
  development
Literature review
  (ongoing)		

1992 **Pilot** _'concept of **survey** caregiving'** →		
1993 **Stage 1 survey**——→	←— Support kit	
	←— GP/Pharmacist	
1994	←— Home-based assessments and Rural	
Stage 2 follow-up—→	pilot	
1995	←— Counselling	
1996 **Stage 3 follow-up**—→		

Since carers identified themselves with a high response rate in a random survey of 26 000 households throughout Victoria, our study participants (976 English-speaking and 35 non-English-speaking) constitute a *representative* sample of carers in all metropolitan, provincial and rural areas of the state. Findings from the survey enabled an accurate profile of family carers in Victoria to be created for the first time and for prevalence rates to be calculated; in fact a family carer was identified in 5% of Victorian households. A comparison group of 219 'non-carers' was also interviewed in order to assess the impact of caregiving on the carer.

The survey was conducted using the computer-assisted telephone interviewing (CATI) system which had been developed by the Australian Institute of Family Studies (AIFS) and used in other community surveys. Interviewing by telephone instead of face to face meant that it was economically possible to include a larger sample of carers, and that respondents could be easily located throughout the state. With its sophisticated programming, the CATI system enabled a *comprehensive* interview with both quantitative and qualitative elements able to be recorded with minimum obtrusiveness. The interview covered socio-demographic characteristics of carers and their relatives, aspects of the care-recipient's disability (including behaviour problems), physical and emotional demands of the caregiving role, support from family and friends, measures of carers' physical health and emotional well-being, effects on employment and family finances, use of and need for formal services. Fifteen months later carers and the comparison group were reinterviewed to assess changes. A third interview was conducted with carers only.

The study examined the following major questions:

- What are the effects of caring for people with disabilities on caregivers' well-being, and what are the scale and distribution of the effects?
- How do characteristics of the caregivers and care-recipients, and their social and environmental setting, influence these effects?
- To what extent do caregivers use available support services? What factors are associated with the use of services and how does this use relate to caregivers' well-being?
- What intervention strategies are most likely to improve the well-being of caregivers or groups of caregivers? How can care-

givers best be helped, and at what point is help best offered in differing circumstances?

• What are the implications of our findings for funding and service development at a federal, state and local level?

In past research stringent criteria have been used to identify caregivers: for example, co-residency, time spent caring, number of activities of daily living for which help is given. Such criteria automatically exclude a large number of carers. As there was *no agreed definition of a caregiver*, we analysed the notion of caregiving through the issues of dependency, responsibility and choice, and in relation to the nature and intensity of caregiving tasks (see Chapter 1). We drew on previous literature, empirical and theoretical, and findings from our exploratory interviews and pilot survey.[5] While maintaining a generic focus, our analysis allowed us to clarify the specific nature of caring for a relative or friend with a disability, and to distinguish this from other caring roles, in particular those of the professional caregiver, the volunteer and the parent.

Since most Australian studies on caregiving had been small-scale and unrepresentative, at the start of our research there was a lack of information about the prevalence and characteristics of caregiving. The Australian Bureau of Statistics' (ABS) 1988 survey of disabled and aged persons provided the most reliable data, but the specific definition of 'caregiver' used by the ABS resulted in the inclusion of co-resident carers only. Even so, to get a picture of caregiving, we used unpublished Victorian data from the 1988 ABS survey *Carers of the Handicapped at Home* (ABS 1990). These formed the basis of a report which profiled co-resident carers and care-recipients, including socio-demographic characteristics, types of disability, sources of income, and activities for which help is provided.[6]

A broad review of caregiving policy and services was undertaken first, to establish the policy context of the VCP, and by implication its current relevance, and second, to identify policy questions which our data should address. The review considered relevant socio-demographic trends and their implications for policies in several areas: the care of people with disabilities; the structure of government and service provision; relevant policy areas (e.g. aged-care strategy, disabled persons, health, housing, ideologies such as deinstitutionalisation); relevant services/benefits and their use. The review is subtitled *The Case of the Invisible and the Invaluable* because it is only in recent years that carers have been mentioned in policy and there remain immense conceptual and practical difficulties in identifying services for them.[7]

Relevant support organisations and service providers were identified and consulted for their expertise and to obtain their continuing input into the VCP, to help in setting up exploratory interviews with carers of people with particular disabilities, and to provide feedback about the VCP's activities.

THE EXPLORATORY INTERVIEWS

To ensure that we were sensitive to the experience of carers and to help develop a survey instrument that would accurately assess the experience of caregiving, we needed a detailed *qualitative* inquiry to start with. As preparation for our major survey and our health promotion strategies, we had to explore the experiences and needs of family carers in a non-statistical way. We were also concerned to explore more than the 'burden' of caring which much of the early work in the area had focused on. In developing our own measure for assessing the experience of caregiving in Australia, we aimed to build on these existing models of caregiving experience. In the first half of 1992 we therefore conducted exploratory interviews with a broad range of family carers: those caring for people with intellectual disability, physical disability, sensory disability, chronic and terminal illness, psychiatric illness, Alzheimer's disease and other dementias, as well as the frail elderly. They included parents, spouses, adult children and other relatives. The interviews, which were recorded and transcribed, were analysed thematically.

Our specific objectives were to:

- determine what it is like to be carer of a person with a disability
- explore the effect of caregiving on the carer's physical and emotional health
- explore the relationship between personal and situational factors and the carer's health
- identify carers' needs
- identify the services required and used by carers
- identify their coping strategies.

Carer organisations across Victoria provided the names of individuals or groups who would be willing to take part; these were then interviewed by telephone. Where carers attended a support group, it was arranged for a team member to conduct the group discussion during a regular meeting. General information about the project and details of interview arrangements were mailed to each participant beforehand.

Clearly this sample is biased towards those who were known to the support organisations. Our subsequent survey revealed that only about 12% of carers are in touch with such organisations. This sample was not, however, intended to be representative of the Victorian population but rather to cover a broad range of caregiving situations so that we could establish our parameters. We tried to represent both female and male carers of a range of ages, residential locations and relationship to the care-recipient, as well as a range of disabilities.

Fourteen group interviews about two hours long and four individual interviews of about one hour were conducted with these caregivers, 60 in all. In most cases participants knew each other through their membership of a support group. Discussions and interviews were facilitated by a member of the VCP research team in a semi-structured way: preliminary discussion was loosely guided by a set of predetermined broad topic areas and probe questions. Questions to start the discussion included:

- What is it like to care for your relative with dementia?
- How do you feel about caregiving?
- What are the most difficult aspects?
- In what ways do you enjoy caregiving?
- How does caregiving affect you?
- How does caregiving affect your life?
- What do you do to make things easier?

Carers were encouraged to initiate and discuss topics of interest, with the facilitator being guided by the participants rather than by a prepared schedule. If specific areas were not raised spontaneously by carers, specific prompts, identified on the basis of past caregiving research, were used towards the end of the discussion, for example:

- What about financial aspects?
- Has caregiving affected your work?

With the consent of all participants, discussions were audio-taped.

Each discussion was transcribed in full and analysed thematically. Responses were clustered into four broad themes:

- the experience of caregiving
- the impacts of caregiving
- ways of coping and mediators of stress, including informal support networks and formal services
- effects on carers' health.

Material from these interviews is presented throughout the book in boxes to give real-life illustrations of our statistical data. The findings from this exploratory work were used in the development of the questionnaire employed in the main telephone survey which was piloted in November 1992. The questionnaire was devised as a generic instrument, where possible using existing scales, with modifications where appropriate. The instrument was programmed for use in a CATI system.

THE PILOT SURVEY

Because of the complexity of the study, a pilot survey was conducted in November 1992 to provide a more accurate estimate of the number of households to be surveyed in the definitive study. This enabled assessment of our method, screening questions and interviews, and helped in the definition of caregiving. Thus, using the CATI system, we conducted a random survey of 2000 telephone numbers. Ninety-one per cent of contacted households agreed to answer the screening question, 72% of identified carers agreed to be interviewed, and 98% of them agreed to be followed up. Data from interviews with 98 carers and 78 non-carers were analysed and published.[8]

THE MAIN RESEARCH STUDY:
DESIGN AND METHOD

The major aims of the research study were to:

- create a socio-demographic profile of carers in the State of Victoria, Australia
- assess the effects of the experience of caregiving on the psychological and physical well-being of carers

- specify the circumstances of caregiving that are especially burdensome or beneficial
- assess the impacts of formal and informal support services, and identify unmet needs for supports
- assess the effects of caregiving over time
- monitor changes in carer status (people ceasing caregiving or becoming carers) over time.

Participants were drawn from a random survey of Victorian households. Since there is no agreed definition of a caregiver in the literature on the experience of caring, caregivers were selected on the basis of self-identification as a person who takes the main responsibility caring for someone who is aged or has a long-term illness or disability. Any type of disability was considered for participation in Stage 1 of the survey.

The CATI system seemed very appropriate to our research needs given the high distribution of telephones in Australian homes, estimated at 95% in 1991, and the advantages of telephone interviews over face-to-face or mailed questionnaires. Research comparing different methods of data-gathering has indicated that telephone interviews are more efficient and generally less expensive without sacrificing validity or reliability.[9] In fact on sensitive issues, responses in telephone interviews have been found to have greater validity than those in face-to-face interviews.[10] And as telephone interviews can be easily monitored for quality control, they are particularly suitable for large-scale surveys involving a team of interviewers.[11] These experiences were borne out in the conduct of the VCP study.

The team of 25 interviewers employed by the AIFS were skilled in this area of work, and our researchers participated in their training and debriefing sessions. From the debriefing and from detailed comments recorded at the end of interviews it appeared that the interviewers found the work demanding but satisfying, getting to know respondents and their situations during the course of interviews lasting from 40 minutes to almost two hours, with an average time of one hour.

The definitive research study, conducted from 1993 to 1996, occurred in three stages.

STAGE 1 STATEWIDE SCREENING SURVEY AND FIRST CAREGIVER INTERVIEW

During August to October 1993, our random survey of 26 000 Victorian telephone numbers identified over 1000 caregivers and a comparison group of over 200 non-carers. Households were initially screened by asking: 'Do you or does anyone in your household take the main responsibility in caring for someone who is aged or has a long-term illness, disability or other problem?' In households where a caregiver was identified further screening questions were designed to ascertain:

- whether any other person or persons in the household provided regular unpaid assistance to someone who was aged or had a long-term illness or disability, living in the same or another household or institution
- the nature of the disability or illness
- basic socio-demographic characteristics of members of the household.

The screening survey enabled us to make an estimate of the numbers and socio-demographic characteristics of caregivers in Victoria.

The screening survey and first caregiver interview took place in the one procedure. If the informant identified as a caregiver, they were then asked if they had a further 45 minutes to answer some questions on their experience of caregiving, their needs and supports. For those willing to participate and who had the time to talk, the interview continued; for those who could not talk at that time, a mutually convenient time was established for the interviewer to call back. If the informant identified someone else as the caregiver, the interviewer asked to speak with that person.

Information gathered from carers included:

- socio-demographic data (age, sex, ethnicity, household composition, education level, employment status, living arrangements)
- effects of caregiving on employment opportunities
- measures of stress
- social support
- physical and emotional well-being
- life satisfaction
- an assessment of the experience of caregiving

- the use of and need for community formal support services
- an assessment of the quality of the relationship between the carer and care-recipient
- care-recipients' age, sex and preferred language
- broad indicators of the diagnostic and functional status of the care-recipient and of behaviour problems.

At the conclusion of the interview, caregivers were asked if they would like further information about the VCP, including a summary of findings from the survey, and if they were willing to be contacted on a later occasion.

The 'non-carers'—respondents who did not fulfil the criteria of caregiver—were also interviewed about their caregiving responsibilities. This comparison group comprised adult females living in households other than single-person or group households. Where there was more than one adult female in a randomly selected household, the female who had the most responsibility for family and household tasks was selected. The interview for these people included questions from the carer interview on household composition, socio-demographic information, responsibility for household tasks, measures of stress, social support, life satisfaction, and physical and emotional well-being.

All non-English-speaking (NES) respondents were screened using the Telephone Interpreter Service. Those identified as carers and willing to be interviewed were asked an abbreviated set of questions from the carer interview using the interpreter service. Questions in the non-English-language interview included socio-demographic information on the carer and care-recipient, household composition, use of services and the following three open-ended questions:

- What support are you getting in caring for (name)?
- What other help would you like?
- How do you feel about your caring role?

STAGE 2 SECOND CAREGIVER INTERVIEW:
MARCH–APRIL 1994 FOLLOW-UP

Carers who were interviewed in Stage 1 and who were willing to be contacted on subsequent occasions were followed up fifteen months after the first interview. The same information was sought as in Stage 1, plus information on changed circumstances and reasons for such changes (for example, the residential status of care-recipient). The same procedures for data-gathering were followed as in Stage 1.

STAGE 3 THIRD CAREGIVER INTERVIEW: 1996 FOLLOW-UP

Similar information was again sought from carers in the Stage 3 follow-up, after another fifteen-month interval and again with the addition of items relating to changed circumstances. There were also more detailed questions on the effects of caregiving on work status, carers' information needs, and carers' use of and need for respite services.

HEALTH PROMOTION INTERVENTIONS

These were developed on the basis of needs identified from our research and introduced with sub-samples of survey participants at various times from Stage 1 onwards. They are described in Chapter 12.

RESPONSE RATES

Stage 1: A 2.26% sample of all telephone numbers in Victoria was selected (30 961). Of these 4623 (14.9%) were either not connected or were business numbers or remained unanswered after fifteen attempts, resulting in an effective sample size of 26 338. Overall, 94% of the 24 705 contacted householders agreed to answer the screening question: carers were identified in 1259 households. There were 976 completed interviews, 38 partial interviews and 245 refusals, giving an overall response rate of 78%. In addition, interviews were completed with 35 NES carers using an interpreter service (see above and see Chapter 4); thirteen were partially completed and five carers refused to be interviewed. A random selection of one in ten households in which a carer was not identified was selected for the non-carer interview until a quota of approximately 200 was filled; 6% of householders refused screening. Of the 353 who declared themselves eligible for the comparison group interview, 75% (219) agreed to be interviewed. After completing the interview, 99% of both carers and non-carers agreed to be contacted again.

Carers were identified in 5.3% of households. We compared this figure with that from a national survey of the Australian Bureau of Statistics (ABS) and with Canadian and British findings. Taking into consideration differences in definition and method, there was a high degree of consistency in reported household prevalence of caregiving between the three sets of data. A detailed account of this comparative study is presented in Howe, Schofield and Herrman (1997). The close correspondence between the VCP and ABS prevalence figures suggests that those who self-identified as carers in the VCP survey imposed quite strict limits on their own definitions of caregiving.

Stage 2: Out of the total of 945 carers interviewed in Stage 1 (i.e. excluding the 30 who had informed us that their relatives had died and the one caregiver who had declined subsequent contact), 802 (85%) were interviewed in Stage 2. These consisted of 608 still caring, 119 (12.5%) no longer caring and a further 80 (8.5%) whose care-recipient had died. The remaining 15% included partial interviews (6%), refusals (7%) and cases where an interview was not possible (7%). Of the 219 non-carers interviewed in Stage 1, 181 (83%) were interviewed in Stage 2. Of the remainder 1% had declined further contact, 12% could not be traced and 5% refused. Thirty of the 35 NES carers were interviewed in Stage 2.

Stage 3: Out of the total of 608 carers interviewed in Stage 2 (i.e. excluding three who declined further contact and two who had informed us that their relatives had died), 514 (85%) were interviewed in Stage 3. These consisted of 399 (66%) still caring, 77 (13%) no longer caring, and 38 whose care-recipient had died. The remaining 15% included refusals (7.5%, in nine of which cases the care-recipient had died) and cases where an interview was not possible (7.5%) because the carer could not be traced, had died, was too ill to be interviewed, or was not available for the duration of the study. Non-carers and NES carers were not followed up in Stage 3.

COUNSELLING SURVEY

Some way into the study, in 1995, we surveyed organisations in the health and disability sectors about direct emotional support available to carers through counselling. This is reported in Chapter 13.

MEASURES

From the questionnaire data reliable scales were constructed to assess various aspects of emotional and physical well-being which are relevant to both caregivers and non-caregivers, and various aspects of the experience of caregiving including both 'subjective' feelings and relatively 'objective' activities. We have also allowed for both positive and negative responses (Table 0.1, p. 255).

Measures relevant to both the caregiver and non-caregiver are aspects of emotional well-being including *life satisfaction*, *positive* and *negative affect*, perceived *social support*, and feelings of *overload*. Those relevant to the caregiver only included changes in perceived *closeness* and *conflict* in the family environment since the onset of caregiving; attitudes to the caregiving role included *satisfaction*, which reflected positive emotional responses; *resentment*, which focused on the negative effects of caregiving on the carer's life, time, opportunities and social relationships; and *anger*, which reflected negative emotional responses like anger, embarrassment and guilt.

Measures of *physical* and *mental* disability in the care-recipient were obtained as well as scales assessing help needed and help provided in various *personal* and *instrumental activities of daily living* (ADLs). Finally, three scales assessed the frequency of *depressive*, *aggressive* and *cognitive behaviour problems* in the care-recipient. For more detail see Schofield, Murphy et al. (1997) and Appendix II.

Importantly, for a sub-sample of 67 participants, carers' ratings of their relatives' disabilities and dependencies were validated against independent and blind ratings by health professionals' assessment made during a home visit. The home visit was made primarily to identify and meet service needs (see Chapter 12), but it allowed carer reports from the interview to be correlated with clinical assessment in three areas: level of disability, level of help needed with ADLs, and level of help provided with ADLs. Details of the validation procedure and results are presented in Appendix II.

PART I

CARERS AND CARE-RECIPIENTS

What do we mean by a family caregiver?

> Caring can be viewed as a species activity that includes everything that we do to maintain, continue, and repair our 'world' so that we can live in it as well as possible. That world includes our bodies, our selves and our environment, all of which we seek to interweave in a complex, life sustaining web. (Fisher & Toronto 1990:40)

We agree with this very general definition of 'caregiving' or 'caring', but for our purposes we need to be more specific. In an overview of recent feminist literature on the concept of caregiving, Hilary Graham (1991) argues for a broadening of this idea. She maintains that gender has been made the key analytical dimension and has resulted in the exclusion of other important aspects such as class and race. The need to expand the concept of caregiving to encompass a broad range of locations and social relations of care is important and has been pursued in various studies.[1] This broad and unified approach has been useful, indeed imperative, at the political level in raising the profile of caregiving and highlighting the gendered division of labour in our society.

A close examination of the concept of caregiving reveals, however, that the term is often too general and does not recognise the complex and variable experiences of caregivers. The existing analyses of the concept are limited when we are attempting to understand the experiences of what we call *family* caregivers—as opposed to the professional and the volunteer—and to assist them in their role. 'Family caregivers' are people who are under a kind of obligation to care because of their close kinship or emotional bond to the care-recipient. They can also, in our definition, be neighbours or friends who are close in the same way. Hence neighbours and friends appear sometimes in the following discussion along with parents, spouses and offspring as caregivers in our sense.

In this chapter we point to the need to understand caregiving in specific contexts. We explore the notion of caregiving through the issues of *responsibility, choice and customary expectations in relationships*. This allows us to clarify the specific nature of caring for a person with a disability,[2] and to distinguish this from other caring roles in our society: parent, spouse, volunteer and the professional carer, which includes nurses, social workers, medical practitioners and allied health workers. To do this we draw on previous caregiving literature, both empirical and theoretical, and use illustrative examples from our exploratory interviews with carers.

THE CONCEPT OF CAREGIVING

'Caregiving' comprises the caring 'activity' and the caring 'emotions'. Graham (1983) has differentiated these two components of caregiving as 'feeling concern for and taking charge of the well being of others', arguing that 'caring demands both love and labour, both identity and activity'. Similarly, Gillian Dalley (1988) distinguishes 'caring' from 'caring about'; 'caring for' refers to the tasks of 'tending', while 'caring about' refers to the carers' feelings for another person. Both writers conceptualise caregiving as some combination of *doing and feeling*.

These distinctions are a useful start but they neither allow a clear understanding of the caregiving experiences nor take into account the caregiving context. Specifically, they do not distinguish 'care for and about a person with a disability' from 'care for and about an independent family member'. Similarly, they do not adequately distinguish 'family caregiving' from volunteer or professional caregiving.

RESPONSIBILITY AND CHOICE

A broad distinction in understanding 'caregiving' concerns the extent to which the recipients of care can look after themselves. In the relationships we are concerned with, one person is physically dependent on the other for certain activities of daily living. In others, one person may be capable of performing the tasks themselves but, because of certain explicit or implicit agreements within the relationship, relies on the other to do tasks such as the 'servicing' work (cooking, cleaning, looking after small children) generally done by women. These are the 'usual' caring tasks performed in households where older children and adults have no physical or mental disability. This is a quite different context from what is meant by 'caregiving'— different in both the nature of the tasks and the carer's motivation for and emotional investment in the caring activities and role.

Where one person is limited in their physical or mental capabilities, there is some degree of *necessary reliance* on the carer by the recipient. The distinction between 'servicing' and 'caregiving' has been explained in terms of *responsibility* for the care-recipient, an aspect regarded as central to the definition of being a carer. The carer of a person with limited or no capacity to look after themselves is responsible for that person's health and well-being; the recipient's survival is dependent on the caregiving of the carer. Because the tasks performed 'go beyond the normal reciprocities between adults' (Twigg et al. 1990:4), this responsibility is over and above that commonly associated with adult relationships. A woman is *not* responsible for her 'well' husband, even though she may take charge of all the

Carers often have such a deep sense of responsibility for the disabled person that they won't, or don't, accept help from other people:

- 'We have always tried to battle through on our own because we believe it is our responsibility.'
- 'We have tried to carry the load ourselves.'
- 'You don't want to bother other people.'

Some acknowledge that this attitude has added to their burden:

- 'We're actually making a rod for our own backs by standing on our own two feet.'

This realisation has led others to accept their own limitations and seek outside assistance:

- 'I think we have to realise that other people can do what we do. You tend to think that you can't trust anybody.'

domestic servicing on his behalf and *feel* responsible for him. A person's capacity or incapacity for self-care is the central notion in distinguishing between 'servicing work' and 'caregiving'.

The idea of *being responsible for* a person is particularly important in explaining the experience of caregiving generically. As has been recognised by Twigg and colleagues (1990:7), the concept of responsibility applies regardless of the nature of the care-recipient's disability and hence regardless of the type or number of tasks performed by the carer. They point out that 'caring for someone with, for example, schizophrenia is often more episodic in character and focused around responsibility for the person, rather than [around] direct care tasks'. Thus even though the tasks performed might be no greater than the services a woman may choose to perform for her well husband, the caregiving role is distinguished by the responsibility required. With the emphasis on responsibility, the concept of caregiving can apply in relationships where the care-recipient still takes charge of their own self-care but where the carer has responsibility for the person's overall well-being. This seems a more useful notion than one which gives sole priority to the nature of the physical tasks performed.

This is not to suggest that the nature and intensity of the tasks themselves are not important in understanding a caregiver's experiences; indeed the results of our research are founded on this importance. Empirical studies have suggested that the nature and intensity of caregiving tasks,[3] as well as the nature and quality of the relationship between carer and care-recipient,[4] can have an impact on the caregiving experience and on the emotional and physical health of carers. Experiences will also vary with other contextual factors such as gender, ethnicity, living arrangements and life-stage.[5]

A further concept in understanding the caregiving context is that of *choice*. This is useful in differentiating family caregiving from caregiving in other contexts, particularly in distinguishing the family carer and the volunteer carer. Rarely is it that the carer of a family member who has an illness or disability is able to choose the onset, intensity or duration of their caregiving. Neither is the carer able to choose freely the time when their caregiving ends, other than through some abdication of their responsibility; the timing usually depends on deterioration in the health of the care-recipient or the carer's own stress. As the word 'volunteer' suggests, the person who takes on volunteer caring outside the family makes a decision to do so and

Carers can find themselves in a dilemma over their relative's conflicting needs for support and independence. Many are uncertain about the amount of help to give.

- One woman was concerned over helping her husband with dressing: 'You don't know whether you should be doing it or letting him do it for himself, but you generally take the easiest way out. I just automatically do it now because that's the easiest way.'
- Another woman caring for her elderly mother confessed that 'I'm not sure whether we're spoiling her by feeding her or whether she's really needing it'. And similarly, a parent said, 'We made the mistake of doing too much for them.'
- There is an even greater sense of uncertainty felt by carers about the future care of their relative: 'What will happen when I'm gone?'
- This is particularly salient for older carers: 'Our problem is what will happen to our daughter when we die. We are both 75 and in poor health. She won't go to anyone else. What will happen to her when we can't stand the strain. She may live for 25 years and we are 75.'
- These fears are not restricted to the elderly. A young single mother explained that 'My biggest fear is if I am in an accident tomorrow'.
- Some hoped that their relative would die before them: 'Sometimes I wish she would die before I do. Nobody is going to look after her like I do.'
- 'I'm getting old and I'm frightened what's going to happen to her when I die . . . I think I might just take her with me.'

has the opportunity to take on demands that are consistent with their capabilities. Studies reveal that many paid volunteers do not work for money but rather seek other rewards such as filling in spare time, reducing social obligation and gaining independence outside their family roles.[6] It could be assumed, then, that the volunteer carer has a personal motive for taking on the caring role and has the choice of discontinuing. Even where the recipient is 'dependent' on the carer, volunteer community caring does not carry the inherent family obligation, or the sense that 'no one else can do it'.

At the same time it is important to recognise that once a volunteer establishes a relationship with the care-recipient they may feel a sense of responsibility and emotional attachment to that person. But there will always be another volunteer to take over the role, which means that the carer in this relationship has the choice of whether to continue. It has been suggested that there is an assumption by care agencies that 'such distant relationships will evaporate should the burden become unacceptable', unlike the familial relationships 'where the individuals are bound by heavy obligations and close attachments' (Twigg et al. 1990:5). This is not to suggest that the emotional involvement is necessarily less for volunteer carers, but that the role is chosen by, rather than imposed on, such carers. (Our study does not concern itself with volunteer carers.)

For the carer of a family member, there is not such a clear choice, because of affectional ties or family obligations. Drawing on empirical studies with carers, Braithwaite (1990:10) suggests that because family carers 'have little choice but to give and give immediately . . . they may be forced to put aside other plans, forego activities and even undertake tasks which are beyond their capabilities'.

In relation to women specifically,

> current community care policies are doing little to alter the supply of freedoms in favour of carers and those for whom they care. Indeed, they are still based on . . . women's 'compulsory altruism' . . . Too many women are not free to choose not to care without either damaging those whom they care about or their own self esteem. (Land 1991:18)

- A woman confronted with the serious debilitating illness of her retired husband described her experience: 'All of a sudden he got sick and we were thrown together . . . I had a terrible lot of resentment because, just as we should be starting to enjoy life, I had to stay at home and look after him.'

- A mother caring for her severely disabled son said: 'I can still say I wish he had never been born. I was unable to get the pregnancy terminated . . . maybe it would have been better if he had died that night.'

Carers' choice has been further limited by trends in government policy over recent decades which have promoted a shift from institutional to home-based care, in Australia, New Zealand and elsewhere.[7]

TRANSGRESSION OF CUSTOMARY EXPECTATIONS

Central to the concept of caregiving is that it goes *beyond the customary expectations within a relationship*, particularly regarding the responsibility one takes and the tasks one performs for another. Caring for a disabled child goes beyond the customary because that child may not ever be able to look after itself; caring for a spouse with dementia turns on its head the customary relationship of equal adults; caring for frail elderly parents reverses the customary relationship of child to parent. It is this transgression of expectations that distinguishes caring for a relative with a disability from, say, bringing up able-bodied dependent children.

Customarily, at the birth of a child, parents expect that they will be responsible for the care of their child for a certain number of years, with diminishing intensity of caring tasks as the child's own self-care abilities develop, perhaps relinquishing responsibility for the well-being of their child once they reach adulthood. The parents of a child with a disability, however, may have to take primary responsibility for the entire lifetime of that child.

- A mother of a middle-aged son with intellectual disability described her role: 'Just damned hard work, and there's no such thing as retirement.'
- A mother of two children with disabilities identified three constant causes of stress which were common to many carers: 'You must wake up every day to the tasks, you have the financial worry and emotionally you can't afford to sit back and relax.'

The constancy of caring can pervade many aspects of a carer's life, with little opportunity for respite.

Valerie Braithwaite has explored the differences between caring for a healthy baby and caring for an elderly person or an adult who is no longer able to care for themselves. She points out that while each experience is accompanied by restrictions in one's social life, work opportunities, finances and freedom, and various disruptions in one's family situation, the two types of caregiving differ in that the dependency involved in caring for a healthy child 'is handled with pride and affection, and rarely interpreted as a burden'. The burden of caregiving is 'most acute where caring does not follow the desired path, where it does not make things better, and where it accompanies losses rather than gains in the well-being of the recipient'. She suggests that the crises of caregiving are concerned with awareness of degeneration, unpredictability, time constraints, the relationship between the caregiver and recipient, and choice restrictions, and argues that 'these crises of decline are either absent or do not assume the same potency in normal child-rearing practice' (Braithwaite 1990:8). These arguments can be extended to include differences between customary child-rearing and caring for a child with a disability.

Just as a spouse or a daughter caring for a relative with dementia suffers loss for the person they once knew, a parent of a child with a congenital disability may have similar feelings of loss for the child they didn't have: 'Grief is the major thing, grief for the child you expected.' The pain does not always dissipate. With each developmental milestone the sorrow is reactivated. 'The comparison with other children is very hard. You never get over it.' 'It's just reliving a tragedy.'

The central concept of caregiving in the sense in which we are using it is then not simply having responsibility for someone else, but *being responsible for that person beyond what might customarily be expected in that relationship.* At the same time it is important to recognise that customary expectations will vary with cultural, historical, class and other contexts.[8]

Dalley (1988:11) has suggested that the difficulty in transgressing expectations is associated with the 'acceptable' social norms which surround specific relationships, and that caregiving can involve 'a transgressing of highly symbolic and significant social norms'.

Caring for an ageing parent may require a reversal of roles: 'You've suddenly become a mother to your mother.' Sensibilities can also be disturbed. A son caring for his mother with dementia noted ruefully: 'You have to do things that a lot of men have never had to do.' The carer is also likely to be grieving for the loss of the mother they had, feeling loss that the 'expected' relationship has not continued.

Whether or not caregiving can be anticipated, and whether or not the transgression of social norms occurs, is possibly dependent on the life-stage of the carer and care-recipient and their relationship. For a couple moving into old age, for example, it might be expected that one partner will at some stage be caring for the other. Younger couples may be less prepared. One carer talked of the difficulties associated with caring for her husband with early-onset dementia, an unexpected turn of events for a couple in their early fifties. Her role as caregiver, and his role as 'dependant', was a transgression of what would be reasonably expected for the couple at that stage in life; their plans and hopes for the future were drastically changed.

A young husband whose wife was severely disabled, physically and neurologically, after a traumatic illness described his loss: 'We had a tremendous marriage. We had a big future, big things and big plans but everything changes . . . tomorrow is not to be the way we planned it.'

Dalley (1988:11) has noted that 'one of the implicit bargains of the marriage contract [is that] spouses are happy to care reciprocally for each other'. We suggest, however, that the age and life-stage and the associated expectations will significantly alter the caregiving context and hence the experiences of the carer.

DIFFERENTIATING FACTORS IN CAREGIVING

In a sense most if not all people throughout their lives or at some time in their lives are involved in caregiving in that they have close relationships with others which entail a special concern for their well-being and feelings of obligation to support and assist them in times of need. This might be as wife, daughter or mother, husband, son or father, as a sibling, friend or neighbour. But this is not what is commonly meant by 'family caregiver'. There are various aspects of the caregiving role or context which distinguish a family caregiver from the broad realm of caring people.

Figure 1.1 is a sketch of the characteristics which broadly define what it is we mean by a carer. Level 1 includes all people, with caregiving defined as a very broad 'species activity'. At Level 2 'paid work' distinguishes the professional caregiving of doctors, nurses and so on from other caregiving. At Level 3 the notion of 'choice' distinguishes the caregiving of volunteers from family caregiving. At Level 4 the notion of 'responsibility' distinguishes caregiving where there is an imbalance in dependency from the reciprocal caregiving

Figure 1.1   Levels and differentiating factors in caring

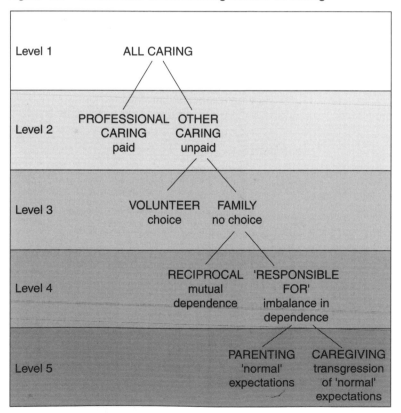

of spouses, siblings, parents with adult offspring, or neighbours. This level recognises the imbalance of dependency and concomitant increased level of responsibility of parents caring for young children or family members caring for someone with a long-term illness or disability. Reciprocal caregiving might include 'servicing' activities or negotiated arrangements about the sharing of household responsibilities. At Level 5 the 'transgression of customary expectations' distinguishes parenting from caring for a person with special needs. This transgression of expectations might involve the loss of a relationship or of an expected child, the duration of care, the nature and intensity of caring tasks.

Theoretical developments about 'caregiving' need to be examined at all five levels, covering both the general and specific aspects of caring. Our analysis goes some way towards clarifying the specific nature of caring for a relative with a disability and how this role differs from other forms of caregiving in our society.

Although much of the discussion in our exploratory interviews centred on difficulties and problems, carers also found satisfaction in the role. Parent carers referred to the feelings of satisfaction gained from seeing their relative achieve a minor goal or make a small improvement:

- 'There's a lot of positives though. You sort your life out as to what's important, and the beautiful bathroom or new kitchen doesn't matter. All that matters is that my son can smile and be happy.'
- 'I find it very rewarding when I see her achieving and I feel gratified by her improvement.'
- Carers of the elderly were particularly satisfied when they saw themselves as 'being able to postpone the nursing-home care'.
- Some emphasised the joy of caring itself: 'I've loved looking after her—it's been no chore to me and never will be.'
- Even though his wife had been unable to speak for about two years, one husband noted that 'sometimes we have lovely times together'.

2

A PROFILE OF CARERS AND CARE-RECIPIENTS

CHARACTERISTICS OF CARERS

The Victorian Carers Program created what was for the time a comprehensive socio-demographic profile of Australian carers.[1] Consistent with this generic focus, the findings of Stage 1 of our survey reflected a heterogeneity of carers and a diversity of caregiving roles and circumstances. There were both men and women carers, but, not surprisingly, women predominated. Caregivers covered a large range of ages from fifteen to 80, but consistent with other research most fell in the middle age-ranges, with two-thirds between 30 and 59. Over three-quarters were married or living with a partner. Although a quarter were employed full-time, most were not in paid employment (Table 2.1, p. 256).

Ethnicity is a key indicator of cultural diversity in caregiving (see Chapter 4). A total of 181 caregivers (18% of the total sample) (including 35 who did not speak English) were born in one of over 35 non-English-speaking countries. This figure compares with 17% of the Victorian population born in such countries.[2] Fifty-nine per cent lived in metropolitan Melbourne, with the remaining 41% spread throughout Victoria, but mainly in provincial cities or large rural towns.

There was diversity in carers' relationship to the person they were looking after. The largest group were adult offspring, mostly daughters, caring for parents. Next came those caring for a spouse or partner of which most were wives caring for their husbands. The next largest group were parents, again mostly mothers, caring for children. The

A recurring theme in our interviews was the constancy of caregiving.

- A woman who had cared for her husband for many years said: 'One thing you get used to is the continual pair of eyes over your shoulder. He can't bear me to be out of his sight, because I'm his security. That's what got me down in the first place—you go to the phone and you lift it up and you've got this pair of eyes, and you can't talk because he's standing right next to you.'
- Carers also described the constant stress and worry: 'You don't relax for any part of the night or day—if there is a noise in the night you think, "Has she fallen?"' 'You've got that tension all the time.'
- The parent of a very active child with intellectual disability explained that 'there is a constant feeling of what's going to happen next? It's absolutely full on, it never stops. He's always trying to run away and he will head off in any type of open environment.'
- The husband of a woman with a psychiatric disorder said, 'you've always got to be on guard that you don't set anything off'.
- After four fires and subsequent removal of all gas knobs from the stove, one adult daughter caring for her father stressed that 'you just can't relax—day and night, 24 hours you have got to be on the alert'.
- A lack of personal freedom in the carer's life often results from this constancy. The mother of a hyperactive child explained: 'I can't go to the toilet when I want to. I have to sit with the door open so that I can see her.'
- Others felt they were unable to get even a couple of days away alone, while another carer described how she was constantly aware of her responsibility: 'It's always in the back of your mind.'

remaining 17% were caring for a range of other relatives including parents-in-law, grandparents, siblings and a tiny handful caring for friends.

Living arrangements were another source of variation. The majority of carers (61%) were 'co-resident', that is, they lived with the person they were caring for. A relatively high 19% were caring for someone who lived alone, 12% for someone in residential care, and 8% for someone who lived with another person (Table 2.2, p. 256), but there were marked differences between relationship groups (see Chapter 7). Not surprisingly, the overwhelming majority of spouse (94%) and parent carers were co-resident (93%). Conversely, daughters and sons were more often caring for a parent who lived elsewhere; only 37% were co-resident.

CHARACTERISTICS OF CARE-RECIPIENTS

Over half the care-recipients were female (Table 2.3, p. 256). They ranged in age from one to 98 years. But whereas there was a concentration of care*givers* in the middle age-ranges, the converse was true for care-*recipients*, who were mainly older, with almost half 75 or over. Consistent with the differential rates of disability between boys and girls, parents were more likely to be caring for a son than a daughter. On the other hand, consistent with the greater longevity of women, adult offspring were more likely to be caring for an ageing mother than for a father (see Chapter 6).

Responses to a series of open-ended questions indicated a wide range of congenital, degenerative and traumatic conditions:

- frailty and age (24%)
- diseases of the circulatory system (19%)
- limb disability or paralysis (15%)
- congenital or developmental disorders (15%)
- dementia (12%)
- sensory impairment (10%)
- rheumatic, inflammatory or arthritic disorders (10%)
- musculoskeletal problems (10%)
- respiratory problems (8%)
- neoplasms (7%)
- endocrine and metabolic disorders (7%)
- neurological disorders (including brain damage) (5%)
- gastrointestinal and urogenital disorders (5%)
- other mental disorders (5%)
- Parkinson's disease (3%).

Carers were also asked whether their relatives had specific impairments, and if so, whether the problem was mild, moderate or severe. Most commonly reported were physical or mobility problems:

a majority (57%) had moderate or severe mobility problems; almost half had moderate or severe sensory loss (45%) and long-term health problems (40%); over a third had difficulties in coordination and intellectual impairment and a little under a third psychiatric or emotional problems (Table 2.4, p. 257). Not surprisingly, those with mobility problems also tended to have problems with motor coordination. Mobility problems were significantly associated with increasing age. Intellectual problems tended to be linked with difficulties in communication and emotional problems.

Overall, 13% of care-recipients had mild impairments only, 19% mainly mental impairments, 25% mainly physical and 43% both physical and mental impairments. Parents were significantly more likely to be caring for someone who was impaired mentally than were other relationship groups.

A common feature of caring for a relative with a long-term illness or disability is dealing with difficult behaviours. Over two-thirds of our carers said their relatives had at least one behaviour problem 'often' exhibited (Table 2.5, p. 257). The most common were the repetition of questions and stories, becoming listless and fatigued, inability to concentrate, being cranky or easily irritated, forgetful or confused. Well over half the carers indicated that their relatives 'often' or 'sometimes' behaved in these ways. Attention-seeking, hyperactivity and uncooperative behaviours were also common, as were depression and fearfulness. Although few carers reported

- A mother of a young boy described how he will 'scream and throw himself about when we are shopping. I am not prepared to take him on a social outing or take him to the park because he heads off and tries to run away in any type of open environment.'
- Behaviour problems were not restricted to the young. One woman caring for her 85-year-old mother commented on how demanding her mother had become and how she wouldn't let anyone else do things for her. She was unable to get out because 'she is not going to behave herself'. Difficult behaviour such as refusal to shower or to eat, or being 'sarcastic and quarrelsome' or 'aggressive' was also a problem for carers.

physically violent behaviour in their relatives, parents reported such behaviour significantly more often than other relationship groups.

Behaviour problems often clustered together. Those who were cranky and easily irritated were more likely to have changeable moods, be aggressive, uncooperative, even suspicious or accusing. Forgetfulness and confusion were linked with an inability to concentrate, the repetition of questions and stories, becoming withdrawn or hardly ever speaking, wandering and getting lost. Overall 38% of carers found these behaviours difficult or very difficult to cope with.

USE OF SERVICES

In view of the shift in emphasis from institutional care to care in the home or community, the use of formal services to help in family caregiving was particularly interesting (see Chapter 10). In our sample (excluding residential care), half the carers received no services, a quarter one service only, and the remainder two or more. Each regular service was used by only a minority of carers (Table 2.6, p. 258). Transport and general home help were the most frequently used, but even so only by a quarter of the carers. Even fewer received specific home help or community nursing. But a third of our participants had had modifications made to their homes to help the disabled person. As an overall need for community services, we calculated the proportion of carers who reported that they needed *any one* of these seven services, or another service they had not been asked about: 54% reported an unmet need for at least one.

Few carers had received any counselling or education about their caregiving role, and only 12% had had respite in the past twelve months. Considering that past research has often been based on samples drawn from support organisations, it is particularly interesting that only 8% of carers belonged to a carers' support group.

In contrast to the use of general services, most care-recipients had seen their general practitioner in the past six months for problems or tests related to their condition, around half had seen a medical specialist, and substantial minorities had seen a physiotherapist, other health professional or social worker. In spite of the predominance of elderly care-recipients, however, only a few had been assessed by an aged care assessment team. Satisfaction with the services was generally high, particularly for medical specialists, allied health professionals and general practitioners.

While information about care-recipients' conditions came mainly from medical professionals, carers' main sources of information about services came roughly equally from general practitioners, allied health professionals, and government agencies. Other main sources were family and friends, medical specialists, a society or support organisation, and the media. But quite a few had received no information at all about carer services and organisations.

Although few carers received support from local services, many were helped by family and friends. Help came from children, partners, siblings, parents, other relatives and friends. This was mainly in the form of friendship, emotional support, entertaining and visiting: many carers reported help with housework, shopping, home repairs and gardening, and a few with the personal care of their relative. While some carers expressed the need for more help from their partners, more wanted more help from other relatives or friends.

EMPLOYMENT AND FINANCES

Caregiving can affect employment opportunities, with obvious financial implications (see Chapter 8). Of the near two-thirds of carers not in paid work, some reported having had to give up a job because of caregiving, and some felt unable to take a job. For those who did have work, their caregiving presented certain difficulties, for example interruptions, less energy, fewer hours, or unpaid leave.

The proportion of carers who were working varied significantly with relationship group: half the adult offspring carers compared with a third of the parents and only a few of spouse carers, to some extent reflecting differences in age and life-stage.

When carers were asked what was the main effect caregiving had had on their financial situation, over half reported no change or only minor change in their finances since caregiving began. About a quarter said it entailed extra expenses, and for some it meant a reduction in income. Of the 425 carers reporting adverse financial effects, over half admitted difficulty in meeting their everyday living costs.

CARER HEALTH AND WELL-BEING

A third of carers reported major problems in their own health over the past year (see Chapter 7). Almost half were on medication and over a quarter rated their overall health as only fair or poor. Over half agreed that they were exhausted when they went to bed at night; around half felt they had more things to do than they could handle and no time just for themselves. At the same time, a high 86% were satisfied or very satisfied with their life as a whole, and around 80% were similarly content with their health, their personal and emotional life, the respect or recognition they get and their independence or freedom; a somewhat lower 67% expressed satisfaction with their financial situation.

The comparison with non-carers (Chapter 5), which was limited to females, showed clear differences between the two groups in physical health and emotional well-being. Thus in spite of the wide range of caregiving roles in our sample, carers were generally more prone to health problems and had poorer self-rated health. Likewise, notwithstanding the 86% just mentioned, diminished life satisfaction was more common in carers than in non-carers, particularly those who felt more overloaded and less cushioned by family and friends.

COMPARISON WITH POPULATION SURVEYS

There were marked differences between our study and the ABS survey on disability and ageing (ABS 1993), in sampling and in the defini-tion of a carer. In the latter the main focus was the aged and people with disabilities. Co-resident carers were identified by the care-recipient according to the type of help provided. Information about the caregiving role was only sought from *principal* carers, that is, those carers who gave the most help in the areas of personal care, mobility, and verbal communication; carers of children under the age of five who had disabilities were not identified. In contrast, our carers were self-identified, not defined by the recipient's age or disability type or by the kind of care they provided. Nevertheless some comparisons between our own survey and that of the ABS are useful.

The ABS survey (1993:1) estimated that 14.2% of the Australian population had a handicap which limited ability to perform ordinary tasks in the areas of 'self-care, mobility, verbal communication, schooling or employment'. For 4.1% of the population this handicap was 'profound' (people always needing help from another person) or 'severe' (sometimes needing help). A further 2.6% had a 'moderate' handicap: they had difficulty performing one or more tasks of daily living but maintained that they needed no help from others. Thus between 4.1% and 6.7% of the population were moderately to profoundly handicapped. The ABS prevalence of principal carers was estimated at 4.2% of the Australian population over the age of fifteen. In our Victorian survey, carers of people with disabilities who were not restricted to these activities of care were identified in 5.2% of contacted households.

Table 2.7 (p. 258) presents the sex and age distributions of carers in each survey. Clearly the age distributions are similar. The higher proportion of women carers in our sample (78% compared with 67% in the ABS sample) may be explained by the differences in sampling and definition noted above, for example the exclusion of care-recipients under the age of five in the ABS survey: the 4% of carers in our survey who were caring for children under five were almost all women. It is interesting to note correspondence between the age distribution of our care-recipients and ABS population estimates of handicap within age-brackets: thus while 4% and 8% of our care-recipients were aged 0–4 and 5–14 respectively, the population estimates of handicap within these age-ranges were, respectively, 4% and 7%. Likewise, while almost half our care-recipients were aged 75 or over, the ABS population estimate of handicap in this age-range was 61%.

Included in the 1985 UK General Household Survey (Green 1988) was a set of items largely aimed at obtaining national estimates of numbers and types of carers. It did not include the assessment of the social, emotional and attitudinal components of caregiving which are an important aspect of our own study. But unlike the ABS survey, the method and sampling of the UK survey were very similar to our own in that carers were self-identified by responding to the broad question:

> Some people have extra family responsibilities because they look after someone who is sick, handicapped or elderly. Is there anyone living with you who is sick, handicapped or elderly whom you look after or give special help to? And how about people not living with you, do you provide some regular service or help for any sick, handicapped or elderly relative, friend or neighbour not living with you?

Table 2.8 (p. 259) presents a comparison between carers identified in our survey as taking the primary responsibility in caregiving and 'main' carers identified in the UK survey. The latter were defined as 'those who took the major responsibility for the care of the dependant' and consisted of 'people who were the sole carers of a dependant or who spent more time than anyone else on the depen-dant' (Green 1988:7).

Clearly, in terms of age distribution, sex by age distribution and marital status of carers as well as breakdown in family type, the two samples are very similar. The fact that our sample contains propor-tionately *more* female carers, *fewer* female care-recipients and *more* younger care-recipients may be explained by our comparatively younger population. Among the younger age-groups there is a pre-dominance of males with disabilities, whereas, because of the greater longevity of women, among the older age-groups there is a predom-inance of women with disabilities. It should be noted that the UK survey of carers was part of a more general household survey.

WHAT THE FINDINGS MEAN

The high response rate to the VCP survey and the fact that almost all interviewed carers agreed to be recontacted attest the effectiveness of the CATI system for identifying and interviewing family caregivers.

The findings attest this also. Their most striking aspect was the diversity of caregiving roles and circumstances—though this diversity to some extent reflects group differences, for example between adult offspring, spouse and parent carers, which may in turn reflect different ages, life-stages and intensity of care. Adult offspring caring for ageing parents were less likely to be co-resident and more likely to be working and hence balancing multiple roles. In contrast, spouses, who were generally older, and to a lesser extent parents, who were gen-erally younger, were less likely to be employed but more likely to have a 'high-intensity' caregiving role. Almost all these carers were co-resident.

There was diversity not only in the carers but also in those cared for: female and male, predominantly in the older age-groups but covering the full range of ages. Illnesses and disabilities in the care-recipients were multifarious: many had more than one impair-ment, and with the disabilities came a variety of behaviour problems. Importantly, carer reports of the severity of disability, level of depend-ency and intensity of care provided were independently validated with a sub-sample of study participants and their relatives through a home-based assessment undertaken with local assessment teams (see Chapter 12).

Most carers felt supported by family and friends. Even though feelings of exhaustion prevailed and health problems in carers were not uncommon, use of specific non-medical services was modest. In fact only a little over half the carers indicated a need for services. It is for this reason that a major aim in our health promotion strategies, including the home-based assessment, was facilitating links to appropriate services.

We set out to sample a broad range of caregiving for two reasons. First, it enabled us to describe the full profile of carers, where they lived, their socio-economic status, and the specific disability they were concerned with, and to describe the range of carers' needs and the intensity of their caregiving. Second, in relation to our health promotion strategies and considering the different intensity of care-giving, it enabled us to explore the best timing for interventions and provision of services. The inclusion of a comparison group of non-carers enabled us to assess differences in the effects of caring for a person with disabilities and those of the caregiving responsibilities of the general population.

Despite the differences in focus, comparisons between our Victorian survey and both the Australian (ABS 1993) and UK (Green 1988) surveys support the validity of our socio-demographic profile of family carers of people with disabilities. Our study with its specific focus on carers goes beyond these surveys in the amount of detailed informa-tion collected on the social, emotional and physical aspects of caregiving, the formal and informal supports received and needed. The representative and detailed nature of the data collected will provide a useful basis for social policy analysis and discussion.

3

PHYSICAL AND EMOTIONAL ASPECTS OF CAREGIVING

For more than a decade there has been extensive investigation of the caregiving experience, particularly the fact or sense of 'burden'. Usually this construct has been assessed using *burden scales*, but understanding of the impacts and experience of caregiving has been limited by inconsistencies in the definitions of burden and in the conceptualisation of caregiving as burdensome. Understandably, burden scales measure only the stressful, difficult aspects of caregiving, so those that give satisfaction have traditionally been ignored.

In the literature 'objective' and 'subjective' burdens are distinguished. The distinction theoretically is that objective burden includes disruptions or changes which are potentially verifiable, whereas subjective burden encompasses carers' personal responses to and feelings about these disruptions or changes.[1] In this chapter we present both the objective or physical and the subjective or emotional aspects of caregiving. The physical aspects we consider are living arrangements, duration and hours of care, help with physical and instrumental activities of daily living, and household tasks. The emotional aspects are carers' attitudes towards the caregiving role and the person they are caring for, the quality of the relationship between carer and recipient, the carer's ease or difficulty in coping with behaviour problems, and changes in the family environment since caregiving started. In each area we have included positive and negative items.

Most obvious through the discussions was carers' agreement that the demands of caregiving are constant and relentless, in terms of both practical assistance and emotional strain and worry. Carers referred to the 24-hour daily commitment, as well as the lifelong ongoing commitment: 'It's just damned hard work and there's no such thing as retirement.'

PHYSICAL ASPECTS OF CAREGIVING

Almost two-thirds of carers **lived with** the person they were caring for. Some care-recipients lived alone, and some were in residential accommodation. A smaller number lived with someone other than their main carer, usually their spouse (Table 3.1, 260).

Living arrangements varied significantly in terms of the relationship between carer and care-recipient. Not surprisingly, those co-residing were most likely to be either spouses caring for their partner or parents caring for their child. In fact almost all spouse and parent carers lived with the person they looked after. Where this person lived alone, lived with someone other than their carer, or lived in residential accommodation, the carer was more likely to be an offspring or 'other relative'. Living arrangements also varied significantly according to the carer's age. Consistent with relationship variations, carers under 35 and over 65 were generally living with their relative, which reflects a preponderance of parent and spouse carers. Where the care-recipient lived alone or with another, the carer was more likely to be in the middle age-range of 35–64. There were no significant differences according to the carer's sex.

The **length of time** people had been providing care for their relatives varied from a month to 50 years. Most had been caring for several years: two-thirds had been caring for over two years, and for a quarter it had been more than ten years (Table 3.2, p. 260).

Duration of care varied significantly according to the relationship between carer and recipient. Compared with other relationship groups, parent carers were more likely to have been caring for ten years or more; 'other' relatives were more likely to have been caring for less than two years. Duration also varied significantly according to the carer's age. Younger carers aged under 35 were more likely than others to have been caring for a long period, from six to ten years, though they were less likely to have been caring for more than ten years. Carers over 65 were the most likely to have been caring for a longer period. Carers in the middle age-group of 35–49 were more likely than others to have been caring for a year or less. There were no significant differences in duration of care according to the carer's sex.

Time spent caring varied from four hours a week in the case of 9% of carers to 24 hours a day seven days a week for 25% of carers. Carers were also asked if this had changed substantially over the period of caring; 60% reported a change and were asked how it had changed (Table 3.3, p. 260).

Altered condition, including conditions related to gradual deterioration or improvement, medical crises and age, was reported as a common cause of changing the time spent caring. *Progressive disability* resulted in increased demand: 'He is becoming more dependent, so the number of hours has increased.' Others reported that *partial recovery or recovery of some abilities* had resulted in a reduction of the workload: 'It has decreased over the period because her walking has improved.' *Medical crises* such as strokes, operations and fractures form a class of events leading to an increased time spent by carers: 'Since she broke her wrist we are doing her shopping, bathing and looking after her wrist.' The element of suddenness distinguishes these from progressive disability.

Age was mentioned as an important factor resulting in both increasing and decreasing time. In the aged the passing of time generally resulted in increased needs, whereas for child care-recipients being older often meant being more capable. This generalisation was not true in all cases, for example: 'Caring has increased as he has become mobile and bigger. He has needed to be taught life.' But more typical of replies mentioning age were 'This last year has been a lot worse due to his age and mine', and conversely, 'It is easier as he is older because he can tell me what he needs.'

Altered circumstances (informal support, residential arrangements, schooling and carer needs) formed another major set of reasons for changes. Obviously the availability of informal support was a large factor in increases and decreases in time spent caring. Helpers come or go for various reasons—changed health, work status and place of residence were all reported. The death of a spouse was cited by a number of carers as a reason for increased caregiving. Typical examples were 'increased since [carer's] mother went into hospital' and 'reduced a bit as the children get older and help more'.

Some carers felt that their physical health had declined over the years of caregiving because of the emotional and physical strains and responsibilities, several suffering high blood pressure, stomach ulcer, 'tension' and 'nerves'.

- One woman who had been caring many years for her husband felt that 'it undermines your own health—you think "I am managing, I am fine" and then something goes wrong with your body'.

Lifting and restraining were the most common causes of physical strain for carers, resulting in back, knee and shoulder injuries and torn muscles and tendons, many of which became chronic and irreparable. Both growing children and elderly relatives often required physical support and as carers aged these tasks became more difficult and the injuries more serious.

- The mother of a 35-year-old son with a severe physical disability had spent every day for years lifting him: 'The lifting was just pulling my stomach like it was ripping the lining off my stomach, just transferring him from bed to chair or toilet.'
- Another mother with a 9-year-old son described the physical difficulties she had just supporting him when on outings: 'I have a hand problem which is just from hanging onto him the whole time. Of course he goes down suddenly and my wrist goes too. That sudden jolt does more damage.'
- Regular treatment of these strain injuries is often required: 'My daughter is getting a lot bigger and I have to watch my back. I go to the chiropractor every three months to be able to lift her because I am lifting her all the time.'

A diverse group of influences on increases and decreases in time revolved around *altered residential or visiting arrangements,* including the care-recipient moving closer to the carer, moving into the carer's home, or moving into residential accommodation. It also includes altered visiting arrangements in hospitals or residential accommodation. On the one hand, 'First three and a half years it was much less hours. When she moved in [to the carer's home] sixteen months ago it's been full-time', and on the other, 'It is less now she has entered a home.'

Schooling encompasses all educational facilities, including kindergarten and adult training, but not day care. A number of carers reported putting in less time since the care-recipient started school and a couple, increased demands since school finished. For example, 'Only when [recipient] started school, reduced from 24-hour care' as against 'Yooralla schooling when he was younger, so I did not care for him as full-time as I do now'.

Changed needs of the carer were also mentioned as an explanation for reduced hours. This was often related to an increase in the time the carers spent in paid employment, but other reasons were given: 'Time with [recipient] has lessened because [carer] now has a baby to look after.'

Overall, collapsing the categories, twice as many carers said that the time had increased (40%) as said it had decreased (19%), while 41% reported no change. Fourteen respondents said that the time varied, usually because of fluctuations in the recipient's condition. Parents more often reported decreased time and less often reported increased time than any other relationship group, while spouse carers showed the strongest tendency towards increasing time spent caring. The reduction in time demanded of parents was indicative of the development seen in many child recipients, in which they attend school and learn independent living skills. Undoubtedly, the increased time demands on spouse carers were connected with progressive deterioration of the care-recipient with increasing age. Men more often reported no change than women. Carers whose relatives were in residential care understandably more often reported a decrease in time spent caring, while those caring for a recipient who lived alone were least likely to report a decrease (Table 3.4, p. 261).

ASSISTANCE WITH ACTIVITIES OF DAILY LIVING

Carers were asked how much assistance their relatives needed (none, some, a lot) in the performance of twelve activities of daily living (Table 3.5, p. 261). On the assumption that help would be provided for young children even in the absence of impairment, this information was not sought where the care-recipient was under six years of age. The tasks for which assistance was most often needed were going out, organising appointments and social services and managing money. Over half the care-recipients required help with medications or dressings, again most of these requiring a lot of help. Almost half needed either a lot or some help with personal tasks of bathing/showering and dressing. Over a third required help with communicating. A smaller number needed help with getting in and out of bed or a chair, moving about, using the toilet, incontinence, and eating.

Factor analysis of the twelve activities yielded two broad functional dependence or 'help needed' scales:

- *Physical* activities of daily living (ADLs) including getting in and out of bed, using the toilet, dressing, moving about, bathing/showering, eating, and incontinence.
- *Instrumental* activities of daily living (IADLs) included organising social services, managing money, communicating, and medication use.

Help needed in performing IADLs differed significantly according to the carer's relationship with the recipient (Table 3.6, p. 261). The amount of help required in IADLs by children of parent carers was higher than that reported for all other relationship groups. Help needed for ADLs did not differ for relationship groups. In contrast, the overall amount of help needed by care-recipients in performing ADLs differed significantly according to the carer's age. In particular, carers aged over 65 reported more ADL help required by their relative than did carers in the middle age-range of 35–49. There were no age differences for IADLs.

Help required with both ADLs and IADLs varied according to living arrangements. Not surprisingly, those looking after people in residential care reported more help needed in both ADLs and IADLs (Table 3.7, p. 262). Carers living with their relative reported the next highest amount of help, which was significantly higher on both scales than in situations where the care-recipient lived with someone else. Consistently, where care-recipients lived alone, carers reported significantly less help needed. Indeed, living arrangements appear to reflect the amount of dependence of the care-recipient. Help needed with ADLs also varied according to the duration of care: those who had been caring for a longer period reported more help required in ADLs. While there was a similar trend for IADLs, the effect was not significant. Help needed did not vary with the carer's sex.

HELP PROVIDED BY CARERS

For each activity, carers were also asked how much help they personally provided: all/most, some, or none of the help required (Table 3.8, p. 262). Carers were most commonly helping with going out, organising social services and managing money, generally providing all or most of the help for those needing it. Almost half were providing help with medications and dressings and over a third with communication, again providing most of the help for those needing it. About a third of carers were providing help with dressing, and bathing/showering. Carers were less commonly providing help with the last five items.

Notably, a sizeable minority of carers whose relative required help with personal-care tasks reported that they provided *none of the assistance themselves*: in particular, a third of those needing help with bathing or showering, a fifth of those needing help with dressing, and a fifth of those needing help with medications or dressings were not receiving it from the main carer but through residential care services,

Incontinence can be a great burden, requiring constant and sensitive attention.

- One woman looking after her father explained frankly that 'somebody who's wetting the bed, is incontinent of bowels, they have got to be showered every day—you can't do it any other way'.
- Another caring at home for her mother explained the difficulties of 'trying to give her dignity and treat her as an adult, and not draw attention to the fact that she is having an accident—it is progressively getting more difficult'.

community support services (specific home help or community nursing), or from the family and/or friends of the carer (Table 3.9, p. 263). Only a handful of those needing help with bathing/showering and/or dressing were not receiving it from these sources: these were three elderly parents being cared for by adult offspring. In each case the care-recipient lived with her spouse who, presumably, was helping with these tasks. Two recipients, both elderly parents living alone, appeared not to be receiving from any source the help they needed with medications or dressings.

VARIATIONS IN HELP PROVIDED BY CARERS

The amount of help provided by carers with ADLs overall differed significantly in terms of the relationship to the care-recipient: in particular, spouse and parent carers were providing more help with ADLs than were offspring and 'other' carers (Table 3.10, p. 263). For IADLs, parents were providing more help than all other groups. 'Other' relative carers were providing less help than all others with ADLs. These differences may reflect a combination of the degree of disability of the care-recipient, living arrangements, and the intimacy within the relationship. In terms of carer age, carers 65 and over were providing more ADL help than were those in the middle age-ranges. For help provided with IADLs, however, there were no differences across age-groups.

Help provided varied according to living arrangements for both ADLs and IADLs (Table 3.11, p. 263). Carers living with their relative were providing more help with ADLs than were all other groups. For IADLs, carers were providing more help if their relative lived with them or lived in residential care. There were no significant differences in help provided in terms of duration of care. As with 'help needed', the amount of help provided did not vary according to the carer's sex.

ASSISTANCE WITH HOUSEHOLD TASKS

Information about help required by care-recipients and help provided by carers in household tasks was sought only from non-resident carers. For such carers these tasks were assumed to be additional to the management of their own household (Table 3.12, p. 264). Non-resident carers commonly reported that their relatives needed help with home repairs (85%), shopping (84%) and general housework (77%). About two-thirds needed help with washing and ironing (63%) and preparing meals (60%). A smaller proportion needed financial support (35%). With living arrangements and dependency so closely linked, it is not surprising that help *required* with these tasks varied significantly according to living arrangements: care-recipients living in residential care were more likely than those living alone to need help with preparing meals, washing and ironing, general housework, and financial support. Those living alone, on the other hand, were more likely than others to require at least some help with home repairs. Assistance required with household tasks did not vary significantly according to carer sex, carer age or the duration of care.

Concerning help *provided* with general household tasks (Table 3.13, p. 265), a large 70% of non-resident carers were providing at least some help with shopping, almost half were providing at least some help with general housework (44%), home repairs (42%) and preparing meals (40%), and over a third were helping with washing and ironing (38%). Fewer were giving financial support (19%). Help provided in household tasks varied significantly according to living arrangements. While care-recipients living in residential accommo-dation were more likely, because of frailty or cognitive decline, to require help with these tasks, they were, not surprisingly, less likely than all others to be receiving the required help from the carer. Specifically, these carers were less likely than others to be helping with preparing meals, washing and ironing, general housework, home repairs and shopping. They were, however, more likely than others to be providing most of the required financial support. In situations where the care-recipient either lived alone or lived with someone other than the carer, about three-quarters of carers were helping with shopping, while around half the carers were providing at least some help with home repairs, general housework, and meal preparation. For help with household tasks, there were no significant differences in terms of carer age, carer sex or the duration of care.

About half of those needing help with home repairs and/or general housework, about a third needing help with washing and ironing and/or meal preparation, and a smaller number needing help with shopping were receiving it from someone other than the carer (Table 3.14, p. 266). In many cases these care-recipients lived in residential care, where presumably much of the required assistance was provided. Others were being helped by other family and friends (specifically with housework, cooking, shopping, and repairs around the home) and by community support services (meal services, general home help and/or home maintenance). Only one care-recipient, an elderly woman who lived alone and was cared for by her daughter, who needed some help with general housework, was not receiving help from any of these sources.

CARERS' RESPONSIBILITIES FOR HOUSEHOLD TASKS

All carers were asked about their general family responsibilities in their own household (Table 3.15, p. 267). Over three-quarters had the main responsibility for cooking or preparing meals, washing and ironing, shopping, light housework, and organising health and social services. About two-thirds had the main responsibility for heavy housework, driving people places, and managing finances. Fewer had the main responsibility for repairs around the home. Not surprisingly, household responsibilities varied significantly in terms of carer sex for almost all tasks. Female carers were more likely than males to report having the main responsibility for cooking, washing and ironing, light housework, shopping, organising health and social services, and heavy housework. Male carers were more likely than females to report main responsibility for home repairs. There were no sex differences for managing finances or driving people places.

Most household responsibilities also varied according to the relationship between carer and recipient. Parents were less likely than other groups to report that someone else had the main responsibility for cooking, washing and ironing, and organising health and social services. Spouse carers were more likely than other groups to report having the main responsibility for home repairs and managing finances. These findings may reflect sex differences, considering the higher proportion of women among the parents than among the spouses.

Household responsibilities also varied in terms of carer age (Table 3.16, p. 269). Compared with older carers, those under 35 were more likely to share the cooking and were more likely than others to report that someone else had the main responsibility for organising health and social services and managing finances. Those over 65 were more likely than others to have the main responsibility for managing finances, and to report that someone else had the main responsibility both for heavy housework and for driving people places.

In terms of living arrangements, carers were less likely to have main responsibility if the care-recipient lived alone: for home repairs, managing finances, and driving people places. Carers' household responsibilities did not differ significantly according to the duration of care.

EMOTIONAL ATTITUDES TO CAREGIVING

Carers were asked for their response to a series of seventeen statements, positive and negative, about how they felt caring for their relative (Table 3.17, p. 270). Overall, most carers acknowledged the satisfaction, reassurance and increased confidence they had gained through caregiving. Most also denied negative feelings about their relative and about the effects of caregiving on their lives in terms of lost opportunities, social contacts and control.

It was also true that responses to half the items differed significantly between relationship groups and that the differences were most evident in the extreme response categories. Parents and spouses were significantly more likely than adult offspring and others to 'strongly agree' that they would be at a loss if their relative were not around. More than twice the proportion of parent carers as other groups strongly acknowledged the satisfaction they got from their relative's accomplishments. Although a minority warmly agreed that caregiving had made them more confident in dealing with others, again this was so for twice the proportion of parents as other relationship groups.

Some carers also gained in self-confidence, while others acquired new skills. Caregiving provided the opportunity for some carers to make new friends or broaden their interests:

- 'Many years ago I wouldn't say boo to a goose, but now I'll have a go at anybody. It's certainly made me more assertive.'
- 'We've been on camps with other families and they're great fun.'
- 'I am now involved with a new lot of people through the support group.'

It is perhaps not surprising that parents were most likely, and 'other' relatives and friends least likely, to worry about who would look after their relative if they were not around and to grieve for the opportunities that disability or illness had denied their relative.

Although most carers rejected negative feelings about caregiving, there were uncomfortable minorities who acknowledged negative effects such as lost opportunities, social contacts and control. Thus one in three regretted the opportunities caregiving had denied them, and almost one in five admitted feelings of embarrassment, guilt and anger over their relative. In these respects there was concord between the relationship groups except in relation to friends not visiting so often: more than twice the proportion of adult offspring as other groups strongly endorsed this negative effect.

There were, too, significant differences between men and women in these attitudes. Women strongly affirmed the satisfaction they received from the recipient's accomplishments (39%, men 29%), their worry over who would care for the recipient if they were not around (34%, men 23%), and their grief over opportunities denied the recipient (24%, men 13%). At the same time, women were more apt to acknowledge anger (16%, with 8% of men strongly agreeing or agreeing, and guilt (18%, with 10% of men strongly agreeing or agreeing).[2]

Not surprisingly, these attitudes clustered together. Thus warm satisfaction with the role went with pride in seeing the recipient accomplish things, enhanced confidence in dealing with others, reassurance that the recipient was getting proper care, and an anticipated sense of loss if the recipient were not around. Conversely, anger in the presence of their relative went with embarrassment over their behaviour, frustration that nothing they, the carer, could do

Carers can get caught up in a cycle of resentment and guilt, feelings they find it difficult to allow and resolve. A man caring for his wife explained that 'you have a sense of guilt, because you love them and yet you feel trapped, so you are torn'. A woman caring for her husband reiterated the cycle: 'You think to yourself, what is this man doing to me? And then you feel very selfish, and then you feel guilty because you've been selfish. Guilt is the biggest killer—you just feel guilty all the time.'

seemed to please, guilt *both* about their relative and, potentially, if they did not provide care. The latter was also linked with regret about their own lost opportunities, friends not visiting so often and time taken up in caregiving at the expense of the rest of the family.[3]

Quality of relationship with the care-recipient Carers were asked about the degree of closeness and tension in their relationship with the care-recipient (Table 3.18, p. 271). Almost everyone considered their relationship as very close or close, with only a few dismissing it as not close. At the same time a little over half indicated that the level of tension in the relationship was moderate, even high. Interestingly, parents were most likely to rate their relationship as very close and the tension as high compared with spouse and adult offspring and, not surprisingly, other relatives and friends. Although men and women did not differ in the closeness of their relationship with the care-recipient, women were more apt to report more tension (16% high and 39% moderate compared with respectively, 10% and 34% for men).

Difficulty in coping Carers were asked how easy or difficult it was coping with their relative's behaviour (Table 3.19, p. 271). Over a third said it was difficult (29%) or very difficult (9%), while over half reported it as easy (41%) or very easy (15%), with 6% unsure. But half the parents reported it as difficult or very difficult to cope compared with around a third of the other relationship groups. Consistently, with increasing age of the recipient, carers found it easier to cope. Understandably, difficulty in coping was more common in those who did not feel close to the recipient and those reporting a high degree of tension in the relationship.

Responses to an open-ended question asking what aspects of the recipient's disability the carer found most difficult to cope with were

- 'You've got to have hope, always hope.'
- 'Keep looking on the bright side of things.'
- 'I give myself a bit of a kick when I go through that depressed stage.'
- 'You don't give in and you fight all the time. It's a challenge to think, "Well damn it all, it's not going to beat me." A lot of us are like that.'

coded into broad response categories. Most frequently mentioned were the care-recipient's emotional and behaviour problems (25%) and demands and dependence (23%), the carer's own emotions, fears and pain witnessing the suffering of the recipient (20%), and the recipient's physical (20%) and intellectual (19%) incapacity.

Emotions/personality/psychiatric problems/behaviour Common problems included not only aggression, stubbornness, tantrums, anger and selfishness but also loneliness, lack of motivation and moodiness.

- 'When he's asked to do something that he doesn't want to do, he becomes very aggressive.'
- 'His naughty behaviour.'
- 'Depression. She doesn't have other friends and her entire focus is on us. We don't know how to break this cycle.'
- 'Her self-pity now. She used to be a very outgoing person.'

Co-operation/demands/dependence/time Problems included not only the constancy of the demands but also recipients' difficulty in knowing and accepting the limits imposed on them by their conditions.

- 'It's ongoing—24 hours a day.'
- 'Constancy.'
- 'Won't accept help. Feels she can manage even if she can't.'

The carer's emotions/worries/fears/recipient's sickness/pain Common problems included lack of support, financial worries, fear of the future, upset over the recipient's suffering, pain and difficulty in breathing.

- 'Not having the support of the rest of the family as they're in [another country].'
- 'I feel helpless that I can't do anything for him.'
- 'Asthma attacks, coughing and temperature, loss of breath and becomes purple colour.'
- 'The continuous pain.'

Physical inability/mobility Common responses included problems related to eating, walking, hearing, eyesight and incontinence.

- 'Toileting and feeding her. Every meal must be prepared and liquefied.'
- 'His not being able to walk, that is very hard.'

The strains and stresses of caregiving seem to depend on the life-stage of carer and recipient, their relationship before caregiving, and the readiness of the carer for the caregiving role. For a couple moving into old age, it might be expected that one partner will at some stage be caring for the other. Others may be less prepared. One woman talked of the difficulties associated with caring for her husband with early-onset dementia, an unexpected turn of events for a couple in their mid-fifties: 'I'm finding all the time that I have to do more and more for him. Sometimes I wonder how I *do* cope with him, but you just keep going, there's nothing you can do about it, it's your responsibility. You try to shield the children from it too, to a certain extent. I tell the kids—well, you can sort of highlight the funny things. I mean, you try to make it funny otherwise you just go under.'

Intellectual incapacity/communication Common problems included lack of concentration and memory, repetition and inability to comprehend what the recipient was saying.

- 'To see that her brain is not ticking over the way it should.'
- 'Not knowing who I am.'
- 'Communication—can't understand what he means or wants to say. That's bad.'
- 'The repetitiveness of her conversation and difficulties people have in getting the message through to her.'

None/no comment/unspecified

- 'None, I don't find it difficult at all.'
- 'We carry on as good as we can.'

It was more often the problems brought about by the disability, especially the recipient's emotions, behaviour and lack of independence, that carers found difficult to cope with, less so the actual physical or intellectual incapacity (Table 3.20, p. 272). Spouses tended to find their own emotions and the sickness, pain and physical inability of the care-recipients the most difficult things to deal with, whereas adult offspring and parents often found the emotional and behavioural aspects of the disability the most trying. Carers in other relationships to the recipient often found physical incapacity difficult to deal with, but these carers were also more apt to report no problems in dealing with the disability. Carers who found the recipient's emotional-behavioural problems, sickness and pain and their own emotional difficulties as the most trying aspect of their situation tended to have higher negative affect scores, whereas those reporting no problems reported the lowest negative affect.

THE FAMILY ENVIRONMENT

Caring for a relative can affect the atmosphere in a family. Carers were asked, generally speaking, whether caregiving had meant more, the same or less of six emotions in their immediate family (Table 3.21, p. 272).[4] The emotions most likely to have increased were compassion and tension; those most likely to have remained unchanged were resentment, conflict and love. But there were

Even within a 'supportive' family, relations can become strained.

- A woman caring for an elderly parent complained of having no time with her spouse: 'We can't even get ten minutes to ourselves.'
- '[My mother] gets stroppy with me because I can't get there early enough in the morning, but I've got a baby to look after. My time is taken up with him early in the morning.'
- 'I find myself getting jealous because he puts so much time in on him. He irritates me and I can't get angry with anybody.'
- 'You stop being a wife to your husband because you are being a mother to your mother.'
- 'My husband lost so much of me. He lost a companion wife due to always having to attend to our daughter's needs. He lost a sexual partner because I was always so tired. I think he's marvellous to be still there.'
- 'It was almost a choice between looking after one member of the family [a boy with severe physical disability] or the others. My husband couldn't handle the situation and the others couldn't cope. I'm now separated and the family's now divided as a result of the circumstances.'

significant differences between relationship groups. More parents and to a lesser extent spouses reported increased compassion, love and closeness in the family since the onset of caregiving than adult offspring, other relatives or friends. At the same time, more parents and to a lesser extent adult offspring reported increased tension, conflict and resentment in the family than spouses or other relatives. Changes in the family environment varied also between men and women. Half the women perceived more tension (cf. a third of the men) and a quarter more resentment (cf. 15% of men).[5]

Family disagreements Carers were asked if there had been any disagreements about the care-recipient with anyone in their immediate family (Table 3.22, p. 272). Overall, 28% reported such disagreements, but proportionately more women than men, and twice the proportion of parents and adult offspring as spouses. Disputes were also more common when the care-recipient was young (39% of those caring for people under fifteen) and when the tension between the carer and care-recipient was high. The presence of family disagreements was also associated with higher negative affect.

Responses to an open-ended question about the issues in dispute were coded. Most fell into eight different categories, although many mentioned more than one thing. Of the 265 carers who responded, 28% mentioned issues around carers and level of care, 19% emotional issues, 14% professional treatment, 13% accommodation, 11% carers' time and dependence of recipient, 9% recipient's behaviour, and 8% money and property. The most commonly volunteered, *emotional issues* and *level of care*, encompassed a wide range of responses.

Emotional issues within the family tended to revolve around independence and interference. Many disputes arose when a care-recipient felt independence was jeopardised or when a carer felt undue interference was coming from other members of the family.

- 'The manner of care—people still have to keep their dignity.'
- 'Other people think he should be treated as a child. He *is* worthwhile.'
- 'Long-distance idealism causing conflict.'

The **level of care** category covered issues about who is going to do what, with whom, and when. Often some people thought of the recipient as being more dependent than others, and this was a cause of conflict.

- 'I wonder if I did too much in the beginning. Now I'm expected to do it.'
- 'Disagreements between [recipient's] sisters over which one is not helping.'

There were disagreements over *professional treatment* of recipients by doctors and hospitals, and over medication, for example whether ongoing drug therapy was effective, useful or necessary. Sometimes there was tension over denial of the recipient's condition by other relatives of the carer.

Disputes over *accommodation* often centred on whether the care-recipient should be in residential care.

- 'Some members want him to go into the aged hostel; others disagree.'
- 'Some people think I should not live where I live, think we should live closer to the city where there are more services.'

Another source of disagreement was the *time* given by, or demanded of, carers. Some carers were told they were doing too much, while others wanted help so that they could do less. Many carers would like a little more help from the rest of their families; often they feel effectively alone in the caregiving role while others could help.

The *care-recipient's behaviour*, with associated embarrassment and trouble, also caused disagreements:

- 'We all get very upset by [her] behaviour sometimes.'
- '[He] has an anxiety activity. [A male relative] did not understand how [his] behaviour affected him. He actually slammed the door on her son.'

Responses in the category *money/property* varied from 'finances' to 'family behaved like vultures and wanted to sell [my mother's] belongings'.

An '*other*' category included a variety of issues mentioned by too few carers to justify separate categories: for example, about the future, politics, food, 'teenage issues', points of law (separation and access), and drinking.

Despite the emphasis on the negative and stressful aspects of caregiving in the literature and despite the evidence from our study that as a group carers have significantly worse physical health and well-being than those with usual family responsibilities (see Chapter 5), carers overwhelmingly endorsed the positive aspects of caregiving, and most rejected its negative effects. Most carers, but particularly parents, confirmed the satisfaction, reassurance and confidence they received from caregiving. Some admitted to negative feelings about the recipient and to adverse effects of caregiving on their lives. While women were more apt than men to acknowledge *both* its positive and negative aspects, adult offspring in particular complained of lost social contacts. Most carers felt close to their relative, but half admitted to tension in the relationship. Parents were more likely to report high levels of both closeness and tension, and more difficulty in coping, particularly with emotional and behavioural problems as well as their own anxieties and fears.

In terms of the family environment, parents and spouses, who were generally living with the recipient and providing more personal

Many carers felt isolated and not understood by others, within and outside the family. In some cases other family members and friends could not cope with the condition, either denying it or feeling embarrassed about it, and would stay away. Social isolation felt worse when it stopped normal leisure activities.

- 'You seem to lose everybody, even your own family. They don't visit as often and things like that.'
- 'There's lots of things you don't tell people. Nobody outside knows what it's like—they *can't* know what it's like.'
- 'You think that you're the only one going through it and you feel different from everybody else.'
- 'You lose contact with all your friends because you just can't go anywhere, and your world gets so small.'
- 'We became very isolated because if someone came to visit I was really too busy to sit down with them, make a cup of tea—my wife needed so much attention.'
- 'I've become the world's biggest liar. I think of an excuse to leave [my mother]. It's the only way I can get out.'

care (see Chapter 7), tended to see the family as enriched by caregiving, bringing it closer together, arousing compassion and love. On the other hand, parents and adult offspring, who were generally younger and more likely to have competing roles, more often witnessed increased tension, resentment and conflict, disagreements over levels of care, emotional issues, professional treatment, residential care and so on.

Research evidence suggests that caregivers' subjective responses to caregiving have a stronger impact on their well-being than the tasks themselves.[6] Our own work confirms that it is often the carers' emotions and perceptions rather than the severity of the disability or the physical demands of caregiving that are more powerful predictors of diminished well-being. Clearly, there is complexity and ambivalence in the emotional aspects of caregiving, and with high-level involvement comes an intensity of emotions both benign—even edifying—and destructive. Be that as it may, our findings confirm the importance of including both positive and negative aspects in assessing the experience of caregiving. Indeed Braithwaite (1992) maintains that the tendency to focus on the negative may overload and possibly distress the respondent.

4

A COMPARISON OF ANGLO AND NON-ANGLO CARERS

As in Australia generally, Victoria has a large and diverse ethnic population, the result of successive Commonwealth immigration policies. In 1991 people born in non-English-speaking (NES) countries represented 17% of the Victorian population.[1] Many others belonged to families with an ethnic identity as second and third-generation offspring of migrants or through intermarriage.

With the increase of age-related disabilities among earlier immigrant groups,[2] and of other disabilities and conditions arising from occupational or settlement risks,[3] there is assumed to be a corresponding growth in caregiving by families of non-English-speaking background (NESB). Compared with Anglo-Australian carers, NESB carers are seen by some researchers to be particularly vulnerable to ill health and burden because of cultural expectations of family care, social isolation, the enduring impact of migration, and unequal access to supportive services in the community.[4]

To date there is little comprehensive or systematic information about non-Anglo caregiving in Victoria. Published findings of the latest national caregiving survey (ABS 1993) did not include information on ethnicity, and other available studies have tended to be small-scale (25–50 NESB carers) and to focus on women. Most are restricted in their treatment of disability type, kin relationship,[5] ethnic group,[6] locality or service type, and have limited dissemination.[7] All have ultimately recruited carers through organisations in contact with NESB clients/members, potentially biasing the sample. While these studies have provided some valuable information, it is not clear how representative their findings are for NESB carers overall, nor what they imply vis-à-vis other carers since studies have rarely included an Anglo-Australian comparison group.

Given these limitations, the VCP survey provides a unique overview of NESB care-dyads and an opportunity for comparison with Anglo-Australian dyads. Our aims were to explore the prevalence of NESB dyads in Victoria and to compare NESB and Anglo-Australian dyads in terms of:

- socio-demographic characteristics
- carers' experiences, health and well-being
- informal and formal supports.

Stage 1 participants included 236 NESB care-dyads, 23% of the total sample. They contained 182 dyads (18%) where the carer was born in a NES country (35 of whom were given the shortened interview through an interpreter). In most of this group the recipient was also described as of NES background, but a fifth were largely spouse and child recipients where intermarriage or upbringing in Australia could have weakened ethnic identification. In the remaining 54 dyads (5%) the care-recipient was of NES background and spoke a language other than English. Carers in this latter group consisted mainly of offspring and members of extended families caring for relatives over 60 years. They were included in our NESB definition in recognition of the impact the care-recipient's ethnic identity and language preference are likely to have on carers' experiences and care-dyads' use of services. The remaining 775 dyads in our total sample are referred to as Anglo-Australian, although strictly speaking some may have distant origins other than Anglo-Celtic.

In all, 40 different NES countries of origin were recorded for ethnic dyads (Table 4.1, p. 273). Most reflected the earlier migration patterns to Victoria from western, southern and central Europe, with smaller numbers of more recent migrants from the Middle East, Asia, South and Central America, and Africa. Seventy-four per cent of recipients had a preferred language other than English, covering 29 languages. As such, the NESB sample is inclusive but heterogeneous. Data on time since migration and English proficiency for either party were not collected, preventing analysis according to acculturation and language factors.

In addition to demographic and factual information such as time spent caring and service use, various measures were used to assess carers' health, well-being and reactions to the caregiving role, as well as the care-recipient's disability level, functional dependencies and behaviour problems.[8]

WHAT WE FOUND

Personal characteristics NESB carers' relationship to the care-recipient was of similar diversity to that of Anglo-Australian carers. The two groups were also comparable in carers' marital status, tertiary qualifications, workforce participation, household income and home-ownership (Table 4.2, p. 274). Recipients were comparable in sex and pensioner status.

In other respects the dyads differed (Table 4.3, p. 275). Although two-thirds of NESB carers were women, the NESB group included significantly more males than did the Anglo group. Age differences for both carer and recipient were evident: NESB carers were more likely to be under 35 and less likely to be over 50; fewer NESB care-recipients were under 20, and a greater proportion were in the range 21–60. NESB carers had less education, though the proportion with only primary schooling was small.

Three-quarters of NESB carers lived in metropolitan Melbourne, a significantly higher rate than for Anglo carers. While NESB and Anglo care-recipients were equally likely to be in institutional care or to be co-resident, overall there were differences in living arrangements: NESB recipients were less likely to live alone, and more often lived with their spouse or other relatives. About a quarter of each group expressed difficulty with their living arrangements.

Given the lower proportion of NESB women and the emphasis placed on them in the literature, it is interesting to note that NESB male and female carers did not differ in age, work status, relationship to the care-recipient, or living arrangements, though fewer men were married (69% cf. 83%).

Disability, dependency and care provided NESB care-recipients had diverse and multiple conditions, as with the Anglo group, the most common primary illnesses being stroke, dementia/memory loss, heart disease, rheumatic and musculoskeletal conditions. NESB carers reported their relative to be 'moderately' or 'severely' impaired in one or more of the following areas: physical mobility (59%), hearing/vision (42%), coordination (40%), long-term health (38%), communication (37%), intellectual (37%) and psychological (33%) functioning. Almost half said their relative was impaired both mentally and physically.

These patterns and the combined severity of cognitive and physical impairments matched those of Anglo care-recipients, with the exception of communication, in which half of NESB recipients compared with a third of Anglo recipients reported impairment, the difference no doubt reflecting language difficulties. The type and amount of assistance needed in personal activities such as bathing, dressing, toileting and moving about were similar between groups, but NESB care-recipients understandably required more assistance with instrumental activities like organising appointments or social services (65% cf. 53% needed a lot of help) and communicating with others (25% cf. 12% needed a lot of help), and significantly more NESB care-recipients needed financial support (20% cf. 8% needed a lot).

In rating a number of potentially difficult behaviours in their relatives, NESB carers reported more frequent depressive behaviours, such as being listless or depressed, than Anglo carers. No differences were found, however, in overall levels of aggressive and cognitive problems.

Hours a week spent caring were spread, with 35% NESB carers providing under ten, 21% 10–30, 16% 31–100 and 28% over 100. This pattern was virtually identical to Anglo carers, as was the duration of caregiving: 41% of both groups had provided care for six or more years. Anglo and NESB carers also gave a comparable amount of help to the recipient in mobility/personal care. Not surprisingly, NESB carers gave more help with the instrumental tasks reported above: communicating (39% cf. 21% all or most help); organising appointments or services (13% cf. 6% most help), and providing financial support (20% cf. 6% some/most help).[9] Among NESB carers, however, women spent more hours a week caring than men and gave more assistance with instrumental needs.

Carer health and well-being While a third of both carer groups reported major health problems in the preceding year, such as arthritis, heart, circulatory and respiratory illnesses, NESB carers rated their own health more poorly, a third compared to a quarter of Anglo carers rating it as fair or poor. NESB female carers also reported poorer health than males (37% cf. 22%).[10]

There were no differences between NESB and Anglo carers on individual or combined emotional well-being measures: feelings of overload, life satisfaction, anxiety and depression, and perceived social support. They were also similar in their reports of family conflict and closeness since caregiving began. About a quarter of each group said there had been more conflict and more resentment within the family, while a half reported more compassion, and two in five greater closeness. NESB carers thus reflected the diversity of emotional and family-relationship impacts reported by carers generally. NESB women carers, however, experienced greater overload and more anxiety/depression than NESB men, although they did not differ on life satisfaction or change in family relationships.

The caregiving role Carers were asked for their responses to a series of statements about their caregiving covering positive and negative feelings (see Table 3.17, p. 270). Overall, NESB and Anglo-Australian carers revealed similar feelings (Table 4.4, p. 276). A high proportion of both groups derived considerable satisfaction from the relationship and the care they gave, though such positive feelings were obviously balanced by more negative ones: over 80% said they would feel very guilty if they did not give the care and over two-thirds worried about what would happen to the recipient if something happened to *them*— an understandable feeling in the light of about half saying they cared 'because no one else can'. The level of negative feeling about the caregiving situation was lower overall, however, than that reported on satisfaction items.

Informal supports Given these concerns about the availability of alternative carers, carers' comments on the help they did receive is interesting. In the full interview carers were asked about help from other family members, friends or neighbours. Two-thirds of NESB carers identified one or two people who shared caring, though a fifth said nobody else helped them. Support most commonly came from siblings (23% of nominated helpers), children (21%), and partners (18%). To a lesser extent their parents (9%), other family members (16%) and non-relatives (13%) also helped.

For each helper identified, carers were asked to describe the type of help they gave. The responses covered thirteen different activities which were grouped into three main categories: household assistance, direct care of the recipient, and emotional support to the carer. Half the secondary carers gave practical help with household tasks such as shopping, home maintenance, financial management and child minding, while four in five helped by visiting, minding or transporting the care-recipient, and to a lesser extent helped with personal care. Only two-fifths of nominated helpers were reported by the carer to provide emotional support. Overall, 45% NESB carers received help from their informal network, with four or more activity areas.

Importantly, there were no significant differences between NESB and Anglo carers in the number of secondary carers reported or their relationship to the carer, nor in the number and range of activities this informal network undertook. Furthermore, both groups expressed a similar need for additional informal help. A third of NESB carers said they would like more help from other family members or friends, and of those with partners, one in six wanted more help from them. Those wanting more help typically wished for greater emotional support and for help through minding or visiting the care-recipient, activities that would give the carer a break and/or provide company for the recipient.

Community services Carers were asked whether they or the recipient used any of seven community services: respite care, general home help, personal-care home help, transport, community nursing, meals services and home maintenance. Excluding carers whose relative was in residential care, only a third (36%) of NESB care-dyads reported using *any one* of the services, a rate significantly lower than for Anglo carers (47%). Consistent with this difference, they used fewer services and reported less use of each individual service (Table 4.5, p. 276), but of those NESB carers who were using home or community services, most (85–100%) expressed satisfaction with each service.

Respite care Almost half the NESB carers had experienced a break of two or more days from caring in the past six months, although over a third reported it was more than two years. This pattern was very similar to that of Anglo carers, but NESB carers were less likely to have used formal respite services in the preceding twelve months. Of eleven NESB respite users, six had used longer-term respite, and only a few received in-home respite or centre day care. Ten were satisfied with the services they did use, a comparable rate to Anglo carers.

Over half of the NESB carers expressed a need for at least one of these respite and community services, the rate and pattern being similar to Anglo carers (Table 4.5, p. 276). The exceptions were a reported higher unmet need by NESB dyads for general home help and transport. Lack of information, recipients not wanting the service, and dissatisfaction with previous use were the main reasons given by NESB carers for unmet need for general home help. Half reported lack of information as the main reason for unmet need for home maintenance, transport, and help with personal care at home. Overall, these reasons mirrored those given by Anglo carers.

There was no difference between the groups in their need for formal respite, or in their pattern of preferred care, which was for longer-term respite (44% of carers' *reported need*) and overnight or weekend care away from home (27%) and at home (25%). But among all 218 carers identifying a need, NESB carers were more likely to report not knowing about respite care as a reason for not receiving it (53% cf. 29%). A quarter cited their relatives' dislike of formal respite as a barrier, although this rate did not differ significantly from Anglo carers.

Information about services There were marked differences between NESB and Anglo carers in their main sources of information about services (Table 4.6, p. 277). More NESB carers had not received information from any source; of those who had, it was more likely through GPs, a traditional source, and less likely through health/welfare professionals or government agencies. NESB carers were less satisfied overall than Anglo carers with information available (27% cf. 19% dissatisfied).

WHAT THE FINDINGS MEAN

These findings suggest that family caregiving is equally prevalent among NESB and Anglo or Australian-born people, since the percentage of overseas-born NESB carers among primary carers in this Victorian sample is proportional to NESB immigrants in the general population. But although the proportion of second-generation NESB immigrants is available, there is no identical population figure for comparison with our broader definition of NESB care-dyads (which includes intermarriage/affiliation and depends on ethnic identification of the recipient by the carer).

Ethnic carers revealed a striking diversity of caregiving roles and circumstances, as did their Anglo counterparts, encompassing a range of relationships, life-stages, working and living arrangements, and care responsibilities. Considered as a group, NESB carers were also socio-economically similar to Anglo carers, and apart from health impacts, results did not indicate that they experienced more hardship or burden than their Anglo counterparts. These findings are of interest, as little past research with NESB carers has been of a systematic, comparative nature.

In socio-demographic characteristics, the predominance of offspring among both NESB and Anglo carers indicates the strength of filial commitment to family care within the general community. But the lower age of ethnic carers and the greater number of care-recipients in the mid-adult age-group suggest an earlier adoption by NESB sons, daughters and others of the carer role. This age difference may reflect a greater need arising from the adverse effects of living and working conditions on adult immigrant health,[11] or it may reflect their assumption of responsibility and negotiation with the wider environment during the family's initial phase of settlement.[12] For example, the greater reported need for NESB carers to give help with communication, social services, finance and the like may be a continuation or compounding of earlier patterns developed through language, economic difficulties or isolation of the care-recipient after migration, rather than something occurring with the onset of disability or old age.

Such patterns of assistance may persist or be re-established despite changes in living arrangements. In contrast to the assumption of co-residency, NESB carers were just as likely as Anglo carers to live apart from the recipient, reflecting perhaps the 'modified extended' family structure reported by Rowland (1986:34) that arises with greater accommodation to the dominant culture norms.

An unexpected finding was the higher proportion of men among NESB than Anglo carers. Previous studies have emphasised a greater involvement of NESB women in caregiving,[13] although Legge and Westbrook (1991) had indicated some ethnic variation, with more Chinese sons assuming responsibility than Greek. Potentially, NESB males who saw themselves with a formal or instrumental role may have responded positively to our screening question of 'main *respon-sibility* in caring'. Our random recruitment procedure, our broad definition of caregiving, and the diversity of NESB groups included, perhaps allowed men to identify themselves more easily as carers. Previously, where male carers generally have been studied, they provide fewer hours and less 'hands-on' assistance than females,[14] but although our NESB males cared for fewer hours, they reported a similar involvement to NESB females in help with personal care and mobility, indicating more than a nominal caring role. This finding calls for greater attention by professionals to potential male carers within NESB families and for further research into gender and ethnic caregiving, such as variations between ethnic communities in attitude and division of care responsibilities, and between immigrants of differing length of residency and English-language proficiency.

Contrary to prior indications,[15] the objective care demands on NESB carers were very similar to those on Anglo carers. Our findings indicated the same diversity of conditions, type and severity of disability, physical dependencies and behaviour problems between NESB and Anglo care-recipients. Differences occurred only in depressive symptoms, a common problem among migrants,[16] and dependency levels in instrumental daily activities, both of which may reflect the migration process with its associated grief, isolation and language problems. Caregiving demands were also matched in terms of duration of care, hours per week, and the proportion of required assistance provided personally by the carer.

This last finding suggests that primary NESB and Anglo carers had similar amounts of support in caregiving, from formal or informal sources. Indeed, the commonly reported assumption that NESB carers have greater access to support from an extended family network[17] is challenged by our findings, there being no difference between the groups in the number of identified secondary carers, their relationship or patterns of assistance provided. Consistently, the perceived amount of informal social support and degree of family closeness were also similar between the two groups.

The majority of NESB and Anglo carers relied on a few secondary helpers, or received no assistance at all. Few of the helpers of either group were reported to provide emotional support, an area commonly identified by carers as their greatest need.[18] While this picture of the 'abandonment' of carers within ethnic communities is not as bleak as that painted by McCallum and Gelfand (1990), a considerable number of both NESB and Anglo carers wanted more help from partners, family and friends.

While substantial satisfaction flowed from caregiving, clearly many NESB and Anglo carers currently saw few alternatives to their providing care and felt their responsibility equally keenly, expressing marked anxiety and guilt at the possibility of relinquishing their role. These findings, together with the minority of both groups who reported resentment at the personal losses caregiving incurred, indicate the need for professionals and service providers to be alert to such issues and to empower carers to resolve them positively. In particular, they need to pay closer attention to the informal networks of NESB carers and to find ways to inform and encourage involvement by other family members about caregiving and carers' needs.

Given these similarities in caregiving experiences, it is not surprising that our results do not support the view that NESB carers are more burdened than Anglo carers, specifically regarding feelings of overload, life satisfaction, anxiety and depression, social support and family conflict. This contrasts with most previous Australian studies which have emphasised isolation, burden, distress, poor health and family conflict among ethnic carers.[19]

Physical health problems were equally prevalent in NESB and Anglo groups, though the former saw their health as significantly worse, a reliable indicator of long-term health status. This discrepancy in health ratings perhaps reflects different expectations, the older Anglo carer group accepting bad health as part of advancing age. The poorer physical health of NESB carers, a younger group overall, may be attributable not only to caregiving but also, as noted earlier, to adverse living and working conditions for immigrants generally. Further research in ethnic communities is needed to clarify the specific impact of caregiving on health, with particular attention being given to NESB women, who in this study reported worse health than males, and significantly greater overload, anxiety and depression.

Similarly, further action is desirable to enhance NESB carers' access to formal supports in the community, despite advances already made under recent ethnic policies.[20] Our findings indicate a lower use of respite, home and community-based services than Anglo dyads, overall and for individual services. This supports the message of low service use in previous NESB carer research[21] rather than recent indications of more equitable service use by NESB clients;[22] such government monitoring reports focus on frail or disabled NESB clients and provide little information about carers' use of services despite their being a specified target group.

Contrary to earlier reports, however, our comparative analysis would not suggest inequity in *access* to services, since the level of unmet need for respite and community services was generally comparable between NESB and Anglo carer groups. The exceptions were a greater need for general home help and transport, the latter perhaps indicative of transport difficulties generally among immigrants. Nonetheless, the unmet need for respite, home help, home maintenance and transport, identified by approximately a fifth of NESB carers, calls for access issues to be addressed, most probably employing different strategies from those applicable to Anglo carers.

The lack of information about services was highlighted by NESB carers as the main barrier to obtaining needed supports, followed by the recipient's dislike of formal services, particularly regarding respite and home help. Their stronger overall dissatisfaction with information available further underlines the presence of knowledge barriers. The recent publication of the Carers' Support Kit in ten community languages is thus an important advance in facilitating culturally relevant information on services, especially since three-quarters of our NESB care-recipients spoke languages other than English.

NESB carers' greater reliance on information from general practitioners, a frequently consulted profession yet one noted for their reluctance to make community referrals,[23] suggests the need to get local doctors to discuss the issues and make more referrals (see Chapter 12), and to diversify sources of information. The need for a variety of formats and approaches has been stressed by the national ethnic consultative body and others.[24] Recommendations include a range of multilingual information *formats* (e.g. written, audiovisual, personal—as in bilingual or access workers) and *approaches* (e.g. ethnic media campaigns, community development, cross-cultural education of mainstream service providers) to promote carer services. Such strategies involve not only information on specific programs but mean broader education about services for all family members, as well as exploring cultural attitudes towards formal support. These seem essential, given the disparity in acceptance of formal services within

NESB dyads found in this study, together with carers' feelings about their care commitment and expressed need for greater assistance from other family members.

While sizeable, our NESB sample is heterogeneous, perhaps masking the greater impact caregiving has on particular subgroups of NESB carers and difficulties in accessing services. Given the range of ethnic communities included in our survey, the small numbers for all but earlier immigrant groups and the lack of specific information on either language proficiency or date of migration, our analysis has been unable to distinguish the interplay of birthplace, settlement and acculturation factors in caregiving experiences. Further community-based research with larger numbers of carers from both recent and established immigrant communities is needed to explore systematically such differences within and between NESB groups. And, as noted above, comparisons with non-carers from within the same ethnic community, as well as socio-demographically comparable Anglo-Australian carers, are necessary to elucidate the distinctive aspects of ethnic caregiving and strategies to enhance carers' well-being.

PART II

THE IMPACT OF CAREGIVING

5

A COMPARISON WITH NON-CARERS

Existing research provides valuable information about certain sub-groups, for example those caring for dementia sufferers and the elderly, which is vital for practice and for providing services. But it is limited in representation and does not establish whether carers, as a group, are substantially different from other community groups, specifically in warranting government priority in allocating resources. The few previous comparisons with non-carers have been limited to a particular disability or age-group, and/or in the size and representativeness of the sample.[1]

To overcome these limitations, our survey included as a comparison a representative sample of 219 'non-carers' drawn at random from the same population as our carers. We assessed differences between carers and non-carers in five areas:

- self-reported physical health
- psychological well-being
- life satisfaction
- social support
- feelings of overload.[2]

Given the preponderance of women carers and the possibility that men and women may experience the role differently,[3] our comparison was limited to women. The comparison group was further restricted to those living with a partner, children or both; that is, women with usual household and/or parenting responsibilities. The aim was to obtain a comparison sample which highlighted differences emanating

Carers often feel constrained; their freedom and activities are limited and life is not as they had planned or imagined.

- 'We can't even go across the road to have a chat—you don't know what they might do, and you can't trust them.'
- An ageing couple whose deaf daughter also suffered from a physically disabling condition explained that 'she gets upset because we go out without her. We're not allowed to go away without her.'
- Such constriction brings feelings of resentment towards their relative: 'sometimes I resent her because we can't do things that we would like to do.'
- Some carers talked of resenting the loss of contact with friends and being unable to take a holiday.

from the *special* circumstances of caring for a person with a disability or long-term illness.

WHAT WE FOUND

The average age of carers (50) was significantly higher than for our non-carer sample (41). Hence in subsequent analyses carers and non-carers are compared within three age-ranges: under 40, 40–59, 60 and over, corresponding to broad life-stages. Within these age-ranges there were no significant differences between carers and non-carers in percentages who had completed secondary education, obtained tertiary qualifications or were Australian-born. Within each age-*group*, however, carers were less likely than non-carers to have partners: in those under 40 years, 75% of carers and 88% of non-carers had partners; the respective percentages were 82% and 94% for 40–59-year-olds, and 82% and 100% for the over-60s. Carers were also less likely to have paid work: 44% compared with 56% of those under 40, and 46% compared with 59% of those 40–59.[4]

In the 40–59 age-range, non-carers (75%) were more likely than carers (58%) to have dependent children in the home, and a greater number of children. But regardless of age or carer status, most women took sole responsibility for meal preparation, washing, ironing, and light and heavy housework. Carers more often than non-carers took responsibility for taking or driving people places: respectively, 74% of carers and 55% of non-carers in the under-40s, 63% and 42% in the 40–59-year-olds, and 52% and 26% in the over-60s. In the under-40s, carers more often than non-carers organised health and social services (86% cf. 74%), likewise in the over-60s. Similarly, managing finances was more commonly the main responsibility of carers than of non-carers in the 40–59 age-bracket (58% cf. 42%) and in the over-60s. Regardless of age, only a minority of women in each group was responsible for home repairs, but twice as many carers as non-carers had assumed this role: this difference was statistically significant in those 40 years and over.

We found that being a carer and not having full-time work were the significant predictors of having major health problems in the past year; age, marital status and number of children did not significantly contribute to this. Being older and being a carer were the significant predictors of using medication; here marital status, work status and number of children did not significantly contribute. Being a carer and being single significantly predicted a fair to poor health rating; age, work status and number of children did not significantly contribute (Table 5.1, p. 277).

While age-groups did not differ on life satisfaction, carers reported lower life satisfaction than non-carers, and partnered women higher life satisfaction than single (Table 5.2, p. 278). Partnered and single women did not differ on either positive or negative affect, but carers' positive affect ratings were lower and their negative affect higher than non-carers; and those 60 and over reported lower positive and negative affect than the younger age-groups, with those under 40 highest on negative affect. Carers felt less supported than non-carers,

Sleeping problems were common among carers of people with a disability. Many needed to attend to their relative many times during the night, while others found that the worry and emotional stress of caregiving disrupted their sleep. This often resulted in extreme fatigue and stress:

- 'We cannot continue the pace we are now. She is still only very young and my level of stress is getting higher and higher. All this is killing me.'

and single women less than women with partners. Carers reported less support than non-carers, but the difference was most marked in those under 40. Carers reported more overload than non-carers, and older age-groups reported less than younger.

In order of importance, the factors most salient in distinguishing carers from non-carers were:

- being older
- being single
- having responsibility for more household tasks
- feeling more overloaded
- having fewer children
- experiencing lower life satisfaction
- having less perceived social support
- having poorer self-rated health.

With the exception of self-rated health, each of these made a significant independent contribution to distinguishing carers from non-carers.[5]

WHAT THE FINDINGS MEAN

Using self-identification to recruit carers in a statewide random survey and not imposing arbitrary exclusion criteria resulted in an immensely diverse sample in terms of age, sex, relationship to care-recipient, time devoted to caregiving, and range of everyday activities for which help was given. Notwithstanding this diversity, which implies varying intensity of care, are there differences between women caring for people with disabilities and women in the general community with usual caregiving responsibilities?

Our findings, which are based on a large representative sample of carers crossing diagnostic boundaries and a representative sample of non-carers from the same population at the same time, add weight to the hypothesised association between caregiving and the poorer physical health of carers. Considering age, working status, marital status and number of children, being a carer was a significant predictor of medication use and the best predictor of major health problems in the past year and of a self-rating of health as fair or poor.[6]

On all measures of well-being as well as potentially intervening factors there were marked contrasts between carers and non-carers.

Regardless of age or marital status, we found less life satisfaction, less positive affect, more negative affect and greater overload among carers compared with non-carers. Among the young, carers reported more social isolation than non-carers.

Given the strength of our design and sample, these findings confirm the consistent association between caregiving and poorer emotional well-being reported in past work, based mostly on less extensive studies of carers from specific disability groups. For example, George and Gwyther (1986) found that, compared with random community samples, dementia carers reported significantly more stress, less life satisfaction, lower levels of affect balance and social participation. Pruchno and Potashnik (1989) compared the physical and mental health of spouse carers of partners with dementia with existing population norms and found that the carers were more depressed, had more symptoms of psychological distress and higher levels of negative affect. Breslau and colleagues (1986) reported significantly more depressive symptoms in mothers of children with disabilities than those in a geographically-based probability sample. Carpiniello and colleagues (1995) reported similar findings comparing parents of children with and without disabilities.[7]

In our study, together with some demographic characteristics, high overload, lower levels of perceived social support, diminished life satisfaction and poorer health rating were linked in differentiating carers from non-carers.

In spite of the fact that women in the comparison group were more likely to be caring for children and a greater number of children, overall they had less responsibility for household tasks. This was particularly notable in relation to less traditionally female tasks such as managing finances and repairs around the house, indicating a need for assistance for carers in these respects: differences were largely confined to the elderly and middle-aged.

To minimise the confounding effects of extraneous variables and allow a more focused comparison, the non-carers were limited to women with usual caregiving responsibilities, that is, women living with a partner, children or both. Carers tended to be older than non-carers and less likely to have a partner. The latter could well be due to the selection criteria for our comparison group, or it may be partly attributable to real differences between carers and non-carers. In Whittick's (1988) comparative study of mothers caring for children with disabilities and daughters caring for parents with dementia, over half the daughters were single. Could it be that single daughters are more likely to assume the responsibility of ageing parents? Brody and colleagues (1994) found that 'never married' and 'widowed' daughters provided more hours of care than married, remarried or divorced carers; moreover, 'never married' daughters were more often the sole carer. While similar findings are reported by Stoller (1983) and Kendig (1988), Jutras and Veilleux (1991a) reported little difference between the hours of care or 'global burden' of daughter carers with and without partners.

Irrespective of whether they were carers or not, women without partners expressed less satisfaction with their lives and more social isolation than those with partners; and elderly women were less likely to feel overloaded and anxious but more apt to be depressed than the young and middle-aged.

Carers of working age were less likely to be in paid employment than non-carers. This difference could be partly explained by the fact that caregiving commitments have meant that some carers have had to give up their job and others have been unable to take a job, but of those in paid employment, well over half found it a welcome relief, perhaps providing respite from their caregiving role as well as needed social support. Full-time employment, irrespective of age or carer status, was associated with fewer major health problems. Consistently, several researchers have found that flexibility at work can act as a buffer against role strain and have argued for the promotion of greater flexibility in the workplace[8] (see Chapter 8).

Undoubtedly, within carers there are subgroups who are more stressed than others. For example, Livingston and colleagues (1996), in a large representative sample of people 65 and over, reported an increased risk of psychological morbidity in carers of people with a psychiatric but not a physical condition, although only in comparisons with other adults living in the household, not with those living alone. In our study,[9] carers with multiple roles of work and parenting were more overloaded than those with fewer roles, and co-resident daughters reported more overload and less life satisfaction than non-resident daughters. However, there would also be particularly stressed subgroups within the non-carer population. We contend that the full range of carers is necessary to demonstrate broad differences between *carers in general* and *non-carers*. Many factors will influence levels of stress within both populations: here we have demonstrated, for policy purposes, differences in well-being between carers, *as a group*, and non-carers.

The poorer health status and emotional well-being of carers, in general, compared with non-carers, and the associations between overload (including greater responsibility for household tasks), diminished life satisfaction and perceived social support and health problems in carers, suggest that interventions of a practical kind are desirable. These may include working with general practitioners and other health professionals (see Chapter 12) to promote an awareness of the potentially deleterious effects that caregiving can have on the health and well-being of their patients and encouraging them to inform carers about community services and make referrals.

The problems of social isolation, anxiety (high negative affect) and depression (low positive affect) in carers point to a need for support beyond that of a practical kind: for example, links with the extended family, neighbours and community groups which call for community education about carers' needs and active participation by service providers to engage these informal supports; and assistance and encouragement to use respite care to enable carers to form and/or maintain friendships and recreational interests. For some carers membership of support organisations, individual or family counselling may be beneficial (see Chapters 10 and 13).

The conclusion from our comparison with non-carers is that in spite of their diversity and the range of their activities and experience, carers clearly differed from non-carers in physical health and emotional well-being. Illness was more common in the carers, particularly in those who felt exhausted and unable to cope with the demands on them and less supported by family and friends.

6

THE RELATIVE BURDEN OF
PHYSICAL AND MENTAL
DISABILITIES

With the increasing need to understand the stressors of family care-giving, and thereby develop and provide appropriate supports, various studies have attempted to identify the aspects of disability that are most emotionally burdensome to carers. Some argue that dealing with cognitive impairment and behavioural disturbance is more stressful than dealing with physical or functional disability.[1] In studies of dementia carers, behavioural and mood disturbance have been found to be closely associated with carer burden and distress[2] and predictive of depression.[3] Moreover, behaviour and mood disturbance in dementia patients is more highly correlated to carer burden than is physical disability in stroke patients;[4] indeed one study found no significant relationship between carer burden and level of physical disability in stroke patients.[5]

Comparing carers from distinct disability groups has been less conclusive. It was found that carers of those with physical disability, but not carers of the elderly with behavioural disability, had greater anxiety and depression and worse self-rated health.[6] A comparable study found no differences in carer burden.[7] Dementia carers have been found to have similar levels of burden or distress to those caring for physically-impaired stroke,[8] cardiac,[9] and cancer patients.[10]

Whether or not cognitive disability has been diagnosed as Alzheimer's disease or other dementia may also affect carer burden. Carers are less likely to interpret behaviour problems as 'misbehaviour or a result of some failure on their own part' when they have knowledge of dementia symptoms (Rabins 1985:81). As Alzheimer's

There was general agreement that 'you need to know what is going to happen, so you understand it better as it is happening'.

- A woman caring for her husband with Alzheimer's disease said: 'I saw a film about the parts of the brain which are affected, and what the results are. It really helped me, more than anything else, because I realised he can't help what he's doing, that he's not just doing this to be difficult.'

onset is 'commonly slow and insidious', diagnosis may be delayed, particularly if the person maintains a social facade (Levin et al. 1989:3).

In this chapter we have:

- compared the health, well-being and experience of carers of people with physical impairment and carers of those with intellectual impairment
- assessed the extent to which care-recipients' physical disability and other factors contribute to burden in carers of people with intellectual impairment
- explored the impact on carer well-being of a diagnosis of intellectual impairment, specifically undiagnosed memory loss as against Alzheimer's disease or other dementia.[11]

WHAT WE FOUND

From our total sample of 976 interviewees, we identified three sub-samples in carers of people 50 years and over.

- Group 1, *physical disabilities* (PD), comprised 186 carers reporting their relatives as being moderately or severely physically impaired but with no intellectual impairment.
- Group 2, *undiagnosed memory loss* (UML), comprised 182 carers who reported an intellectual impairment in their relatives that was described as memory loss or short-term memory loss, with no mention of Alzheimer's disease or dementia.
- Group 3, *dementia* (DEM), comprised 117 carers who reported intellectual impairment in their relatives that was described as Alzheimer's disease, dementia or senile dementia. Being mainly

elderly, most care-recipients in Groups 2 and 3 also had some physical impairment.

Carer characteristics Carers were mainly women, most of them married and not in paid employment. A third had completed second-ary education. They tended to be in the middle to older age-ranges, with over 70% aged between 35 and 64. A little over half were adult offspring (mostly daughters) caring for aged parents, a quarter spouses (mostly wives) caring for partners, and 21% for 'other' relatives or friends. Twenty-two per cent had been caring for more than ten years, 46% for three to nine years, and the remainder two years. Excluding those whose relatives were in residential care, almost a third had had no break at all or no break in over two years. In relationship to care-recipient, duration of care and time since having a break, there were no differences between the three groups.

Care-recipient characteristics, disabilities and behaviour problems While most care-recipients were women, there were proportionately more women in the DEM group (77%) than in the PD (68%) or UML (60%) groups. Higher proportions of DEM carers (93%) were aged over 70 than were UML (76%) or PD (77%) carers. Moreover, care-recipients with DEM (36%) were more likely to be living in residential care than those with PD (9%) or UML (11%); conversely, those with UML (56%) and PD (48%) tended to be living with their carers; the remainder in each group lived alone, with partners or another person.

Physical disability care-recipients were more physically disabled and less mentally disabled than the other groups (Table 6.1, p. 279). DEM care-recipients were higher on the severity of mental disability than UML recipients. The groups differed also on each behaviour-problem scale, the PD group reporting less cognitive, aggressive and depressive behaviour problems in their relatives than the other groups. Most notable was the higher frequency of cognitive behaviour problems in the DEM group.

Carer health and well-being In terms of self-rated health and various indices of emotional well-being, consistent differences between the groups favoured PD carers. While these carers were more likely to rate their health as excellent (27%) than the other groups (17–18%), DEM carers were more apt to rate it as fair or poor (36% cf. 19%

PD and 27% UML). And compared with both UML and DEM carers, PD carers reported higher life satisfaction and lower overload. Similarly, these carers expressed less negative affect, particularly in comparison with UML carers. But the groups did not differ on positive affect.

Physical aspects of the caregiving role Time spent caring did not differ between the groups, but excluding those in residential care, over half the DEM care-recipients were unable to be left alone compared with a quarter of UML and 13% of PD recipients. DEM carers reported higher ADL and IADL dependence and corresponding IADL care provision than did the other groups (Table 6.1). Similarly, UML carers reported both more IADL dependence and care provision than PD carers. The groups did not differ in the provision of ADL care.

Emotional aspects of the caregiving role PD carers were less likely than other groups to report anger and resentment, but UML carers

With the cognitive decline and personality changes of dementia and old age, carers of the elderly were often adjusting to the loss of a previously fulfilling or positive relationship with their relative.

- 'They are not the person that you have known as a child, so you are adjusting to having a stranger in your house.'
- 'It's terrible, it's soul-destroying, watching someone that you love go downhill.'
- 'Our relationship has changed. Before he got sick our marriage wasn't too close because he was away a lot and we grew apart. All of a sudden he got sick and we were thrown together . . . I had a terrible lot of resentment because just as we should be starting to enjoy life, I had to stay at home and look after him.'
- 'He's never asked me to do anything in all our 35 years of married life and now he finds that he's got to and that's the worst thing.'
- A man caring for his wife felt that 'if you're feeding them three times a day, and you're standing there for two hours every meal, you start getting very uptight yourself.'

expressed more resentment than PD and DEM carers; the groups did not differ in satisfaction. Concerning the quality of the relationship with their relatives, PD carers were more likely to rate their relationship as 'very close' (71%) than were UML (52%) and DEM (53%) carers, and the level of tension in that relationship as 'low' (62% cf. 41% UML and 49% DEM). Higher proportions of PD carers also reported it as 'very easy' to cope with their relatives' behaviour (36% cf. 6% UML and 3% DEM); conversely, fewer reported it as 'very difficult'. PD carers were less likely to report increasing conflict in the family after the onset of caregiving compared with the other groups. The groups did not differ on family closeness, but social support was higher for the PD carers than the DEM and UML carers.

Informal support Compared with the other groups, PD carers were less likely to report increasing conflict in the family after the onset of caregiving. The groups did not significantly differ on family closeness, but perceived social support was higher in the PD carers than the DEM and UML carers (Table 6.1, p. 279).

Formal support Use and need for assistance from formal services differed between the groups. Higher proportions of DEM carers (23%) had received counselling on their relatives' condition than UML (9%) or PD (7%) carers. Conversely, higher proportions of PD carers (44%) than UML (30%) and DEM (34%) carers had received home modifications in the past.

Excluding carers of those in residential care, DEM carers were more likely to both use (17% cf. 11% UML and 7% PD) and need respite care (47% cf. 27% UML and 19% PD). Although the groups did not differ on the proportions *getting* one or more of the six regular community services (general home help, specific home help, community nursing, meals, home maintenance and transport) fewer of the PD carers reported *needing* one or more of these services (34% cf. 49% UML and 47% DEM).

Predicting carer 'burden' and carer resentment Given the diminished well-being of carers of people with intellectual impairment and the *similarity* between the undiagnosed and diagnosed groups in this respect, we did an analysis to explore the importance of various factors in predicting a composite measure of burden (combined scores for negative affect, overload, life satisfaction and social support, with scores inverted on the positive dimensions) in the two groups.

Included in the analysis were *care-recipient* physical disabilities scale and mental disabilities scale, ADL and IADL dependence, aggressive, depressive and cognitive behaviour problems, *carer* anger and resentment, difficulty in coping with behaviour problems, closeness and tension in the relationship with the care-recipient, family conflict, recipient in residential care, and carer group (UML, DEM). In order of importance, carer resentment, followed by increased family conflict, depression in the care-recipient, close relationship and anger predicted burden; the other variables including care-recipient disability dropped from the equation (Table 6.2, p. 279).

Using the same set of predictors, with the addition of social support and excluding carer resentment, a further analysis was used to explore factors contributing to carer resentment. Low social support, anger, difficulty in coping with behaviour problems, being in the UML rather than the DEM group emerged in the significant equation predicting carer resentment; the remaining variables dropped from the equation (Table 6.2).

Living arrangements There is some evidence that co-resident carers are more stressed than those whose relative is living elsewhere or in residential care (Table 6.3, p. 280).[12] We therefore did an analysis to check whether differences in living arrangements might account for differences in well-being between the groups. We found that anger, social support, overload and negative affect did not differ with living arrangements, but that *regardless of carer group*, co-resident carers expressed both more satisfaction and more resentment than those looking after someone living alone, with another, or in residential care. These reported higher levels of positive affect and life satisfaction than co-resident carers.

Three groups of carers were delineated from a representative sample. In summary, PD carers clearly expressed a greater sense of well-being than those caring for people with intellectual disabilities, reporting better health, more life satisfaction and less overload and negative affect.[13]

WHAT THE FINDINGS MEAN

Our findings support the link established in caregiver studies of dementia between intellectual/behavioural impairment and carer burden and depression and provide insights into contributory factors.

With intellectually-impaired care-recipients there were more aggressive, depressive, forgetful and confused behaviours, and greater dependence in ADLs and IADLs. With their carers, not surprisingly, there were greater difficulties coping with these behaviours, more family conflict, less perceived support from family and friends, higher resentment about the negative effects of caregiving on their lives, and more anger and tension and less intimacy in relating to their relative. The latter findings support Livingston and colleagues' (1996:155) speculation that the increased prevalence of depression in carers of people with a psychiatric disorder 'may be mediated by the lack of a confiding relationship', especially as caring for physically-disabled people appeared to be protective.

> Cognitive problems often led to communication difficulties—forgetfulness and confusion, lack of concentration and lack of recognition.
>
> - Speaking of her husband, a carer said: 'Some days he doesn't know who I am and other days he can't put a sentence together, so I just can't talk to him.'
> - The 'continual questions' and 'repeated stories' caused further pressure for many carers: 'When it is repeated 60 times a day it drives you up the wall.'

Importantly, from our predictive analyses, neither variations in care-recipients' physical or mental disability nor the level of dependency in personal care contributed to the burden experienced by carers of people with intellectual impairment in our study. More salient were the complex emotional responses of the carers: in an atmosphere of increased family conflict they expressed resentment about the negative effects of caregiving on their lives, felt anger and guilt, but at the same time had a close bond with a recipient who was depressed, fearful and withdrawn.

Despite greater mental and behavioural disturbance and dependency in the DEM care-recipients compared with the UML, carers in the latter group were more resentful about the negative effects of caregiving. Main factors associated with burden in these two groups were resentment about the negative effects of caregiving and increased family conflict. The fact that major predictors of resentment were not having a diagnosis, linked with feeling little support from family and friends, anger (including embarrassment and guilt) and difficulty coping with behaviour problems, supports the importance of early diagnosis. The effects on carers of greater care-recipient impairment in the DEM group may be ameliorated by a diagnosis, perhaps bringing with it increased understanding, tolerance or resignation.

Dementia carers were also more likely to have received counselling on their relatives' condition, perhaps at the time of or following diagnosis. There is some evidence that counselling can reduce carer burden and depression.[14] Dementia carers were also more likely to have used respite care, and hence to have had a break from caregiving, than the UML carers. There is some evidence that use of respite care can also reduce carer burden.[15] It was also true that proportionately more dementia carers wanted more respite care, perhaps reflecting their greater awareness of respite care services. Clipp and George (1989) found that even knowing support is available gives carers relief. Although differences in the use of community services were few, they lend indirect support to the benefits of having a diagnosis. Moreover, unmet need for services was higher in carers of those with dementia (in our study including UML) than in those without.

Finally, negative feelings predictive of burden may be subject to intervention, which might provide:

- information about the condition to promote understanding of the relative's symptoms and behaviour
- counselling or therapy to deal with negative feelings, mobilise support and resolve conflict in the family
- training in how to deal with behaviour problems and physical aspects of caregiving
- community services including respite care to reduce overload.

In conclusion, caring for an elderly intellectually-impaired relative is more stressful than caring for one who is physically impaired but intellectually intact: carers of the latter consistently express a greater sense of well-being. In carers of people with intellectual impairment, while variations in the care-recipient's physical disability do not contribute to carer burden, having a diagnosis of dementia, despite greater mental impairment, appears to ameliorate resentment and, hence, burden.

7

CARERS' WELL-BEING: DIFFERENCES BETWEEN WOMEN AND MEN, ADULT OFFSPRING, PARENTS AND SPOUSES

Very few studies compare the experiences of men and women carers and those belonging to different relationship groups. Those that do, tend to divide into two groups: studies focusing on caring for a relative who is aged or has dementia, which may include wives, husbands, daughters and sons, and those focusing on caring for children with disabilities, which are mostly limited to parents. Among the first group, George and Gwyther (1986) in the United States in exploring the physical and mental health of those caring for memory-impaired older adults concluded that characteristics of the caregiving situation were more closely related to the carer's well-being than were the characteristics of the care-recipient's illness. They note that the carer–recipient relationship was important and that, even with age differences controlled, compared with adult offspring and more particularly 'other' carers, spouse carers expressed lower physical health, mental health, financial resources and social participation.[1]

Among the second group of studies, Beckman (1991) compared the perceptions of parents caring for young children with and without disabilities and ranging in age from 18 months to six years. Stress was significantly linked with parenting children with disabilities and lack of informal support. Mothers generally reported more stress than fathers. Romans-Clarkson and colleagues (1986), focusing on the mental health of parents of pre-school children, found that mothers of children with physical and mental disabilities had more psychiatric problems than did mothers of healthy children, but fathers in the

- Some carers treated themselves to simple privileges which gave them pleasure and respite from their day-to-day pressures: 'I sit in the Regency room in Georges and have a nice cup of coffee and whatever I fancy, and I'm waited on. There's a tablecloth on the table, silver, china and everything. I might sit there for about half an hour and then get up and walk out and go home. That's my outlet.'
- Several noted that doing 'little things to spoil yourself' can make the pressures more bearable.
- Others took up hobbies. A mother with a disabled son living at home said: 'I started a craft class and thoroughly enjoy that because I mix with someone different.'

two groups did not differ significantly. Similarly, in a comparison of mothers and fathers of children ranging from one to 30 years old with and without disabilities or chronic illness, Kazak (1987) found that only mothers of children with disabilities reported higher levels of stress than did comparison parents.[2]

Few studies have examined the differential impact of caring for parents or spouses or children with disabilities. Whittick (1988) compared levels of emotional distress in daughters caring for a co-resident parent with dementia, mothers caring for children with intellectual disabilities, and those caring for adult children similarly disabled. Daughters reported significantly higher distress than both groups of mothers. Allen and associates (1994) compared the burden experienced by spouse and parent carers of relatives with traumatic brain injury: while parents received more personal reward from caregiving than did spouses, they also reported greater burden.

In this chapter we explore the differential impact of the caregiving experience on the psychological and physical well-being of:

- male and female carers
- adult offspring, spouse and parent carers.[3]

Findings are limited to the three main groups of carers: adult offspring, spouses and parents. The small numbers of daughters and sons-in-law (43), siblings (23), grandchildren (19), 'other' relatives (51) and friends (33), together comprising 17% of the total sample, have been excluded.

- The mother of an adult son with physical and intellectual disability described her daily routine: 'You get him up, toilet him, dress him, get him ready for the centre, wait for the bus—and those bloody buses come any time between quarter to eight and half past nine so you're looking out all the time—and when he gets home at night it's the same thing. You can't go to bed until he's in bed. You've got to toilet, undress, shower and get him into bed before you can even think about getting into the shower yourself.'
- The father of a severely physically- and intellectually-disabled daughter commented: 'She has to be turned every two and a half hours otherwise she gets bedsores. Your day starts at five o'clock in the morning and doesn't finish until five o'clock the next morning.'

WHAT WE FOUND

Almost half the carers were adult offspring caring for parents, about a quarter were spouses caring for their partners, and a similar proportion were parents caring for children (Table 7.1, p. 281). Women predominated in each relationship group, but this was particularly the case in parent carers and less so in spouse carers. There were also significant age differences between the relationship groups, reflecting different life-stages: spouse carers tended to be older than other groups and parent carers younger. In view of their older age, spouse carers were also least likely to have paid work, with only 15% working compared with over half the adult offspring and a third of the parents. Men were more often working than women. While the sexes did not differ in marital status, almost a third of the adult offspring did not have a partner, compared with 18% of parents.

Men were mostly caring for female relatives (particularly husbands caring for wives and sons caring for mothers), whereas women were caring for almost as many male as female relatives. It follows that men were also caring mainly for older people, as were adult offspring and, to a lesser extent, spouses. In view of the greater longevity of women and the higher incidence of disability in male children, it is not surprising that over three-quarters of the adult offspring were caring for mothers and almost two-thirds of the parents were caring for sons.

The sexes did not differ on where the care-recipient lives, but there were predictable differences in relationship groups. Spouse carers generally lived with their partners; a few looked after a partner in residential care. Likewise parent carers had their children living with them. In contrast, almost as many adult offspring were caring for a parent who lived alone as with them.

There were no significant differences between male and female carers in their self-reported health status. Spouses (43%) were significantly more likely to report major health problems than were adult offspring (30%) or parent carers (26%). Likewise there was a higher use of medication in spouses (65% cf. 39% of adult offspring and parents). But differential rates of reported health problems were largely accounted for by differential work status, with working carers less likely to report such problems; and differential rates of medication use by differences in age, with carers 45 and over twice as likely to be using medication as those under 45. The relationship groups did not differ, however, in self-rated health regardless of sex or relationship, 22% of carers rated their health as excellent, 51% as good and 27% as fair or poor.[4]

EMOTIONAL WELL-BEING

We assessed the effects of carer sex and relationship and (given the significant age difference between relationship groups) carer age on all measures of emotional well-being. While men and women did not differ significantly in *life satisfaction or positive affect*, women were significantly higher on *negative affect, anxiety/depression*, and *overload* (Table 7.2, p. 282).[5] While the relationship groups did not differ in *life satisfaction, negative affect* or *anxiety/depression*, spouse carers were lower on *positive affect* and *overload* than parents and adult offspring. While the age-groups did not significantly differ on *anxiety/depression*, those over 60 reported significantly higher *life satisfaction* than those under 60, and increasing age was associated with less *positive affect*, less *negative affect*, and less *overload*.

Given the significant variation in living arrangements between the relationship groups, we assessed the effects of relationship independent of living arrangements by examining differences in co-resident carers only.[6] There were significant main effects for relationship on

77

life satisfaction, *negative affect*, and *overload*. Adult offspring expressed less *life satisfaction* than spouse or parent carers; spouse carers less *negative affect* than parents, and less *overload* than both parents and adult offspring (Table 7.3, p. 283).[7]

SOCIAL SUPPORT AND FAMILY ENVIRONMENT

We also assessed the effects of gender, relationship and carer age on perceived *social support* and aspects of the family environment. While perceived family *closeness* did not differentiate between men and women or between age-groups, parents and spouses reported more *closeness* in their family than did adult offspring. Moreover, family *conflict* was higher in women than in men, and in adult offspring and parents than in spouses (Table 7.2, p. 282).

When analyses were limited to co-resident carers, the significant relationship effects on *family closeness* and *family conflict* were confirmed. No significant effect on perceived *social support* was observed (Table 7.3, p. 283).

EMOTIONAL ASPECTS OF THE CAREGIVING ROLE

Women reported more *anger* than men did; parents reported more *satisfaction* than spouses, who reported more than adult offspring; and younger and older carers reported more satisfaction than middle-aged (Table 7.2). However, men and women did not differ in role satisfaction or resentment; parents, adult offspring and spouses did not differ in role anger or resentment; and anger and resentment did not vary with age-group.

Analyses limited to co-resident carers confirmed the significant relationship effect on role *satisfaction*, with parents significantly higher than spouses, who were in turn significantly higher than adult offspring. There was also a significant relationship effect on resentment, with adult offspring expressing more resentment than spouses, who expressed more than parents (Table 7.3).

CARE-RECIPIENTS' DISABILITIES AND DEPENDENCIES

Men and women did not differ significantly in relation to the severity of their relative's *mental* or *physical* disabilities. Nor did they differ in help provided with activities of daily living. But women gave more help with *instrumental* activities than men did. Spouse and adult

Many carers need emotional outlets for their frustration and sadness: 'You need to get it out of your system', they explained, suggesting strategies of 'screaming and yelling', 'going off crook at someone', or 'blaspheming to myself'. Several felt that 'just having someone who will listen' can release the tension.

- One mother said: 'I need an outlet and my outlet is music and exercise. I find that I do switch off, I have to switch off, but it has taken a long time to get over that guilty feeling. Now I am able to cry and scream and not feel too bad afterwards.'

In contrast, some try to cope by denying the strain:

- 'I prefer to hold it all in—it's the ostrich approach.'
- 'I don't let go—I bottle things up and the blood pressure goes up.'
- One mother of a 4-year-old with severe disabilities remarked, 'If I could yell out I might be a lot better off.'

offspring reported greater *physical disability* in their relatives than parents did, whereas parents reported more *mental disabilities* than spouses, who reported more than adult offspring. While spouses and parents provided more ADL assistance than adult offspring, parents provided more IADL assistance than spouses and adult offspring (Table 7.4, p. 284).

While there were no significant differences between carer age-groups in recipients' mental disability, or help with ADLs or IADLs, carers under 45 reported lower physical disability in their recipients than those 45 and over.

Analyses limited to co-resident carers confirmed the significant relationship effects on *physical* and *mental disabilities* and on IADLs (Table 7.3).

BEHAVIOUR PROBLEMS

Another common feature of caring for a relative with a disability or long-term illness is dealing with difficult behaviours. Women reported more *aggressive* and *cognitive* behaviour problems. Likewise, parents reported more *aggressive* behaviour in their relatives, and together with adult offspring, more *cognitive* behaviour problems. On the other hand, spouse and adult offspring carers reported more *depressive* behaviours in their relatives than parents. While there were no significant carer age effects on *depressive* or *cognitive* behaviour problems, young carers reported more *aggressive* problems in their recipients than middle-aged and old carers (Table 7.4).

Analyses limited to co-resident carers confirmed the significant effects of relationship on *aggressive*, *depressive*, and *cognitive* behaviour problems (Table 7.3).

QUALITY OF RELATIONSHIP WITH CARE-RECIPIENT

Carers were asked about the closeness of and degree of tension in their relationship with their relative. Irrespective of sex or relationship, two-thirds of the carers felt very close to their relative, but around twice the proportion of parent carers (26%) as adult offspring (13%) or spouses (14%) indicated that the tension in the relationship was great.[8] Degree of tension was unrelated to living arrangements, carer age, partner or work status.

Carers were also asked about help received from family and friends. Irrespective of sex or relationship, most carers (84%) received some informal assistance, but almost twice the proportion of adult offspring and parent carers (38%) as spouses (20%) expressed the need for more help.[9] Need for informal help was unrelated to living arrangements or carer age.

EFFECTS ON EMPLOYMENT

Carers were divided into four groups on the basis of reported effects of caregiving on work status. Of the total, 26% reported at least one adverse effect on their work such as working fewer hours or refusing promotion and were labelled *affected workers*; 12% were working with no reported adverse effects (*unaffected workers*); 36% were not working, but did not attribute this to caregiving (*traditional non-worker/retired*); and 27% were unable to work or had resigned because of caregiving (*excluded non-workers*).

As there were both sex and relationship differences in work effects, relationship differences are presented separately for women and men (Table 7.5, p. 285). Of women carers, more than half the wives, compared with under a third of mothers and daughters, were *traditional non-workers or retired*; over a third of wives and mothers, compared with a fifth of daughters, had quit work or were unable to work; compared with wives, daughters and mothers were more often *affected workers*; and daughters were more often *unaffected workers* than both mothers and the handful of wives who fell in this category. Of the men, husbands were most likely to be retired or to have quit work, fathers were more often affected workers, and sons affected or unaffected workers. Marital status did not differentiate between the work effect groups; and significant carer age differences disappeared when the sample was limited to those of workforce age.

FINANCIAL EFFECTS

Carers were divided into three groups on the basis of adverse financial effects of caregiving (loss of income or extra expenses) on their financial situation (see Chapter 8). Of the total, 52% reported no adverse effects (*No effect*); 20% adverse effects but no difficulty in meeting living expenses (*Effect, no difficulty*); and 28% adverse effects and difficulty meeting living expenses (*Effect, difficulty*). While there were no significant differences based on carer sex, work or marital status, relationship and age-groups differed in reported financial effects.

Within each age-group most adult offspring reported no adverse effects and in those aged 60 and over a majority of parents also reported no adverse effects. In those under 45, most of the spouses and half the parents reported adverse effects and difficulty in meeting living costs. In those 45–59 years, almost half the spouse and parent carers had difficulty compared with a small minority of adult offspring. In those 60 and over, spouse carers were more likely than others to report adverse effects *without* difficulty in meeting living costs (Table 7.6, p. 285).

WHAT THE FINDINGS MEAN

Sex differences The caregiving role in families has been assigned traditionally to women.[10] In our study, women felt more overloaded, less able to cope with the demands on them, and more angry about the person they were looking after. They saw themselves as having to deal with more aggressive, depressive and cognitive behaviour problems and as providing more assistance with instrumental activities of daily living. More anxiety and depression in women, compared with men, is an understandable corollary. In their linear structural modelling of caregiver burden in spouse and adult offspring caring for the elderly, Miller, McFall and Montgomery (1991:517) found that women carers reported higher stress and personal and interpersonal burden. Since these effects were mainly direct, the authors speculated that 'gender socialisation and role attributes may be more important than attributes of the caregiving situation'. Likewise, Hinrichsen (1991) reported a significant association between being female and greater caregiver burden and relationship strain in a study of spouse and adult offspring carers of depressed elderly. Indeed, irrespective of disability, age of recipient, carer–recipient relationship or measure of burden/psychological distress, much past research has indicated that women carers experience significantly more distress than do men.[11]

Relationship differences Although her study did not include parent carers, Cantor's concept of centrality, both kinship and functional, seems particularly pertinent to our findings on relationship groups. In her study of caring for the elderly, she found that the adverse effects of caring were greatest among co-resident spouses, followed by adult offspring, other relatives and friends. She argued that emotional strain seemed clearly linked to 'the closeness of the kinship bond and the availability of the caregiver for continual involvement' (Cantor 1983:601). She also reported a negative correlation between carers feeling close to the care-recipient and being able to get along well. Strain was associated with women, and worry over the caregiving situation. Using a measure of the importance of familism, she found that feelings of 'responsibility for and involvement in the family' and perceiving that as a positive value were important in predicting caregiver strain.

Like Cantor's spouse carers, both parents and spouses in our study were high in terms of centrality of kinship and function. They were caring within their family of procreation and, unlike adult offspring, were mostly co-resident. Compared with adult offspring, both groups reported more closeness in the family and more role satisfaction. This satisfaction was particularly strong in parents, who also reported more involvement in instrumental care, more family conflict and more tension in their relationship with the care-recipient. With this greater involvement of parents and spouses came increased financial difficulties through added expenses or loss of income, particularly in the younger age-groups.

Even though spouse carers reported more ill health in themselves than did other relationship groups and, with adult offspring, were caring for relatives with greater physical disability and more depressive behaviours, the response of parents—both positive and negative— seemed more intense. Of course there was a close correspondence between relationship and age-groups. That this intensity was related to a different life-stage was also borne out by other findings: specifically, overload and negative affect as well as satisfaction with the caregiving role were more common in younger carers. Notably, parents, and young carers generally, were also caring for people with a greater mental disability and concomitant aggressive behaviours.

In contrast with parents and spouses, adult offspring *as a group* appeared lower in centrality of kinship and function. However, in a more detailed study focusing on the daughter carers in our sample,[12] it is clear that there is a diversity of centrality in adult offspring. If daughters lived with their relative, compared with other daughter groups they provided more hours of care and were less likely to have a partner or responsibilities to a family of their own. Consistent with Harper and Lund (1990), Murphy and colleagues (1997) found that co-resident daughters were higher on overload and reported more resentment and less life satisfaction than non-resident daughters.

The comparisons between relationship groups presented in this chapter, limited to co-resident carers, indicate that co-resident daughter carers were similar to spouse and parent carers in centrality of kinship and function, but compared with spouse and parent carers expressed less life satisfaction and more resentment about the negative effects of caring on their lives. Whittick's (1988) daughter carers, who were significantly higher on a measure of psychological distress than mothers caring for children with intellectual disabilities, were all co-resident and over half had no partner. Brody and colleagues (1992) found that having a partner was the only factor significantly associated with enhanced life satisfaction and perceived social support.

Being in paid employment was clearly protective, being associated with fewer major health problems and, we have found, with higher life satisfaction and less resentment. Of course, with multiple roles, working carers have also reported higher overload. These findings agree with past research, associating work on the one hand, with burden, given the demands of multiple roles,[13] and on the other, with beneficial effects, for example, in providing respite.[14] Among women, mothers had more often relinquished their work role, while daughters had more often maintained their paid employment, with the greater likelihood of conflict in roles.

Given the traditional sexual division of labour assigning women the primary responsibility for caring for those who cannot take care of themselves, it is not surprising that our carers were predominantly women and that women were more adversely affected than their male counterparts in emotional well-being and employment opportunities.

At a community level, education is needed to promote the social value of caregiving and an awareness of the demands and impacts of the caring role. A greater emphasis on the importance of sharing special care responsibilities within families is needed to challenge current gender stereotypes,[15] to ameliorate the isolation of many high-intensity carers, to enhance options, provide emotional support and reduce the burden of care.

Some carers stressed the intensity of reaction to the birth of a child with a disability:

- 'You are angry and grieving and terrified of the unknown.'
- 'You are denying it. You don't want it. You feel that you don't deserve it.'

For many parents, these feelings did not dissipate. Throughout the child's life, at health centres or school entry, they were reminded again and again of their child's deficiencies:

- 'The comparison with other children is very hard. You never get over it. It's just reliving a tragedy.'

In depressed moments these sentiments can lead to wishing for the problems and suffering to end:

- 'Sometimes you wish them dead and it's the truth.'
- 'I can still say I wish he had never been born. I was unable to get the pregnancy terminated . . . maybe it would have been better if he had died that night.'

Community education of doctors, health professionals and service providers is particularly desirable given their key role in carers' access to practical support. A better appreciation of the potential distress experienced by carers with high-intensity roles and close kinship bonds is crucial for more timely discussion and mobilisation of supports.

The toll of caring on mothers, younger wives and co-resident daughters especially suggests the need for programs which reduce the intensity of care and/or help carers to deal with its emotional concomitants. Respite care is seen by many high-intensity carers as the most important service here (see Chapter 10).[16] Information about various respite options, and the availability of affordable, reliable and flexible programs which can manage behaviour problems, appear to be high priorities in enhancing carer well-being, especially for parent carers. Furthermore, for carers to stay in the workforce more permanent day-care arrangements would be needed than current respite options provide.

Complementing respite and day care with other services may also be of benefit to high-intensity carers. These would include relief from caregiving tasks (such as escorting or personal care) and support in coping with the recipient or their role through information lines, educational programs (e.g. managing difficult behaviours, problem-solving skills), support groups (providing both information and emotional support) and where appropriate, family or individual counselling. For some carers, especially parents, desired services may be those directed towards their dependent relative, providing social contact, employment and recreation.[17]

Clearly, there is a need for more flexible employment arrangements to reduce work conflict and give both women and men greater options in combining paid employment with caregiving. For women especially, carer-sensitive policies are needed to help maintain job skills and workforce participation (with its associated long-term financial security), and to create an employment context in which men can participate more equitably in caregiving.

Given the range of caregiving situations (relationship, life-stage, disability type, employment status) a diversity of services is needed to accommodate individual needs, either through direct provision by the health and social services sector or by subsidy of private services.

8

THE IMPACT ON CARERS' EMPLOYMENT AND FINANCES

Some people found paid employment a way to get respite from caregiving: 'It has helped me to go out working. I feel I need to have somewhere I can go independently and at work I can close the door on everything.' But the constancy of caregiving and the lack of respite facilities precluded that option for some.

The adverse financial impacts of caregiving have been frequently raised and reported in the literature across a variety of caregiving situations.[1] Findings on the proportion of carers who experience financial strain and its extent, differ depending on the focus of the study: that is, expenditure directly related to care (e.g. community care, medical or residential services, household equipment), current indirect costs (e.g. income forgone, relocation expenses and damage to property) or, especially for women carers, the lifetime opportunity costs of reduced participation in the workforce.

Financial hardship can affect carers' emotional well-being and reduce the capacity to buy services and other practical items which help in caregiving, as well as the social, therapeutic and recreational resources which enhance the quality of life of the carer, care-recipient and other family members.[2]

Federal Government policies have tried to help carers financially in the ongoing care of their dependent relatives. Health care coverage through Medicare, public hospital treatment and pharmaceutical listings reduce the medical costs associated with caring for someone with a long-term illness or disability, and there are additional concessions for pensioners. Direct subsidy of nursing homes and approval of private health cover rebates also make residential and medical care more affordable. The taxation system offers limited relief through rebates allowable for care of a frail parent, invalid relative or dependent spouse, and for medical expenses where defined conditions and income thresholds are met.

Among the programs specifically developed to support carers, various financial entitlements have also been provided including the Carers' Pension (CP), the Domiciliary Nursing Care Benefit (DNCB) and the Child Disability Allowance (CDA). The CP is an income-support measure aimed at 'high-intensity' carers of people over sixteen years where both parties have limited means. The DNCB provides an allowance to co-resident carers of people over sixteen whose illness or disability would otherwise place them in a nursing home. Similarly, the CDA is a payment to co-resident parent carers of chronically ill or disabled children and young people. Together they complement other existing income security measures (such as the Aged, Invalid or Sole Parent pensions) which some carers may have received. But Australian studies indicate that few carers have taken up these entitlements. The 1993 national survey of disability, ageing and carers (ABS 1993) reported that only 7.4% of carers received a carers'/wives' pension, 2.2% the DNCB, and 4.3% the CDA. The adequacy of these various measures and options has thus been the subject of recent debate.

One of the many issues raised is the question of whether carers' current and long-term financial needs are best addressed by restructuring pensions and benefits or, particularly for women, by other ways of offsetting adverse effects of caregiving on their working life, and hence on their financial resources. Increasingly more mid-life women are in paid work,[3] and these working women are as likely as their non-working counterparts to become carers for elderly relatives.[4]

Because of the demands of caregiving, working carers sometimes have to reduce their working hours, use various leave entitlements, or take unpaid leave. They may also have to take less responsible jobs or miss training or opportunities for promotion.[5] Such strains can make people consider quitting their job. Some eventually resign to care full-time, especially where there have been frequent work adjustments.[6] Thus, for some, the point comes where caregiving is given precedence over employment. But this traditional view that they do, has recently been challenged by Moen and colleagues (1994), who found that women with both caregiving and work roles are more likely over a lifetime to cease caregiving than to leave their jobs, reflecting the growing economic and social significance of paid work in women's lives.

A number of researchers have explored the factors related to the decisions and adjustments carers make in trying to balance their work and caregiving roles: carers' gender and age, their education and occupation, their relationship to the care-recipient, the nature of the care-recipient's disability and amount of care required, as well as the availability of secondary help. Consistently, women have been found to experience greater conflict between caregiving and paid work than men, more often making work adjustments or quitting the workforce.[7] Differential impacts on work adjustments and resignation have also been reported according to carers' educational and/or occupational level.[8]

Compared with other relationship groups, spouse carers have been found to be relatively more affected by the competing demands of work and caregiving, though few studies have included a full range of relationship groups, being mainly focused on the care of the elderly.[9] Similarly, in several studies greater adverse effects emerged in people whose caregiving was very demanding, either because of the nature of the recipient's disability or need for supervision or the hours of care required.[10] As well as this, the availability of secondary help, formal or informal, has been found to influence whether a carer makes work adjustments or quits.[11]

Findings on the effects of work on caregivers' emotional health have been inconsistent. Several studies have shown extra strain and lower well-being among employed carers,[12] while others have reported work as a source of respite, resources and enhanced competency.[13] Some more detailed studies have suggested that only where increased work pressures and conflict between the two roles exist (e.g. the carer has to reduce hours, take unpaid leave, or be absent from work) do employed carers experience greater emotional distress and overload.[14] Furthermore, with a longer life-course perspective, Moen and colleagues (1994) found that for women who had ever been caregivers, paid work brought enhanced life satisfaction, mastery and self-esteem.

Such findings suggest that carers need viable choices across their lifespan about their preferred combination of work and caregiving.

WHAT WE FOUND

EMPLOYMENT STATUS AND IMPACTS OF CAREGIVING ON WORK

Considering the *employment status* of the full sample of carers, almost two-thirds (62%) were not in the paid workforce, 23% were in full-time employment, and 15% worked part-time. Taking only those of workforce age (800 carers under 65), these figures adjust to 54% not in the workforce, 28% working full-time and 18% working part-time. Compared with the non-carer sample of workforce age, women carers showed a significantly different pattern. They were more likely not to be in paid employment (59% cf. 44%), and where employed were less likely to be working full-time (20% cf. 29%); part-time rates were more comparable (21% cf. 27%).[15]

All carers were asked about the impact of their caregiving on work. Of the 601 *not in paid work*, 17% reported having to give up work because of their caregiving, and 34% felt currently unable to take a job. These figures understandably were slightly higher for the 430 carers of workforce age (21% and 40%). With an overlap between these two responses, a total of 46% of non-working carers of workforce age reported that caregiving prevented them from taking paid work. A minority (16%) were currently looking for work.

Although work was a source of relief and other interest for over half of all 375 carers *in paid employment*, it was also for many a source of competing pressures. Over half worried about their relative while they were at work, and almost a third reported that their caregiving responsibilities meant repeated interruptions at work, having less energy for work, and having to work fewer hours. For a fifth, caregiving also meant having to take periods of unpaid leave, and for over one in ten carers, settling for a less responsible job, refusing promotion, working from home or changing jobs. In total, three-quarters (77%) of those in employment reported that caregiving adversely affected their work situation in one way or another.

On the basis of these reported effects, the sample can be divided into four groups outlined in Chapter 7:

- 9% were working without any negative effects (*unaffected workers*)
- 30% reported an adverse impact on at least one aspect of their current job (*affected workers*)
- 24% suffered detrimental effects to their work status (having to quit or not take work—*excluded non-workers*)
- 37% were not working for reasons other than caregiving (perhaps because of retirement, general family commitments, unemployment—*traditional or other non-workers*).

These groups constitute an 'overall work impact' variable.

DIFFERENTIAL IMPACTS OF CAREGIVING ON EMPLOYMENT

Given the diversity of carers surveyed, we explored whether the effects of caregiving on work were experienced differentially among carers, in particular according to their gender, relationship to the care-recipient, and the nature of the recipient's disability.

Perhaps not unexpectedly, there was a *sex difference* in employment status, with male carers being more likely than women to work full-time when in paid employment (Table 8.1, p. 286). Consistent with this, employed women were more likely to have had to adjust their work schedules to accommodate caregiving—reducing the hours worked or level of responsibility held, taking unpaid leave, and changing jobs. There were no sex differences in day-to-day impacts such as interruptions at work, loss of energy and worry about their relative while at work, though women carers more often found work a source of relief than men.

Considering the effect of caregiving on workforce participation, among 430 *non-employed carers of workforce age* there was no sex difference in having had to quit work or being unable to work. Nevertheless, women were more likely than men to report being out of the workforce for one or other of these reasons. Overall, for *all carers*, men were more likely to belong to the unaffected worker group than women, and less likely to have been excluded from the workforce because of their caregiving.

Consistent with their older age, spouse carers were less likely to be in paid employment than other groups (Table 8.1). Considering therefore the impact of caregiving on workforce participation for 430 *non-employed carers of working age*, carers with a less central relationship to the care-recipient (i.e. 'other' carers) were less likely to report adverse effects: proportionally fewer had had to quit work, especially compared with spouse carers, or were unable to take a job, especially in contrast to parent carers. For one or other of these reasons, parent and spouse carers were most likely to be excluded from the workforce by their caregiving, which is consistent with the greater exclusion reported also by co-resident carers. Compared with carers of people who lived alone or in another household, and to a lesser extent in residential care, co-resident carers were more likely to indicate having quit and/or being unable to take a job (57% cf 26% alone, 16% other household, and 35% residential care).

Of all 375 *employed carers*, parents were the group most likely to report that caregiving restricted their work opportunities. Thus significantly more parents, compared with adult offspring, spouse and other carers, reported having to work fewer hours or take an unpaid or less responsible job. And parents along with spouse carers were more likely to have refused promotion and changed jobs to accommodate caregiving.

These latter adverse effects experienced by parent carers are consistent with and reinforced by similar work adjustments reported by carers of people under 21. Compared with carers of other age-groups, proportionally more carers of children and young people reported having to work fewer hours, take unpaid leave, take a less responsible job, refuse promotion, or change jobs. Given the positive association between duration of care and parent-carer status (see Chapter 7), the work adjustments required by parents may also reflect their longer caregiving career. In particular, carers of ten or more years were more likely to report adverse impacts on promotion, level of responsibility and the need to change jobs.

Regarding the day-to-day impacts of caregiving on work, such as reduced energy, interruptions and the like, no differences were found between the relationship groups or on other characteristics. Overall, the working lives of adult offspring and other carers appeared least adversely affected, yet these two groups were less likely to see work as a source of relief than parent and spouse carers, perhaps reflecting their less intense caregiving role.

Finally, considering *all carers* on the combined work impact variable, there were significant differences between the relationship groups. Parent carers were more likely to be excluded non-workers, while spouse carers were over-represented in both the excluded and traditional non-worker groupings. In contrast, adult offspring were more likely to fall into the affected worker category, whereas other carers were more likely to be unaffected workers.

We were also interested to explore the impact on work of the *nature of the care-recipient's disability* (Table 8.2, p. 287). Using our combined disability variable which covers both severity and type of impairment, we found that carers of a relative with moderate to severe mental *and* physical disability were less likely to be in full-time employment than those caring for other disability groups. Of carers *in paid employment*, those looking after a relative with both mental and physical disabilities were more likely than others to report having had to make adjustments to their working life, especially to hours and level of responsibility. This same group of carers also claimed greater negative impacts on their work—interruptions, worry about their relative and having less energy for the job. Despite this, they were more likely to find work a source of relief and outside interest than carers of other disability groups. In addition, carers of people with both mental and physical disabilities were more likely to report adverse impacts of caregiving on their workforce participation. Taking *non-employed carers of workforce age*, proportionally more of these carers had needed to quit work and/or were unable to take a job because of caregiving, particularly compared with carers of people with minor or mainly physical disabilities.

Not surprisingly, then, differences in the overall work impact of caregiving were evident on the basis of the recipient's disability type. For the full sample, where recipients had both types of disability, their carers were more likely to be excluded from the workforce and least likely to belong to the unaffected worker group. In contrast, carers of people with minor or mainly physical disabilities were more likely to continue working unaffected by caregiving and least likely to fall into the excluded group.

Carers reporting adverse effects (namely affected and excluded workers) revealed poorer *emotional health* on several well-being measures. Both groups reported greater negative affect and feelings of overload than unaffected workers and traditional non-workers/retired, as well as lower well-being on the combined index (Table 8.3, p. 287). Additionally, the excluded group indicated significantly lower life satisfaction than the traditional non-workers and unaffected workers, and lower social support than all other groups. In contrast, the unaffected workers scored higher on both measures compared with all other groups. Affected workers did, however, report greater positive affect than excluded workers and traditional non-workers, suggesting some buffering by employment against carer depression despite the conflicts experienced.

CARERS' PREFERENCES ON PARTICIPATION IN THE WORKFORCE

Given the association found between adverse impacts on work and well-being and carers' financial situation (see below), information on carers' employment preferences was sought at the Stage 3 interview. Carers under 65 whose relative lived in the community were asked their preferences about working, about what assistance was required to let them enter or re-enter the workforce, either while caregiving or on stopping it. Additionally, for those in paid employment, factors which have enabled them to combine caregiving and paid work were explored. It should be noted that carers in full-time employment were not asked whether they wanted to work less or stop working.

Figure 8.1 presents a profile of the sample of carers in terms of current work status and desired increases in workforce participation, showing within-group percentages for each subgroup (shown in boxes) as well as overall percentages for the total sample (shown in italics below boxes). Of the sample of 274 carers, almost half (47%) were currently in paid work: 27% were full-time and 20% part-time. The remaining 53% did not have paid work.

Of 145 non-employed carers asked whether they would like to be in paid work while caregiving, 46% said that they would. The remaining 78 non-employed carers were asked whether they would like to be in paid work after their caregiving ceased: 38% of this group said yes. In total then, a high two-thirds (67%) of all non-employed carers wanted to enter or re-enter the workforce, either while caregiving or after their caregiving stopped. This group constitutes 36% of all carers.

Of 56 carers in part-time paid work asked whether they would like to increase their hours while caregiving, eleven (20%) said yes. The remaining 45 were asked whether they would like to increase their work hours after their caregiving ceased; 33% said that they would. In total then, almost half (46%) of carers in part-time employment wanted to increase their work hours, during or after caregiving.

This group constitutes 9% of all carers. Overall, 38% of carers were in full-time employment; 28% wanted work or increased work while caregiving, 17% wanted this after their caregiving ceased, and 17% wanted to remain out of the workforce.

Carers wanting to increase their workforce participation (indicated by shading in Figure 8.1) were compared in terms of the characteristics of carers, care-recipients, and the care situation. Because of the small number of part-time carers, the eleven wanting to increase their work hours while caring and the fifteen wanting to increase their hours after caring ceased were combined. Thus three groups were compared: 30 non-employed carers wanting to work when caring ceased; 67 non-employed carers wanting to work while caring;

Figure 8.1   Profile of carers' work status and intentions to increase workforce participation (N = 274)

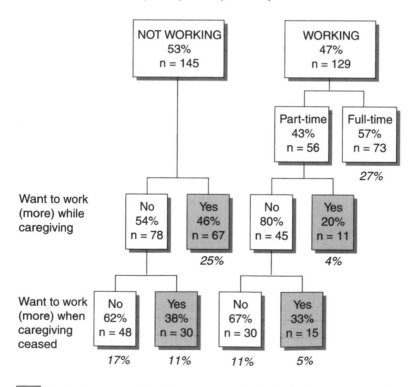

and 26 part-time workers wanting to work more hours while caring or when it ceased.

There were no differences between the three groups in terms of the carer (age, sex, level of schooling, tertiary qualifications, geographic location, combined income, country of birth), the care-recipient (age, sex, nature of disability, dependencies in activities of daily living), or the care situation (living arrangements, relationship between carer and care-recipient, hours of care, years of caring, informal support available, use of formal respite or community services). That is, regardless of their current employment status (unemployed or part-time) and regardless of when they wanted the change (either during or after caregiving), the characteristics of those wanting to increase workforce participation did not differ.

Because of this, these carers were then combined to represent all 123 carers wanting work or increased work. This group was compared with 48 non-employed carers wanting to remain out of the workforce and 103 employed carers (73 full-time workers and 30 part-time workers who wanted to stay as they were). We compared the three groups in terms of carer characteristics (Table 8.4, p. 288), care-recipient characteristics (Table 8.5, p. 288), and characteristics of the care situation (Table 8.6, p. 289).

Carer characteristics Male carers were more likely than females to be working and wanting to maintain their level of work, whereas females were more likely than males to want to increase it (Table 8.4). Carers with a higher level of schooling were more likely to want to maintain their current level of work. Older carers aged 50–64 were more likely than younger ones to be non-workers wanting to remain out of the workforce. Not surprisingly, carers with a household income over $60 000 were most likely working and not wanting a change, while those earning less than $20 000 were less likely to be in this group. There were no differences between the groups in terms of geographic location or country of birth.

Care-recipient characteristics Those caring for females were more likely to be content with their current workforce participation than those caring for males (Table 8.5). Those caring for people aged under 20—a reflection of the carer's age—were more likely than others to want an increase in work hours, either during or after caregiving. Those caring for someone living alone were more likely than others to be content with their current work arrangement and less likely to want an increase in work hours. There were no differences in desire for work in terms of the nature of the care-recipient's disability.

Characteristics of the care situation In terms of relationship, those caring for their partner were more likely than others to want to stay out of the workforce, while offspring caring for parents were more likely than others to be in the workforce and wanting no change from this (Table 8.6). Parents caring for children were more likely than others to want to increase participation, during or after caregiving, again reflecting a difference according to the carer's age. Not surprisingly, carers providing less than ten hours a week in special care were more likely than higher-intensity carers to be working and to be content with their current work participation, and were less likely to be wanting an increase in hours. Consistently, those providing over 30 hours of care a week were less likely to be working, with no desire for change. There were no differences between the three groups according to the years of care provided, the reliance on informal support in caregiving, the use of formal respite care, or the use of community services.

Assistance required in combining caregiving and paid work Carers wishing to enter the workforce or increase their working hours while continuing in their caregiving role were asked whether they would need any of four types of assistance in order to do so (Table 8.7, p. 289). Most carers reported that flexible work conditions would be necessary, while around half said that alternative arrangements for their care-recipient and/or training and education for themselves would be necessary. Financial assistance to cover the costs of care was less commonly endorsed. Carers wishing to enter or re-enter the workforce or increase their working hours after their caregiving ceased were similarly asked about the same four factors. Almost three-quarters (71%) said that flexible work conditions would be necessary, while two-thirds needed training and education. Carers in full-time paid employment were asked which of the four factors, if any, had been important in enabling them to continue working full-time while caring. Around half reported that flexible work conditions had been helpful, while around a third said that alternative care arrangements had helped. Financial assistance to cover costs and training/education were less commonly endorsed.

CARERS' FINANCIAL SITUATION

Carers were asked about their income, the impacts of caregiving on their financial situation, and their access to financial entitlements or coverage to offset any loss of income or increased costs.

Income level Most of the total 939 carers reported relatively low income: 15% said they had no income, 50% had an income under $15 000, a further 17% were between $15 001 and $25 000, with the remaining 18% above this (Table 8.8, p. 290). Where the carer had a partner, a combined income level was constructed taking the mid-point of the range identified as applicable to each individually. On this basis, a third of carer households had an income of less than $15 000 and over half less than $35 000.

This combined level was associated with several characteristics of carer and recipient, in particular their age, their relationship, and the recipient's living arrangements. Spouse-carer households were more likely to fall into the lowest category, which is consistent with households of carers over 65 and with co-resident dyads also being over-represented in the under $15 000 level. In contrast, parent-carer households were more likely to be in the middle-income brackets, consistent with a similar association for recipients aged under twenty and carers under 35. Offspring-carer households were proportionally more likely to be in the highest income bracket, perhaps reflecting the preponderance of middle-aged carer households at this level, and the association between highest income and care-recipients' independent living arrangements. Undoubtedly these patterns are associated with differential rates of employment, with spouse carers least likely to be in paid employment, and offspring most likely.

Given these variations across the whole carer sample, it is important to note that for those under 60, women carers and their partners had significantly lower combined incomes than non-carer households. In particular, they were more likely to fall into the under $15 000 category, in contrast to non-carer households who were overrepresented over $55 000. The greater likely age of carers may to some extent account for this, given decreasing rates of employment in women over the age of 45.

Effects on well-being Over half (56%) of all carers reported that caregiving had no substantial impact on their financial situation (Table 8.9, p. 290). But 26% said it had mainly meant extra costs, while 18% emphasised the loss of income it entailed. Of the 44%

reporting such adverse effects, over half (25% of the total sample) said they had consequent difficulty in meeting everyday living costs. This group also showed significantly worse emotional health than other carers: they were more likely to report greater negative affect and overload, as well as lower life satisfaction and social support. It is also worth noting that the 19% of carers who reported adverse financial effects without associated difficulties in meeting daily costs also showed lower life satisfaction and greater overload than those reporting no adverse financial impacts.

FINANCIAL IMPACTS OF CAREGIVING

These impacts were evidently linked to reported employment impacts (Table 8.10, p. 291). In particular, carers who were 'excluded' from the workforce by their caregiving were more likely than other carers to report financial difficulties, whereas traditional non-workers and unaffected workers were over-represented in the 'nil/minor financial change' category.

This finding is consistent with significant differences in financial impacts according to the age of carer and recipient, their relationship, and the recipient's living arrangements. Parent carers especially reported financial difficulties, while spouses experienced financial impacts without everyday difficulties. Both groups presented a contrast to offspring and other carers, who were more likely to report no overall adverse financial effects and least likely to experience negative effects on employment status, as noted earlier. In line with this result, co-resident carers were more likely to report adverse financial impacts, both with and without associated difficulties in living costs, whereas those whose recipient lived alone or in another household disproportionately reported no financial effects. As well as this, younger carers and those looking after people under 60 reported greater difficulty in meeting everyday living costs, perhaps reflecting differing life-stage responsibilities and financial commitments. Somewhat surprisingly, carer sex and the duration of care were not significantly related to the financial impacts of caregiving.

FINANCIAL ENTITLEMENT AND ASSISTANCE
TO ADDRESS FINANCIAL EFFECTS

Given the financial impacts of caregiving claimed by almost half our carers, to what extent did other financial resources offset expenses and income forgone? In terms of *carer benefits and entitlements* available from the Federal Government, only 9% of the full sample of carers were receiving the CP. A similarly small proportion (8%) were getting the DNCB and only a further 6% of carers the CDA. Thus, overall, relatively few carers received entitlements specifically related to their caregiving. When asked why they were not getting the CP or the DNCB, about half in each case said they did not know about the benefit, and a further third regarded themselves as ineligible. Ineligibility for the CP is likely since a number of carers were receiving other entitlements, such as the Aged Pension (17%), the Disability/Invalid Pension (5%), the Sole Parent Pension (2%), unemployment benefits (Newstart/JobSearch 2%), Austudy (1%) and Veteran Service Pensions (2%).

Considering some of the *expenses* associated with caring for an impaired relative, carers were asked whether the health and medical services used by their relative were covered wholly or in part by various options. The majority (80%) said that the care-recipient was covered by government benefits such as the health care card, while almost half (44%) had private health insurance. A sizeable minority were covered by accident/sickness insurance (19%) or war service benefits (10%). Overall, 97% care-recipients were covered by one or more of these subsidy/reimbursement measures.

At the Stage 2 interview, carers were asked additional questions about various extra expenses they might have incurred during the preceding year, and about any assistance they had had in meeting such care-related costs. Around a quarter said they had incurred additional costs for household items such as heating, laundry, telephone (26%), and providing transport (23%). Pharmaceutical and nutritional expenses were reported also by 17% and 13%, respectively. One in ten nominated extra expenses relating to each of housing/home modifications, ongoing nursing and personal equipment (such as continence aids, asthma pumps), one-off aids or equipment (such as a wheelchair, hearing aid), respite care, and holidays. For 81 carers with a relative in residential care, 16% reported extra expenses in meeting the cost of this.

In total, 58% of carers indicated bearing one or more of these additional expenses. Of these 354 carers, only 23% had received financial assistance from any source (such as government concessions and allowances, accident compensation, and family members) although the majority of those who had (82%) were satisfied with the help received. As with the carer entitlements noted above, the main reasons given by the 272 not receiving help were not knowing about any assistance (40%) and believing themselves ineligible (26%).

WHAT THE FINDINGS MEAN

For a majority of carers, caregiving had an adverse impact on their paid work, and for many a related effect on their household's financial situation. Our findings on carers' employment rates are remarkably similar to those reported by the ABS survey (1995): 38% cf. 41% respectively, of all carers were found to be in paid employment and 46% cf. 50% of carers under 65. Carers appear less likely to be employed than all Australians of workforce age, with comparative percentages of 41% and 54% for women and 66% and 74% for men.[16]

That this difference in workforce participation is partly attributable to special care responsibilities was borne out by almost half our non-employed carers under 65 saying that their caregiving made them quit their job or remain out of paid work. Carers who were most markedly disadvantaged here were high-intensity women carers, that is, co-resident carers, parents and spouses, and those looking after a relative with combined physical and mental disabilities. These findings support and extend factors identified by other researchers as impinging on employment, in particular gender, relationship and impairment.

It is not surprising that carers in such circumstances may be more often 'excluded' from the workforce. Where the severity and pervasiveness of the recipient's disability required considerable care and supervision, the centrality of the relationship and living arrangements between carer and recipient, combined with gender expectations of the caregiving role, may have offered few alternatives to the carer but to withdraw from the workforce. In comparison, offspring and 'other' carers were less likely to live with the recipient, suggesting either a less serious disability and/or the availability of someone able to help at the recipient's home, circumstances which may make combining caregiving and paid employment more possible.

Nevertheless, carers of workforce age *generally* wanted to work, as evidenced by our Stage 3 findings: 27% were working full-time,

45% wanted to work or increase their hours (29% while caregiving and 16% after it has ended) (Figure 8.1). This finding suggests the importance of paid work in accessing the personal, economic and social resources noted by other researchers.[17]

Importantly, carers wanting to work or increase their work hours reflected many of the same characteristics as those currently excluded from work, and were typically in a phase of family consolidation. Women, parent carers and, consistently, those looking after younger males were more likely to want an increase in work, while those giving fewer hours of care to non-resident relatives intended continuing with their existing working hours. In line with community employment patterns (ABS 1994), younger carers were more likely to want to maintain or increase their workforce participation compared with those aged over 50, who presumably felt less pressure on financial and career consolidation. Better qualified and educated carers were most likely to intend maintaining their current working hours, suggesting a greater existing workforce involvement, in contrast to carers with lower household incomes (under $30 000) who were least desirous of working the same hours in the long term.

Since 72% of workforce-age carers have or want paid work while caring, our findings on the highly adverse impacts of caregiving on work schedules and productivity (through interruptions, worry, lower energy) warrant serious consideration. In particular, the substantial work adjustments (such as declining promotion, reducing hours, taking unpaid leave and the like) made by half the employed carers are noteworthy. Consistent with those excluded from paid work, carers making these accommodations were again more likely to be women, parent and spouse carers, especially of younger and/or both mentally- and physically-disabled care-recipients, with a long history of providing care, thus highlighting the group of carers most disadvantaged overall in employment.

Not only were mothers and wives adversely affected in work, but by virtue of being more often excluded from working they were also more likely than all other carers to report lower emotional well-being and financial difficulties. These findings underline the need for policy-makers to develop strategies which will facilitate carers' desired participation in the workforce.

Our findings that *conflict* between caregiving and work (both work adjustments/interferences and exclusion) was negatively associated with carer well-being, support those of earlier research on this issue.[18] Importantly, only a small 9% of all carers fell into the category of unaffected worker, the group reporting highest life satisfaction, social support and combined emotional well-being. It is therefore essential that initiatives to facilitate greater carer employment (status or hours worked) should address the conflicts reported by employed carers if carers' well-being overall is to be enhanced.

In line with this, researchers both in Australia and overseas have concluded that flexibility at work is a buffer against role strain and enables carers to maintain work skills, social networks and income resources, and have called on policy-makers to promote flexible work arrangements.[19] Indeed, in their comprehensive study of employed caregivers, Scharlach's group (1991) found that where there was job flexibility, work conflict and carer strain were less likely. Where carers could, for example, receive personal phone calls, adjust their work routines and take work home, they less often had to miss work or related career opportunities. Furthermore, they speculated that carers had a greater capacity to take on care-related tasks or respond to crises without loss of work productivity. Importantly, it is this very factor of job flexibility that carers in our Stage 3 interviews identified as most important to allow their greater workforce participation, both during and after caregiving.

Flexibility in work schedules is an approach shown to have beneficial effects for employees with other family responsibilities and could be extended to cover family carers. The AIFS study of living standards[20] has identified supportive work practices variously available to employed parents, including flexible work hours, hourly leave for personal reasons, telephone access for personal calls, parental leave, accruing time in lieu, and determining one's own work pace. Part-time or job-sharing arrangements also obviate the need to give up work completely. Importantly, the interest, personal satisfaction, social and financial benefits derived from work itself underscore the importance of enabling carers to maintain this role where desired.

In their review of North American workplace initiatives, Wagner and Neal (1994) identify a range of carer-specific programs as well as general work policies and benefits applicable to all employees. There are specific programs for carers of the elderly:

- informational programs on ageing
- community resources (seminars, books/videos, company newsletters)

- resource and referral programs (individualised information and referral services provided in-house or by external contract)
- direct service programs (assessment and case management, carer support groups, on-site adult day care)
- reimbursement programs (cash reimbursement for purchased community services).

The authors conclude that workplace programs may not be the answer for all employees with caregiving responsibilities but can play an important part alongside general work policies and benefits for current and anticipatory caregivers.

Indeed, approximately half of our carers wishing to increase workforce participation while caring said they needed alternative day care and help with the associated costs, indicating the need for developing complementary direct services, whether in the workplace or the wider community. The need for formal care has been noted by other researchers[21] and requires policy-makers to devise a range of strategies and services such as has been achieved in the child-care sector over recent decades.

Equally important, however, was carers' identified need for training and education programs, particularly among those intending to increase workforce participation after caregiving ceased. A more detailed analysis of those carers needing training (VCP 1996) found that they were more likely to have been caring longer, to have been out of the workforce longer and to have less education than carers not identifying this prerequisite condition. Similar concerns about their limited experience and education, age and time out of the workforce were expressed by carers in the ABS survey (1995). The value of maintaining skills through continuing work and the need for help with training and job placement are thus evident.

Although nearly three-quarters of working-age carers intended to increase or maintain their employment while caring, many, if given the choice, might also have expressed a desire for better financial assistance in their caregiving role from other sources. Clearly, carer households had relatively low incomes (58% less than $35 000), which partly reflected the number of older retired spouse carers in the sample and in the lowest income bracket, but also the household's reduced earning capacity, especially for younger parent carers.

In the VCP study the proportion of carers reporting income loss as the main effect of caregiving on their financial situation was comparable to that in the ABS survey (1995): 18% and 13% respectively. A somewhat higher percentage (26% cf. 17%) reported extra expenses as the main effect, suggesting that Victorian carers overall perceived worse financial impacts from caregiving. For a quarter, this entailed difficulties in meeting everyday living costs, a similar proportion to the 23% of dementia carers reported to experience considerable financial strain.[22]

Given the diversity of caring situations included in our study, the characteristics of carers experiencing greatest financial strain warrant attention by policy-makers. Unlike some previous studies,[23] the degree of care-recipient impairment was not crucial, whereas life-stage factors were: parents, younger carers and those looking after a younger relative were most affected, as were co-resident carers who more possibly felt the direct impact of lost income and additional costs as spelt out by carers in our Stage 2 interview. Consistent with these factors, carers who were 'excluded' from the workforce were also more likely to have financial difficulties.

These findings raise questions about the availability and adequacy of financial measures to support vulnerable carer groups. While parent carers are likely to receive the CDA, the amount itself is modest, and they are ineligible for the CP until their child turns sixteen. At this point not all are automatically eligible to transfer to the DNCB. Moreover, fewer parent and younger carers of people over sixteen appear eligible for the CP because of means-testing of partner income and assets.[24] Indeed, Graham's (1987) costs study of families with disabled teenagers found that a third of mothers had quit work and many needed to make constant adaptations between work and caregiving that had little to do with the seriousness of their child's disability. Graham estimated that this reduced the family income between $12 000 and $25 000 per annum, with families on lower incomes being less able to afford items or activities that increased the child's or carer's quality of life. A considerable number of parent and younger spouse carers would thus appear to be under considerable financial strain. As such, the recent debate on carers' allowances, entitlements, subsidies and alternative strategies for financial relief via taxation or insurance cover is welcome and timely.

9

THE EFFECTS OF
CAREGIVING OVER TIME

Most past research has been cross-sectional, providing a snapshot of caregivers' experiences, health and well-being at a particular point in time. With data gathered at one such point inferences about changes over time cannot be drawn. Does stress increase, decrease, fluctuate or remain the same with the passage of time? Does this vary with relationship group? What changes occur in carers' health and well-being when they stop caregiving?

Our study was longitudinal, allowing us to answer these questions. Participating carers were interviewed at roughly fifteen-month intervals in 1993, 1995 and 1996. Non-carers were followed up in 1995 only. In this chapter we report the changes apparent over these two intervals:

- differential change in caregiver status (still caring, care-recipient died, and no longer caring) according to major socio-demographic and situational characteristics
- differential change in the health and well-being of those still caring and those no longer caring
- differential change between carers and non-carers in physical health, emotional well-being and mediating factors.

WHAT WE FOUND

CHANGE IN CAREGIVER STATUS

Fifteen months after the Stage 1 interview, approximately two-thirds of the 976 carers from Stage 1 were still caring for their recipient ('continuing carers'), likewise at the second follow-up interview 30 months on (Table 9.1, p. 291). In around 10% of cases at each follow-up interview the care-recipient had died. A similar proportion at each stage were no longer caring for a variety of reasons:

- the recipient had moved into residential care and the participant no longer identified as a carer
- the participant was still providing care but for less than four hours a week and so was ineligible for the carer interview
- someone else had taken over the caregiving role
- the recipient's condition had improved to the extent that care was no longer needed.

Our comparison group of women with usual family responsibilities was also contacted after fifteen months; 181 (83%) were reinterviewed; of these, nineteen (10%) had taken on the role of primary caregiver since the Stage 1 interview. There were eight adult offspring caring for parents, five spouses caring for partners, and four parents caring for children, as well as a grandparent and a non-relative caring for a friend. Hours spent caring ranged from one to 105; over half the respondents spent over twenty hours a week; 63% were providing care seven days a week. Twelve (most) of these recipients were female; they ranged in age from two to 85 and more than half were over 60. Disabling conditions included stroke, chronic asthma, Parkinson's disease, muscular distrophy, cancer and heart problems. Interestingly, in terms of relationship, time spent caring and care-recipient characteristics, these new carers were similar in profile and diversity to the original sample.

The sample of reinterviewed carers (819 in Stage 2, 725 in Stage 3) was divided on the basis of carer status at Stages 2 and 3 and the groups compared in terms of carer and care-recipient characteristics and aspects of the caring situation reported in Stage 1. This provided a profile of who was still caring fifteen months and then 30 months later, who was no longer caring, and whose care-recipient had died.

Carer characteristics There were no differences between the carer status groups according to carer sex, marital or employment status, nor on the basis of country of birth. But at each later time, living in country Victoria rather than metropolitan Melbourne was associated with continuing care (Table 9.2, p. 292).

At Stage 2 more carers over 50, compared with those under 50, reported that their relatives had died; conversely, younger carers, particularly those under 35, were more likely to have ceased caregiving for other reasons. Even so, regardless of age, around three-quarters of those interviewed were still giving care. Similar patterns were evident at Stage 3, but understandably the changes were more marked, with only half the carers aged 50 and over still caring; the relatives of almost a third of these older carers had died. Indeed, with the carers' increasing age came a greater likelihood that their relative had died, whereas decreasing age was associated with greater likelihood of caregiving ceasing for other reasons.

Undoubtedly these findings are associated with carer and recipient age differences between relationship groups. Thus most parents (who were generally younger than other relationship groups) were still caring fifteen months on and none of their recipients had died; conversely, the recipients of spouses, who were generally older, were more likely than other recipients to have died. Not surprisingly, 'other relatives and friends', that is, those with less intense kinship bonds, were most likely to have ceased caregiving for reasons other than the recipient's death. A similar pattern was evident at Stage 3, but by this time a third of spouse recipients and a quarter of the recipients of adult offspring had died; only half these carers were still caring compared with the vast majority of parents.

Care-recipient characteristics Expected differences between care-recipient age-groups were observed (Table 9.3, p. 293). No recipients under 21 had died between Stages 1 and 2 compared with one in five of those over 80, and almost all carers with a recipient under 21 were still caring after fifteen months, compared with a relatively low 70% of those whose recipient was over 60. After 30 months the pattern was similar, but by that time only half those caring for someone over 60 were still caring, compared with 81% of those caring for someone under 21. Consistently, recipients over 60 were more likely to have died—over a quarter, compared with less than one in ten of younger recipients.

Living arrangements were another source of variation. Co-resident carers were more likely than others to have maintained their caregiving role at Stage 2; those caring for someone living with a partner or another person at Stage 1 were more likely to have ceased caregiving, while those caring for someone in residential care at

Stage 1 more often reported that that person had died by the time of the second interview. The pattern was again similar at Stage 3, and again the differences were more marked: twice the proportion of co-resident carers as carers of people in residential care or living with someone else at Stage 1 were still caring at Stage 3; over half those caring for a person living with someone else at Stage 1 had ceased caring by Stage 3, compared with less than a third of other groups; and those in residential care at Stage 1 were more likely than others to have died by Stage 3. Neither the recipient's sex nor the nature of the disability differentially related to change in carer status.

Characteristics of the care situation Although neither reported formal support (that is, number of community services received) nor informal support at Stage 1 was associated with carer status at Stages 2 or 3, hours of care and duration of care were (Table 9.4, p. 294). Those who had been caring less than ten hours a week had more often stopped caring at the time of the second interview, particularly compared with those who had been caring for more than 30 hours a week. Likewise, at Stage 3, less than half those caring under ten hours were still caring, compared with two-thirds of those giving more than 30 hours from the outset; those providing more than 100 hours a week had less often relinquished their role. In terms of duration of care, those who had been caring more than six years were least likely to have ceased caregiving by Stage 2; conversely those who had been caring for one year or less were most likely to have ceased, because their recipient had died or for other reasons.

CHANGE IN HEALTH AND WELL-BEING: CONTINUING AND NO LONGER CARERS

Comparisons were made on changes in health and well-being among those still caring and those no longer caring. Those whose recipient had died were excluded from these analyses as information about their physical health and emotional well-being was not gathered in either follow-up interview. Scale scores measuring overload, life satisfaction, positive affect, negative affect, social support, family conflict and self-reported health were used in these analyses, as were categorical measures of the presence of a major illness and regular use of medication. Carers who had stopped caregiving before Stage 2 were not reinterviewed at Stage 3.

Some carers had, over time, adjusted to the caregiving role and come to accept it. Initially 'wondering how I would cope', one woman caring for her mother said that her way of coping had improved over the eighteen months of caregiving: 'When I first knew she had it I felt frightened for her, but I also felt as though someone had done me an injustice. I thought, "Oh gee, I don't know what I'll do", and I ate myself silly. But now I'm starting to take action and I'm starting to feel better about me, and about her situation. I feel I can cope.'

We explored changes in health and well-being between the Stage 1 interview (Time 1) and the Stage 2 interview (Time 2), focusing on whether changes differed between people who were still carers and those no longer caring and whether relationship group affected these changes. Differential changes between Time 1 and Time 3 (Stage 3 interview) were also assessed. Analyses were limited to the three major relationship groups (spouses, offspring and parents). Findings need to be interpreted with caution because of the relatively low numbers in the no longer carer groups, particularly spouse and parent. It should also be noted that age was associated with relationship (almost two-thirds of spouse carers were 60 or older, half the adult offspring were between 45 and 60 and almost two-thirds of the parents were 45 or under): 'relationship' effects, then, need to be interpreted in the light of these age differences.[1]

Overload Regardless of relationship, those who had ceased caring by Time 2 showed a significant reduction in overload between Time 1 and Time 2, whereas those still caring reported similar levels at each time. Interestingly, those no longer caring at Time 2 had a relatively higher overload at Time 1 (Figure 9.1). Despite this decrease between Times 1 and 2, the Times 1 to 3 comparison showed no significant differences in overload between the carer status groups, relationship groups or across time.[2]

Life satisfaction Life satisfaction did not vary across time regardless of relationship group or carer status. However, between Times 1 and 3 it had decreased for those still caring and increased for those no longer doing so (Figure 9.2).[3]

Figure 9.1   Differential change in feelings of overload

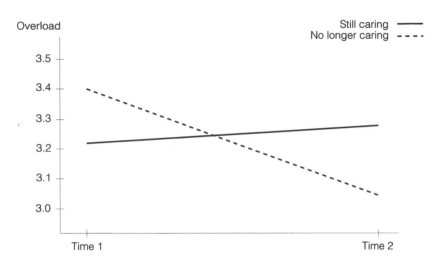

Figure 9.2   Differential change in life satisfaction

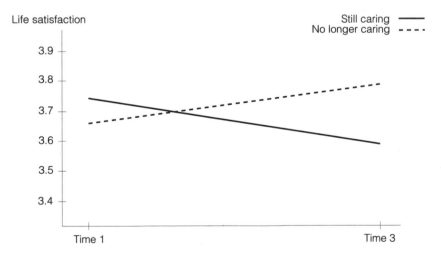

Positive and negative affect There was no *differential* change in either positive or negative affect between Times 1 and 2 or between Times 1 and 3, although spouses reported lower positive affect than parents and offspring, and spouse no longer carers were lower in positive affect than spouse continuing carers at both time-points (Figure 9.3).

Figure 9.3 Differential change in positive affect

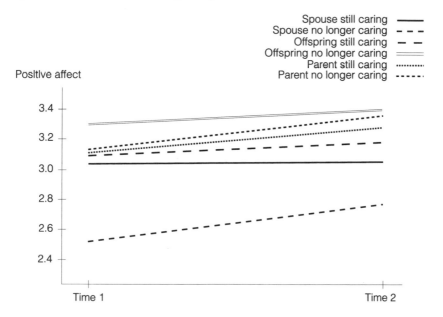

Social support Regardless of relationship group, perceived social support increased between Times 1 and 2, but this increase was more marked in no longer carers (Figure 9.4).[4]

Family conflict For those no longer caring, family conflict decreased in both the Times 1 to 2 and Times 1 to 3 comparisons (Figures 9.5 (p. 112) and 9.6 (p. 113)). Those still caring showed no change over time. All participants showed similar patterns of family conflict at Time 1.[5]

Self-reported health rating For continuing carers, health rating was similar in all relationship groups and did not change over time (Figure 9.7 (p. 113)). While parents and adult offspring who ceased caregiving had similar health ratings to continuing carers, spouses who ceased had a relatively low health rating at Time 1, but a rating which improved to the level of continuing carers at Time 2. These effects were not evident in the Times 1 to 3 analysis.[6]

Health problems and medication At each interview (Times 1, 2 and 3) participants were asked whether they had had a major health problem in the past year and whether they used medication. For each

Figure 9.4   Differential change in perceived social support

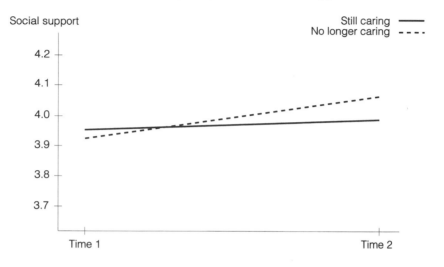

Figure 9.5   Differential change in family conflict over 15 months

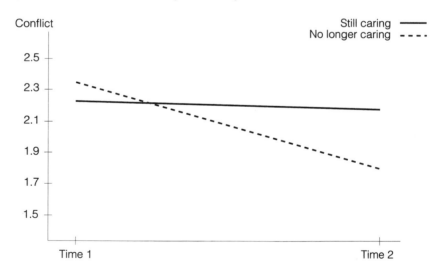

of these variables, four groups were created representing change in either health problems or medication use across time-points. Thus for major health problems, this distinguished those who had continuing health problems, those who no longer had health problems, those who had newly developed problems and those who had no

Figure 9.6   Differential change in family conflict over 30 months

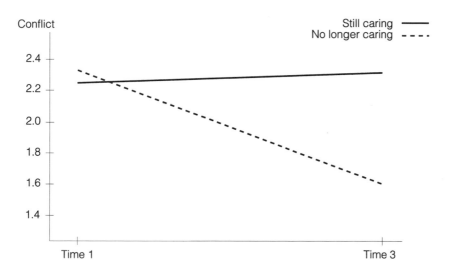

Figure 9.7   Differential change in health rating

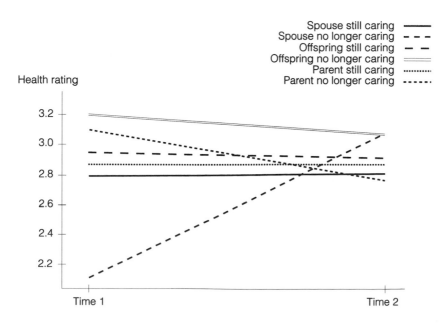

problems at either Times 1 to 2 or Times 2 to 3. For medication use, this distinguished those who continued medication, those who stopped medication, those who started medication and those who did not use medication at Times 1, 2 or 3.

The analysis predicting change (between Times 1 and 2) in the presence of major health problems from carer status and relationship showed that compared with those still caring, those no longer caring had a higher chance of being in the group whose health improved over time.[7] Spouses had a higher chance of continued health problems than did other relationship groups.[8] This latter finding may reflect the age difference in the relationship groups, with the spouse carers being considerably older than the other two groups. The change in health problems between Times 1 and 3 indicated that spouse carers were significantly more likely than other groups to be in poor health at both times.[9]

The analysis predicting change in medication use between Times 1 and 2 showed no significant effect of carer status but did show spouse carers significantly over-represented in the group on continued medication[10] and under-represented in the group who stopped taking medication by Time 2.[11] In the Times 1 to 3 analysis, while there were no differences in use of medication across carer groups, spouse carers (including no longer carers) were more likely to be using medication regularly at both time-points.[12]

CHANGE IN WELL-BEING AND HEALTH: CARERS AND NON-CARERS

We explored differential change in emotional well-being and physical health between female carers and non-carers. On average we found that non-carers were significantly younger than carers. Since carer age was found to be highly associated with carer relationship group, age-categories reflecting relevant life-stage differences were used as a factor in these analyses.

Although there was no *differential* change in perceived emotional well-being or physical health between carers and non-carers over time, carers reported less life satisfaction than non-carers at both time-points, and the life satisfaction of both groups reduced over time. Interestingly, regardless of carer status or age-group, perceived social support increased with time. Not surprisingly, at both time-points, carers reported higher overload than non-carers, and those in the younger age-group were more overloaded than older respondents. On self-rated health, regardless of time or age, carers rated their health as significantly poorer than non-carers (Table 9.5, p. 295).

In each interview (Stages 1 and 2) non-carers, like carers, were asked whether they had had a major health problem in the past year and whether they had used medication. As in the 'continuing carer' and 'no longer carer' comparisons, four groups were created representing change in either health problems or medication use across time-points. Thus, for major health problems, this distinguished those who had continuing problems, those who no longer had problems, those who had newly developed problems, and those who had no problems at either time. For medication use, this distinguished those who continued medication, those who stopped it, those who started it, and those who did not use it at either time.

We analysed changes in the presence of major health problems and use of medication and found that carers were more likely to have persisting health problems than non-carers.[13] Although there was no differential change in medication use in carers and non-carers, those under 45 were least likely to be in the group using medication at both time-points.[14]

WHAT THE FINDINGS MEAN

Our study was longitudinal, assessing the health and well-being of carers three times in two and a half years, exploring changes in carer status, that is, in the numbers continuing to care and discontinuing for various reasons, and the factors associated with these changes. We were therefore able to investigate differential change in the health and well-being of continuing carers and no longer carers. The health and well-being of our comparison group of non-carers, that is, women with usual family responsibilities, were assessed twice, enabling us to look also at the differential change in health and well-being of continuing carers and non-carers.

Change in caregiver status Excluding those carers whose recipient had died and those lost to the study, two-thirds of the people who were carers in 1993 were still providing care after two and a half years. Moreover, 10% of our comparison group of non-carers had become carers within fifteen months of initial contact. Continuance was associated with propinquity in the relationship between carer and care-recipient, with parents most likely and 'other' relatives and friends least likely to have maintained their caring role. Consistently, continuance was also associated with a young care-recipient, a caring role of high intensity and longer duration, and co-residency. Understandably, relinquishing the caring role because of the death of the care-recipient was more likely in adult offspring and spouses who were mainly caring for elderly relatives.

Changes in health and well-being: continuing and no longer carers
The few studies which have compared the health and well-being of continuing and no longer carers are of those looking after dementia patients or the elderly, and definitions of continuing and no longer carers differ from each other and from our own. In our study, with its generic focus, the category of no longer carers excluded those whose relatives had died and includes other reasons, besides institutional placement, for discontinuing; continuing carers included a small number whose recipient had moved into residential care, where they continued to identify as the primary caregiver and spent a minimum of four hours a week giving care. Nevertheless, some comparisons will be made.

Gold and colleagues (1995) surveyed 157 dementia carers over two years. They found that carers who had stopped caring because of residential placement or death reported reduced burden, improved quality of life and better health than continuing home carers, despite the latter having originally functioned better. All carers became more satisfied with social support over time. Despite differences in sampling and definition, these findings accord with our own in that no longer carers in our study expressed more life satisfaction than did continuing carers, and spouses who had relinquished care reported better health than those continuing. Perceived social support increased with time overall, but particularly in those who had given up their caregiving. Moreover, feelings of overload and family conflict decreased in no longer carers. These findings are consistent with those of Zarit and Whitlatch (1993), who reported reduced overload and tension in carers whose relative had moved into residential care during the two-year study period, as compared with continuing carers, while other indicators of stress, such as evaluations of their role and emotional well-being, remained stable. Again this accords with our findings where no differential change in *positive or negative affect* was observed between the continuing and no longer carers.

It is, however, important to note that in our study those who subsequently ceased caring were relatively overloaded and had diminished life satisfaction *at Time 1*, and that spouses who relinquished care also reported poorer health *at Time 1*. Their improvement after relinquishing care underscores the deleterious effects caregiving had had on their health. This is further emphasised by the decreasing life satisfaction of continuing carers.

Interestingly, Bodnar and Kiecolt-Glaser (1994) compared those still caring with those whose relative had died, finding that the two groups did not differ in terms of carer depression. In our study we did not gather information about the well-being of those whose recipient had died for compassionate reasons, not wanting to burden them with the full structured telephone interview. A further consideration was the potential difficulty in interpreting findings with the complex emotions surrounding bereavement and cessation of the caregiving role.

Change in health and well-being: continuing carers and non-carers

There have been several longitudinal studies assessing changes in carers' stress and well-being, ranging in follow-up period from as little as two months to several years. But only a handful have included a non-carer comparison group.[15] Most of these studies have focused on comparisons between dementia carers and controls.

In our generic study, there were no *differential* changes in health and well-being between carers and our comparison group of non-carers after fifteen months. But the differences between the groups evident at Time 1 did not dissipate with time. Thus, regardless of time, compared with non-carers, continuing carers were more prone to health problems and had lower self-rated health; they expressed less life satisfaction, less perceived social support and more overload. It was also the case that, for both groups, life satisfaction decreased with time and perceived social support increased. Given the buffering effects of perceived social support in the long term,[16] the latter may to some extent account for similar levels of positive and negative affect in the two groups. In their study of 86 dementia carers, with a comparison group of 95 family members of cataract patients, Baumgarten and colleagues (1994) found that carers were somewhat more likely than non-carers to experience an increase in depression and physical symptoms during the one-year study period, but the increases were small and the differences not statistically significant.

Only a few studies have examined differential change for carers of relatives with other disabilities. Using a comparison sample of parents of children without disabilities, Dyson (1993) examined parental stress and family functioning over four years in families of children with disabilities. While both groups showed relatively stable parental stress and family functioning over time, parents of children with disabilities were significantly more stressed than comparison parents at both time-points. Schulz et al. (1988) found that carers of stroke patients showed higher rates of depressive symptoms than those found among middle-aged and elderly populations, but again no differential change over time. In a cohort of 55-year-olds, Taylor and colleagues (1995) compared the health of carers and non-carers and examined changes in health and caring over a three-year period. While there was a suggestion that high-intensity carers experienced more strain than did low-intensity carers, there was no systematic evidence of the deleterious effects of caring on health and functioning. The findings even tended to be in the reverse direction. The authors point out that carer selection and self-selection may account to some extent for the absence of morbidity effects in the expected direction. That is, those with deteriorating health are more likely to relinquish the role than the more robust. Moreover, in this study of elder caregiving, the authors also report a high volatility in carer status. Certainly, in our study longer duration caregiving was associated with young care recipients.

Many of the early studies have been criticised for including carers of patients with low levels of impairment. We argue that demonstration of lower well-being among the full range of carers (even low-intensity carers) compared with non-carers lends greater support to the argument that caregiving is associated with deterioration in carers' physical and emotional health. Of course, within both carer and non-carer samples, there will be subgroups who are at risk of increased stress, such as those with competing roles[17] and those in younger age-groups (see Chapter 7).

In sum, changeableness in the caregiving role was associated with lack of propinquity (other relatives and friends) and with older carers (spouse and adult offspring with their mainly older care-recipients); continuance was associated with familial closeness in the carer-recipient relationship, being a parent, and having a high-intensity and long-duration caregiving role. Volatility was also evident in our sample of non-carers, 10% of whom had taken on a caregiving role at the time of the second interview. With relinquishment came improved physical health, enhanced life satisfaction and perceived social support, and diminished overload and family conflict. While the well-being of carers did not deteriorate further relative to that of non-carers, the poorer physical health and well-being of carers evident at the first interview did not dissipate with time.

PART III

SUPPORTS AND SERVICES

10

SUPPORTS FOR THE CARER AND CARE-RECIPIENT

The literature about family carers has highlighted the stress and social isolation many of them suffer, their employment and financial difficulties, as well as diverse emotional and health problems.[1] All of these are borne out by our survey findings. This chapter looks at the various supports available, of a formal or an informal kind. We start with the informal support of family and friends because this is the 'service' just about everyone uses.

INFORMAL HELP FROM FAMILY AND FRIENDS

Although our study has focused on the main or primary carer, the extent to which other family and friends lend support is very important. Previous studies have provided equivocal findings, emphasising both carers' isolation and stress and the strength of family bonds. Our study shows that this informal support is what carers mainly want, more so than the formal services described below. Consistent

- 'Having visitors and company makes a big difference.'
- 'Having friends and neighbours close by—they're always there if you need them.'
- 'Just knowing that you're not alone, that in a crisis there'd be someone to turn to.'

with this, the ABS (1993) found that elderly and other people with disabilities are typically helped not by formal services but by an informal network of family members and friends.

WHAT WE FOUND[2]

Carers gave their responses to a set of statements (Table 10.1, p. 295). Clearly *most* people felt supported and esteemed by their family and friends. The differences lie more in the strength of their belief in that support, and there is also an uncomfortable minority who were *not* confident that they could rely on their family and who feel alone with friends. These are the items that make up our perceived social support scale. Although there were no differences between men and women, spouses, offspring or parents in perceived social support (Chapter 7), carers felt less supported than non-carers (Chapter 5), and perceived social support was lower in those who had been excluded from employment because of their caregiving commitments and in carers who were finding it difficult to meet living costs.

A large majority (84%) of carers reported that they had help from, on average, two other people. The number of secondary carers was related to a number of socio-demographic factors (Table 10.2, p. 296). Larger networks were found where carers were female, parents or adult offspring and worked part-time (especially compared with non-workers); similarly for female care-recipients and those under 20 (especially compared with young adult and middle-aged recipients). The size of the support network was not associated with the care-recipient's living arrangements, type or severity of condition or the amount of help they required with everyday activities. Nor was it related to the amount of help or the years of care provided by the primary carer. The presence of a supporting network appears to be linked to carers' stage of life rather than the amount or type of help they might need.

Interestingly, the larger the support network, the greater was reported life satisfaction and *perceived* support from family and friends; consistently, the smaller the network the more resentment and anger regarding their caregiving role, particularly in carers identifying no secondary helpers (Table 10.3, p. 296). But the carer's self-rated health, feelings of overload, anxiety and depression were unrelated to the number of helpers.

In all, 1770 secondary carers were identified covering a wide range of family relationships. (Table 10.4, p. 297).

Not surprisingly, this relationship between carer and nominated helper appeared linked to the relationship between carer and recipient (Table 10.5, p. 297). For example, 75% of sibling assistance came when the carer looked after their mutual parent, whereas offspring support was geared mainly towards helping with the care of their own parent (carer's spouse) or grandparent (carer's parent). In contrast, help from the carer's parent-in-law was largely directed to care of a grandchild and to a lesser degree their own child (carer's spouse).

The assistance reported by the primary carer was coded into eleven activities:

- visiting
- taking out
- minding or escorting the recipient
- providing personal care
- child-minding
- home repairs
- housework
- help with transport
- help with business/legal/medical matters
- financial support
- emotional support.

On average, secondary carers helped with two of these. The amount of help individually provided was associated with the closeness of their family relationship to the primary carer, partners providing the most, followed by siblings, parents, offspring, other relatives and non-relatives. The greater the extent of the secondary network, the more help the primary carer received. Thus more activities were also related to care-recipients' younger age, being a parent or adult offspring carer, and part-time employment status (Table 10.2). In addition, younger carers and those whose relative lived apart from them with a spouse or other relative received more help.

For convenience the eleven activities were grouped into three broad categories:

- *direct support* involving the care-recipient (visiting, taking out, minding or escorting the recipient, and providing personal care)

125

- *indirect support* to the carer (child-minding, home repairs, house-work, help with transport, help with business/legal/medical matters, and financial support)
- *emotional support* to the carer.

For each category it was determined if each secondary carer provided *any* help. Overall, four in five helpers helped directly with the recipient, a half indirectly and two-fifths through emotional support to the carer. The nature of support seemed to vary according to the relationship of the secondary carer, with partners providing assistance more broadly across the three main categories (Table 10.6, p. 297).

Spouses were significantly more likely to give emotional support than others, especially siblings and other relatives. Spouses and the carer's parents were more likely to provide greater indirect help. Spouses and siblings provided a greater variety of direct help with the care-recipient than other groups. Overall, the amount of personal care was low, with spouses and the carer's parents providing most of this type of care.

Emotional support was also more likely to be given where the primary carer reported greater resentment about caregiving and greater anxiety and depression (Table 10.7, p. 297). Receiving a greater amount of direct assistance was related to higher life satisfaction and positive affect in primary carers, while the absence of direct help was linked to greater negative affect and resentment.

Carers were asked if they would like more help from partners (where appropriate) or other relatives and friends, and what kind of help.

Support from spouses Excluding spouse carers, 100 (19%) carers with partners said they would like more help from their partners. The main areas where they wanted support were emotional (39%), household chores (29%), minding (21%) and taking out the disabled person (15%). Those reporting a desire for more help were more likely to have no current secondary helpers and to feel less social support (Tables 10.8 and 10.9, p. 298). They were more likely to be female, under 35, parent carers (rather than adult offspring), and to work part-time. Their dependent relative was more likely to live with them, to show aggressive and cognitive behaviour problems and to need more help with instrumental activities of daily living. In turn, these carers reported feeling greater overload, anxiety and depression,

> Mothers of children with disabilities found support from husbands crucial. Some appreciated their attitude and practical assistance; others found them unhelpful.
>
> - 'My husband is practical and pragmatic. He helps me a lot.'
> - 'My husband has helped. He has accepted that he has a daughter like this.'
> - 'My husband would come home and have a temper tantrum, but I needed support from him.'

resentment and anger at their role and lower life satisfaction generally. But the wish for more support from spouses was not associated with the type or severity of the recipients' condition, the extent of their dependency in everyday activities, or the use of formal community services.

Support from other relatives and friends Nearly a third (298) of all carers reported that they would like more support from other informal sources, in particular direct help with the care-recipient, especially visiting (43%), minding (28%), taking out (26%) and driving the recipient places (18%), emotional support (33%) and help with household chores (12%).

The factors associated with the need for greater help from family members and friends closely resembled those reported above for spouse assistance, with the following exceptions. While carer age was again significant, it was the 35–50-year-old group who indicated a greater need, especially compared to carers over 65 (Tables 10.8 and 10.9). In turn, adult offspring carers were more likely than spouse carers to want help from other relatives. Their employment status and the care-recipient's living arrangements were not associated with an expressed need, although the severity of the recipient's condition and the presence of depressive troublesome behaviours were.

WHAT THE FINDINGS MEAN

Our findings indicate that most primary carers in Victoria have a small network of family members who assist them in caregiving, the percentage reporting assistance (84%) roughly corresponding to overseas carer surveys.[3] For the most part these secondary carers are close

> Talking to relatives or friends was an outlet for carers. One woman said that she could talk on the phone to different friends about different things which gave her varied interests and relief. Another described the benefits of talking about her caregiving experiences and had found the interview valuable: 'This is the first conversation I have ever had in my whole life about the experience. Even if you are describing negative things it is freeing. It's nice to actually be able to joke about it. It seems to empower you with a bit of renewed perspective, a breath of fresh air. Analysing it is an energy source.'

relatives, the actual composition of the support network being influenced by the recipient's relationship and place in the extended family. Only a minority of nominated helpers were non-kin; their involvement did not follow any particular recipient-relationship pattern and few offered help with personal care.

The widest and most consistent range of back-up support came from carers' partners, reflecting perhaps both co-residency and the closeness of the marital bond. Although generally other secondary carers were less likely than spouses to provide emotional support to the carer, those with a particular closeness (such as offspring, friends and parents) commonly did, in addition to a variety of direct and indirect help with the recipient. Notably, many secondary carers helped by providing social stimulus and contact for the recipient through visits and outings (rather than through help with everyday activities), an intangible but valuable form of support that can enhance recipients' morale and reduce the social isolation of the care-dyad.

The number of secondary helpers available and the number of support activities a carer received varied with some consistency. Spouse carers were least likely to receive secondary support, perhaps reflecting a more independent attitude to their caregiving role, and/or a diminishing informal network with ageing (including of course the 'central' spousal relationship). Female carers identified a greater number of secondary helpers. This may suggest differing perceptions of support between men and women, or a greater maintenance of family bonds by women.

It is perhaps surprising that available assistance related to demographic characteristics of the care-dyad rather than severity of the disability or functional dependencies in personal or instrumental activities.[4] It may be that the level of disability and needs affect other components of informal support such as hours of assistance provided.

The interaction between available informal support and carers' well-being and feelings about caregiving is interesting. Carers without any secondary support were clearly more resentful and angry about their role, whereas larger informal networks were linked to greater feelings of life satisfaction, of social support and more positive emotions.[5] That the size of the network did not mitigate the carers' feelings of overload or negative affect may indicate that secondary assistance is minor compared with the many and ongoing caregiving tasks undertaken by the primary carer,[6] and that it seldom relieves the carer of the responsibility of care. For example, from the UK study it was evident that only 14% of primary carers had another person who *equally* shared the caregiving responsibility. But the association between carer negative affect and role resentment and receiving greater emotional support does suggest that people are responsive to the emotional difficulties engendered by caregiving.

Indeed it was carers who expressed resentment, anger, lower emotional well-being (i.e. higher overload and negative affect, lower life satisfaction and social support) who indicated the need for additional informal support, from partners, family and friends. Importantly, the need for extra secondary assistance was also related to greater dependency in instrumental activities, the presence of behaviour problems and, in the case of spouse support, the severity of the disability. Since existing support was not associated with such indicators of objective care, these findings would suggest the need to direct support to those carers with such high demands and distress.

Professionals and service providers therefore need to explore and mobilise informal networks that could provide help with social contact, minding, transport, and household chores. The lack of association found between the availability of secondary carers and the overall use of formal services suggests that formal supports may supplement rather than be a substitute for care from family and friends,[7] and so provide an opportunity for emotional as well as practical support to carers. While the need for emotional support in carers[8] is arguably a typical expectation within family networks, it should nevertheless be considered an integral component of formal services if they are to be accepted and used.

HOME AND COMMUNITY SERVICES

In the past decade a diversity of formal programs and services has developed in Australia to support carers in the community. The services can be broadly divided into two types:

- those specifically designed to assist carers in their role, such as respite care, counselling and education programs, support groups, Social Security benefits and information kits
- those mainly aimed at people with disabilities which also help their carer, such as home care, disability aids, day care and companionship programs.

But as Twigg et al. (1990:11) point out, 'there is a sense in which any help that is given to the dependent also helps the carer . . . There is a need to appreciate their interdependence, while not precluding conflicts of interest that may arise.'

- For people living in rural areas the location of services often made them geographically impractical. One family with a quadriplegic son was required to travel for two hours to obtain respite help for one day. The benefits of this service were very limited and made the task of getting to and from a major excursion in itself, and an added burden.
- The mother of an adolescent boy who became paralysed after an accident expressed her need for counselling immediately after the trauma. This was unavailable in her area at the time and yet she felt that counselling might have prevented many of her family's later problems.
- Several people complained that services did not meet their relative's specific need. For example there seemed to be few services for young adults with severe physical disabilities. Once they had grown out of the education system where integration or special education services had been available, there were few appropriate placements: 'Once they've finished that educational age there's nothing. And they cannot tap into respite because they haven't got a day service. If they don't have a day service therefore they are ineligible for respite care.'

This commonality of interest has been recognised nationally in the *Home and Community Care Act 1985* (Cth) which included carers as a target of the various funded services for the frail aged and for younger people with disabilities. These Home and Community Care (HACC) services provided through local government and non-government organisations in Victoria include general home help, personal care given in the home, home maintenance and modifications, meals, community nursing, transport and respite and various less common programs.[9]

The extent to which these formal supports for care-recipients have been taken up by carers within the general community is largely unknown. To date, research has been limited on the use of and unmet need for such services. Such information would form the crucial basis for developing policy and services.

USAGE RATES OF HOME AND COMMUNITY SERVICES

Two sources of information, albeit limited, are available nationally: the annual HACC Activity Report for each state and the ABS survey of disability, ageing and carers (ABS 1993). The report on Victorian HACC programs in 1993 indicates that '61,400 carers benefited directly from the provision of HACC funded services', 52% of HACC users having a carer. Clients with a *co-resident* carer were more likely to use Specific Home Help (the Victorian personal-care service for parent carers), whereas use of other services was more closely related to the care-recipient's age, gender, pensioner status and living alone. The report does not clearly indicate the percentage of carers helped for each service nor whether having a carer affected the total number of services received, but it does show that apart from home help, clients with higher needs 'more often live with others or have a carer but they *do not* receive a higher level of service' (H&CS 1995:19). While acknowledging the help carers give to relatives who might otherwise be in residential care, the report does not indicate whether less use of services is through the carer's choice or reflects an unmet need for formal assistance.

The ABS survey shows that the use of formal services as the main source of help with everyday tasks is exceptionally low. But the survey does not allow an estimate of the extent to which informal care is supplemented by formal services in each area. A later analysis of the same data for handicapped people (ABS 1995) indicates that a mix of formal and informal care is provided to a third of people needing assistance, although no breakdown is given for types of service.

Previous HACC reports and other smaller Australian studies indicate that carers and their disabled relatives seldom use a range of formal services. Numerous Australian studies are available that profile service users, describe their satisfaction and patterns of use, or identify unmet needs.[10] While informative, such studies do not always clearly identify carers' participation and are limited in applying only to a specific geographic area, age-group, disability type or type of service.[11] Although important for service provision to specific communities, they cannot give a representative or comprehensive picture of carers' use of or need for services in the general community, which is essential for planning and resource allocation.

USE OF SERVICES

Alongside issues about the extent to which services are used or needed, is the question of who currently receives services and who is missing out. Given the limited resources for subsidised services and the objective of needs-based access (HACC Guidelines 1991), what factors appear to be affecting the use of services? For funded HACC programs, national guidelines specify a set of 'high need' indicators by which relative need should be assessed (HACC 1995). These include the care-recipient's difficulty in activities of daily living, living alone, social or geographic isolation, and financial disadvantage, as well as the frailty, poor health and distress of co-resident carers.

The Australian studies noted above tend to indicate that for most recipient-oriented community services, advanced age, gender and living alone are the main determinants of access to services, with some suggestion that younger disabled people, non-English-speaking immigrants and co-resident carers are less well served.[12] This question has received more systematic attention overseas. Anderson and Newman (1973) propose that service use results from an interaction of a person's predisposition to use services, other factors which enable them to access needed services, and perceived need.

- *Predisposing factors* include socio-demographic variables such as age, sex, relationships, household composition and ethnicity, as well as attitudes towards health and formal services.

- *Enabling factors* are the conditions that must exist to obtain services, regardless of a person's predisposition or need: community resources, especially the availability of services, referral pathways, geographic location and family finances, social supports, and knowledge of services.
- *Need factors*, viewed as the most immediate cause of using services, are typically measured by the care-recipient's health and cognitive impairment, as well as the carer's stress, burden and intensity of care.

The importance of living arrangements in determining service use has been established: community studies of the elderly and their carers found that co-residency reduces the likelihood of using formal services, particularly for spouse carers.[13]

Care-recipients' needs have been reported to be strongly correlated with the use of formal services.[14] Penning (1995) found that high cognitive impairment was linked with low use of home-care services, while high functional disability (ADLs and IADLs) was linked with the use of personal care, home nursing and therapeutic services. Recipients receiving in-home services only were reported[15] to have more functional (ADL) impairments than those using out-of-home services such as day care, group meals, transport, or a mix of both. But those using no services were also more highly impaired. The inconsistency of findings suggests the operation of service barriers such as eligibility criteria.

Additionally, enabling factors associated with the service system or family resources have been reported in several studies, including geographic locality/service availability, residential stability, the use of existing services, higher income, possession of a health card, and knowledge of services.[16]

UNMET NEED FOR SERVICES

While the relative importance and interrelationship of factors influencing service use is thus far from clear, there is even less information available on the unmet need for services. In Australia, outstanding needs have been indicated for transport, general and personal home care, home modifications, paramedical services, and Specific Home Help.[17] But given the specific disability or geographic focus, small size and biased recruitment procedures of these studies, the extent and profile of unmet need within the general community remains unclear.

The ABS survey (1993) provided some limited information. The 1995 analysis reports that 37% of handicapped people said their need for help was not fully met, though again there is no indication of what areas of help this meant, nor what provider these people would have preferred. They did, however, say why they did not try to get formal help, identifying as barriers perception of need (30%), lack of knowledge (26%), personal reluctance (24%), a service being unavailable (11%), and difficulties in arranging access to it (10%). Various reasons for unmet service needs and low service use have been proffered elsewhere in the literature, for example unavailability/rationing, costs, assessment procedures, and language and cultural relevance of services. The importance of negative or conflicting attitudes to service use has received increasing attention.[18]

WHAT WE FOUND

Given the lack of systematic Australian data on these major issues, the aims of our study were threefold:

- to describe carers' use of home and community care services, including a description of the extent of service use in the general community and a profile of users
- to identify the extent of unmet need and factors associated with it
- to explore the role of predisposing, enabling and need factors in the use of and unmet need for services.[19]

Carers were asked various questions relating to their current use of and need for six community care services which can be accessed regularly:

- general home help
- personal home care
- community nursing service
- meal services
- home maintenance
- transport services.

Excluding those whose relative was in residential care, 862 carers were asked whether they or their relative currently used any of these six regular community care services. As a measure of unmet need, non-users were asked if they needed or wanted the service. Just over half (51%) were not receiving any of these services, 25% were receiving one only, 14% were receiving two, and the remaining 10% were receiving three or more. An unmet need for at least one of these services was reported by 39%. The percentage of carers using ('Met need'), needing but not using ('Unmet need'), and not needing ('Don't need') each service is presented in Table 10.10a (p. 299).

General home help and transport were the most commonly used, followed by community nursing and personal home care; meals and home maintenance were the least commonly used. For each service there was some *unmet need* reported by carers, particularly so for home maintenance, less so for meals and community nursing. Importantly, unmet need was comparable to met need for several services, and higher than met need for home maintenance. Notably, for each service, most carers reported *not needing* the service.

For almost all services, use and unmet need varied according to predisposing factors such as care-recipient age, the carer–recipient relationship, and living arrangements (Table 10.10b, p. 300), as well as need factors such as the care-recipient's disability, behaviour problems and functional dependencies, and carer overload (Table 10.11, p. 301).

The use of *general home help* was most likely by adult offspring carers and older carers, whereas parent carers were unlikely users. The care-recipient was more likely to be female and older and to live alone. Similarly, unmet need was most likely where the care-recipient lived alone. Those with an unmet need also had more severe disability, higher functional dependencies and more frequent aggressive and depressive behaviour problems than those not needing the service, and more frequent behaviour problems than those currently using it. These carers also reported more overload than those using or not needing it.

Those using *personal home care* were more likely to be parents caring for people under 21. These young people had more severe disability, greater dependencies and more frequent aggressive behaviour, and the carers reported more overload, than those not needing the service. Those with unmet needs had more severe disability, higher functional dependencies, and more aggressive, depressive and cognitive behaviour problems, and the carers reported more overload, than those not needing the service. They also had more depressive behaviours than those currently using the service.

Users of *community nursing* were older carers, and were unlikely to be parent carers. Their care-recipients were most likely over 80, with more severe disability and higher functional dependencies than those not needing the service. Unmet need for community nursing was most common for adult offspring carers and when the recipient lived with someone other than the carer. Again, care-recipients with an unmet need had more severe disabilities and greater functional dependencies than those not needing the service. Carers with an unmet need reported more overload than those either using or not needing the service. There were no differences in terms of behaviour problems.

Like general home help, users of *meal services* were most commonly adult offspring carers, with care-recipients over 80 and living alone. Female recipients in this category were more likely than others to have an unmet need for meals. They also had more frequent depressive problems than those either receiving or not needing the service, and more frequent cognitive problems than those not needing it. Carers needing meal services were more overloaded than those receiving the service. There were no differences in terms of severity or functional dependencies.

As with community nursing, users of *home maintenance services* were most likely to be older, non-parent carers; their relatives were older and commonly lived alone. Spouse carers and recipients living alone were more likely than others to have an unmet need for home maintenance. These recipients also had more severe disability than those not needing the service, but did not differ in behaviour problems or functional dependencies. Carers either using or needing home maintenance reported more overload than those not needing it. Importantly, unmet need for this service was greater than met need across all relationship groups and living situations.

Use of *transport services* did not vary by relationship or living arrangements, although it was more common among older carers, older care-recipients, and recipients with more severe disability and higher functional dependencies. Those who had been caring for longer than ten years were more likely than others to be using transport services. There were no significant differences in unmet need on the basis of predisposing factors, although in terms of need factors those with an unmet need had more severe disability and more frequent aggressive and depressive behaviours than those not needing the services, and more depressive behaviours than those already using them. While use and need did not vary in terms of carer overload, carers with an unmet need reported lower social support than those either receiving or not needing transport services.

REASONS FOR UNMET NEED

Unmet need ranged from a low 6% for community nursing to 17% for home maintenance (Table 10.12, p. 302). The most common hindrance was lack of awareness of available services, particularly about home maintenance, transport, and personal home care. Concern that the care-recipient would not want the service was a major deterrent for carers in taking up community nursing, meal services, general home help, and personal home care. Understandably, the more personal and intimate the help offered, the more likely that there was concern about resistance from the care-recipient. The less intimate tasks of home maintenance and transport, which do not require others being in the house with the disabled person, seem to evoke less resistance. Dissatisfaction with service received in the past was another disincentive for carers' use of meal services. Importantly, these percentages need to be interpreted with caution since they represent only a small proportion of carers overall.

All 976 carers, including those whose relative was in residential care, were asked whether they had ever had any home modifications done. A relatively high 32% had. Spouse carers (48% cf. 34% offspring and 18% parents), male carers (44% cf. 29% females), and carers over 65 years (50% cf. 19% of carers under 35, and 31% 36–64) were more likely to have had modifications done. Consistently, the care-recipient was more likely to be over 60 (39% cf. 15% under 21 and 26% 21–60) and to live with the carer (38% cf. 13% living alone and 23% living elsewhere).[20] In terms of need factors, these people had more severe disability and greater functional dependencies, and more depressive and cognitive behaviour problems, although there were no differences in relation to carer overload or social support (Table 10.13, p. 302).

SATISFACTION WITH SERVICES

About 90% of users were either satisfied or very satisfied with the services they received (Table 10.14, p. 302). The few carers dissatisfied with general home help, personal home care and community nursing reported that the service was not frequent enough, that the job was poorly done, or that the staff were unreliable. Those dissatisfied with meals said that their relative had complained about the quality of the food and the small servings. Those who reported dissatisfaction with transport were concerned that taxi-drivers were unhelpful and insensitive to the needs of people with disabilities, and that the services were unreliable. Those dissatisfied with home modifications reported that the work had been badly done or that the cost had been unreasonably high. Since the percentage of carers dissatisfied with any service represents only a handful of the full sample, caution is again required in interpreting these findings.

WHAT THE FINDINGS MEAN

The most notable aspect of these findings is the low use reported by carers of services oriented to the care-recipient, either private or subsidised through the HACC program, to assist in the community care of such people. This echoes the findings of major community studies overseas[21] and other studies cited earlier. Less than half our care-dyads used any one of the included services, seldom as a package of supports, and for each individual service, use was comparatively low. While such figures may suggest a limited reach of available formal supports to targeted carers in the community, only about a third indicated an unmet need for any of these services, and a majority of carers (two-thirds or more) reported having no need for each specific service. Clearly, as reported in other studies,[22] the informal care network appears to provide most of the help frail or disabled people may require with daily living.

Combining use and unmet need, the demand for regular formal services was greatest in the areas of general home help and transport (approximately a third), followed by home maintenance and personal home care (a quarter), with least call for community nursing and meals (under 20%). This pattern of demand is generally reflected in the usage rate of individual services, with the exception of home maintenance (where the unmet need is more than twice the usage rate) and community nursing (where the usage is more than twice the unmet need). Interestingly, with the exception of general home help (highest use), care-dyads' pattern of use differs from that

One carer complained: 'I had to pay to have the bathroom altered because I couldn't get it through the government services. You've got to wait for appliances and usually they make you grovel. You really feel like a second-class citizen and you've just got to wait until they're ready to give it to you.' In contrast, another parent had received prompt service from a government agency: 'The Federal Government fixed up all these things and it was the quickest thing I ever got.'

reported for general HACC clients for the same year (HACC 1995), where community nursing and personal home care outranked meals and home maintenance services. This difference may arise from definitional issues (home modifications were separated from maintenance in our survey, while personal care was broader than that provided through Specific Home Help), or it may lie in actual need, co-resident carers providing meals and repairs as part of the household routine but requiring external help with more skilled medical and personal-care tasks.

Overall, the extent of unmet need for these services (6%–17%) appears to be modest, though it must be noted that care-dyads receiving a service were not asked about the adequacy of service 'intensity' (how many hours or how frequent), something raised by a small number of carers commenting on their satisfaction with services. Unmet need was highest in home maintenance, the service carers most frequently said they didn't get because they didn't know about it. A low-intensity service, the costs of promoting and meeting this outstanding need through subsidised providers may be low relative to meeting carers' need for general home help, the second largest identified gap. The proportion of carers with unmet needs for general home help and transport was about half those already receiving each service, indicating a 50% increase in present use to meet this demand.

What distinguished those people using services from those with unmet needs? First, considering service users, factors associated with receipt of services were mainly *predisposing* factors of carers' and recipients' age, relationship and, to a lesser extent, living arrangements. *Need* factors indicated by severity of the recipient's condition were also consistently associated. Other *need* factors such as impairment in instrumental activities and behavioural problems, or carers' ill health, stress, social isolation or intensity of care had remarkably little association with service use.

Identified factors thus depict users as typically older care-recipients with considerable impairment who live alone, generally cared for by either offspring or an older spouse carer. Younger recipients and parent carers were more likely to use Specific Home Help and less likely to use other home-based services. Co-resident parent carers possibly see these latter tasks as among their usual responsibilities and are more likely than other groups to receive help with them from their spouse.

In contrast, overload in the carer was significantly associated with *unmet need for services*, as was the presence of behaviour problems, a high correlate of overload. Other recipient *need* factors (severity, ADLs and IADLs) were similarly associated with unmet need in at least half the services, these need variables often being equal to if not higher than the levels for care-dyads *receiving* a particular service. For example, carers needing home help experienced significantly higher overload and more aggressive and depressive behaviour problems in their relative, and were caring for people of equal disability and functional dependence than those receiving the service. Predisposing variables were less evident in distinguishing care-dyads with unmet need, though living arrangements showed significance for four services, perhaps confirming the importance of this factor in determining relative need. But it should be noted that, as with use of services, it was not always the recipient's living alone that was the decisive indicator: a higher unmet need for community nursing was evident where the recipient lived elsewhere with others such as an equally frail partner.

These findings suggest that although small in number, there remain care-dyads in the community with an expressed wish for support whose need is as great, if not greater, than those already using services. Similar conclusions have been reached elsewhere.[23] Regarding dementia carers, for example, several researchers[24] suggest that various behavioural problems displayed by sufferers may cause them to be excluded by certain programs despite their dependency needs and the distress of their carers, or may create reluctance in either party to get outside help. Our findings indicate a need for service providers to acknowledge the stresses such behaviours, including depression, create for carers generally and to improve access to services.

The identification of *predisposing attitudes*, specifically care-recipients' reluctance to accept the more personal of the home services, is one of our significant findings. If carers are to have access to needed services, professionals and service providers need to be responsive to these difficulties. By setting up a trusted relationship and ongoing encouragement they can help to lessen such attitudinal barriers and help carers to negotiate services. But the issue is complex and requires further qualitative research.

With the exception of community nursing and meals services, however, *enabling factors* outweighed attitudinal factors as barriers to service use. Having information about services appears more critical to the general carer population than availability or other issues such as cost, quality or waiting lists, which have been reported in the more focused Australian studies cited earlier. Our findings suggest the continued need to consider how best to inform carers about available services.

Our exploratory interviews found that despite some problems, the benefits of services and organisations were acknowledged by many carers, particularly in regard to parent support groups, advocacy people, women's clinics, societies for various disability groups, and some government agencies. The number and types of services provided seemed to vary across regions. While some people had relatively easy access to respite care, others found it impossible to get. Some doctors provided an excellent quality of care for families of people with disability, while others were insensitive to their needs. In some districts there were ample services for people of certain ages or with certain types of disabilities, but these were sometimes inappropriate for others who required help. One participant described it as a lack of coherent support, while others found the lack of coordination confusing and resulting in gross inequities in service provision.

RESPITE CARE

Respite care is designed to temporarily relieve the family carer of their usual caregiving arrangement by providing regular or occasional alternative care. Respite models, variously funded by government bodies, include:

- in-home care
- centre-based day respite
- respite with another family or short-term stay in a residential facility, such as a hostel, Community Residential Unit, hospital or nursing home.

- With her mother at day care, one carer felt relief at having time for her own needs: 'You know that you have got that day. You can go and shop, or you can be sick, or you can do anything you want to do—you can have a bit of time for yourself.' Day care also enhanced her mother's independence: 'It's something that is theirs, that we are not manipulating and doing for them and arranging.'
- Despite their needs, many carers found it difficult to ask for help: 'It's the hardest thing to do, because you've coped all your life without having to ask for help.'
- A man who had been looking after his wife for many years said his decision to seek respite care was 'very, very difficult because you don't want to put them there but you know that you have to have respite. I was glad when the week was up so that I could get her back home again.'
- Some carers complained that respite care confuses and disorients the recipient: 'Every time you move them they do become very disoriented—for a while she gets quite miserable.'
- 'It's not worth it, for my sanity—it takes days for her to calm down if she gets upset and that only upsets me.'
- So carers often preferred in-home respite care. One carer had specific home help with showering and dressing her father: 'It's a lot better, it's a lot easier on the carer, and it's a lot easier on the patient than respite outside the home.'

Care can range from a few hours a day to several weeks at a time.

Respite can reduce carers' burden[25] and is greatly valued by those who use it.[26] Indeed, carers and service providers alike identify it as sorely needed in our society.[27] In particular, the need for more hours, overnight and weekend care, home-based care, flexibility in respite arrangements, and accessible information about respite options have been cited in the literature.

In assessing the need for respite in the general community, most local studies are limited by their focus on a specific disability group, such as dementia;[28] age-group, such as young children;[29] ethnic community; geographic locality, for example rural or inner urban;[30] and by the recruitment of participants through service providers. With its representative sample and generic focus, the VCP survey enabled more accurate assessment of the use of and need for formal respite among Victorian carers.

Most data presented in this section are from the Stage 1 survey, and involve 862 community-based carers. Findings are presented separately for carers of younger and older people because of their differing policy and service sectors. The data presented in the final section are based on the Stage 3 survey, involving a sub-sample of 399 carers, in which additional questions on informal respite were included.

WHAT WE FOUND

Profile of carers In reporting these findings, the full sample of 862 carers is divided into two groups: 333 people caring for someone under 65 and 529 caring for someone 65 or over. Naturally the profiles of these two groups differ. Those looking after younger people were more likely to be parent carers, younger, more often co-resident, providing more hours of care, and had been caring for a longer time. Consistent with higher rates of disability among boys, the younger care-recipients were more often males. Regardless of group, however, carers were predominantly women, most had partners, and just over a third had paid work (Table 10.15, p. 303).

While the groups did not differ in severity of disability, frequency of depressive or cognitive behaviour problems, or dependency in instrumental activities, the younger care-recipients had more aggressive behaviour problems and needed more help with physical activities. Consistently, carers of younger people provided more help with physical activities than did carers of the older group.[31]

Time since having a break Almost half the carers had had a break of two days or more within the past six months, although a third had not had a break from caregiving for over two years. Those caring for younger people were the more likely to have gone over two years without a break, partly a reflection of their longer duration of caregiving (Table 10.16, p. 303).

Use of and need for respite Only 12% of carers overall had used respite care in the previous twelve months, with use a slightly higher 15% for carers of younger people. Just over a quarter of carers reported that they would like (more) respite care, with no difference between the two groups (Table 10.16). Carer reports of respite use in the past year and need for respite in the future were combined to give an indication of met and unmet need for respite services (Table 10.17, p. 304). Overall, most carers had neither used respite nor needed it (*No need*). Very few had used it and did not report further need (*Met need*). A few more had used it and said they would like more respite in the future (*Partly met need*). The remainder needed respite and had not used it in the past (*Unmet need*). Carers of younger people were more likely than others to report a 'met need', although the overall 'met need' was relatively low.

Type of respite used and needed The 101 carers who had used respite care in the past year were asked what type of service they had used. Regardless of care-recipient age, *long-term respite* was the most commonly used (Table 10.18, p. 304). Carers of younger people were more likely than others to have used *away-from-home overnight/weekend* respite services.

The 222 carers who reported wanting respite in the future were asked what type they would like, being able to select any number from a range of options given. Carers of younger people most often requested *in-home overnight/weekend* and *away-from-home overnight/weekend* respite. Carers of older people were more likely to ask for *longer respite*.

Satisfaction with services used All who had used *in-home* respite care were satisfied or very satisfied, as were those few who had used *away-from-home daytime* respite. Four of the 25 carers who had received *away-from-home overnight/weekend* respite were dissatisfied with it, while five of the 63 carers who had received *longer* respite were dissatisfied. Importantly, this represents only a handful of the total sample of carers. The main cause of dissatisfaction was professional carers being unfamiliar with the needs of the care-recipient, so giving inappropriate or insufficient care. So few carers are represented here that this finding needs to be interpreted with caution.

Reasons for unmet need The 152 carers who reported wanting, but not receiving, respite care were asked why they were not presently getting it (Table 10.19, p. 304). Again caution is needed in interpreting these findings, given the small proportion of carers represented. Regardless of group, lack of awareness of available services was the main reason. Carers of older people were also deterred by the belief that the care-recipient would not like respite care, whereas carers of younger people reported that suitable services were not available.

Well-being of carers needing respite Carers wanting respite, for the first time or after having used it previously, were more stressed and burdened than those not in need; they expressed significantly more overload and negative affect, and significantly less social support and life satisfaction (Table 10.20, p. 305). The fact that respite had been used in the past made no difference to the present well-being of these carers. Well-being also varied between the two age-groups: carers of younger people reported more overload and negative affect, and less life satisfaction and social support.[32]

FACTORS ASSOCIATED WITH THE USE OF RESPITE CARE

We explored which of the following factors were most strongly related to the use of respite care:[33]

- carer age
- carer sex
- relationship to care-recipient
- work status
- living arrangements
- geographic location (metropolitan/country)
- hours of care
- duration of care

- care-recipient age
- care-recipient sex
- ADL and IADL dependencies
- aggressive, depressive and cognitive behaviour problems
- nature of disability (physical/intellectual/both)
- household type (partner and/or children at home)
- the amount of informal support in caregiving and household tasks (measured by the number of tasks where help is given by family and friends).

Analyses were made separately for carers of younger and older people.

Of the full sample of 333 carers of younger people, 15% reported using respite care. The main factor in their use was *aggressive behaviour problems* in the recipient: the reported use of respite was 24% among the 150 caring for people with frequent aggressive behaviour problems and a low 7% among the 180 caring for people without, or with only infrequent, aggressive behaviours. The second factor was *hours of care provided:* among the sub-sample of 150 carers of people with frequent aggressive behaviours, respite use was a high 33% for the 93 caring more than 30 hours a week but only 9% for the 57 caring fewer hours (Figure 10.1, p. 147).

Of the full sample of 529 carers of older people, 10% reported using respite care. Here the main factor was *ADL dependencies:* the reported use of respite was a higher 20% among the 186 people caring for relatives with high ADL dependencies and a low 5% among the 336 caring for those with moderate or low ADL dependencies. The second factor was carer *sex:* among the sub-sample of 186 caring for people with high ADL dependencies, respite use was 23% for the 135 female carers, but a low 10% for the 51 male carers (Figure 10.2, p. 148).

FACTORS ASSOCIATED WITH THE NEED FOR RESPITE

Using the same set of variables, of the full sample of 333 carers of younger people, 25% reported a need for respite care. The main factor was *relationship between carer and care-recipient:* of 209 parent and 'other' carers, 33% needed respite, whereas of 113 spouse and offspring carers, only 11% needed it. The second associated factor was *amount of informal help:* among 209 parents and 'other' relatives,

**Figure 10.1   Factors associated with respite use: carers of recipients
< 65 years**

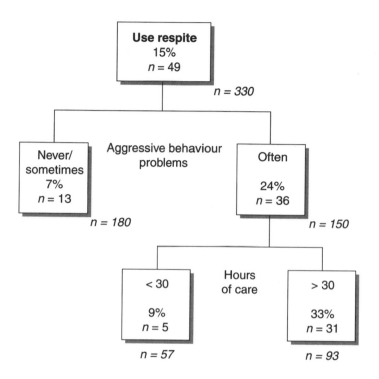

respite use was a high 44% for the 111 people receiving help with
fewer than five tasks, and a low 19% for the 98 receiving help with
five or more tasks (Figure 10.3, p. 149).

Of the full sample of 529 carers of older people, 27% reported a
need for respite care. The main factor was *ADL dependencies*: for the
186 caring for people with high ADL dependencies, respite need was
a high 44%, whereas for those caring for relatives with only moderate
(118) or mild (217) ADL dependencies respite need was only 24%
and 14% respectively. The second associated factor was *frequency of
aggressive behaviour problems*: among the sub-sample of 186 caring for
people with high ADL dependencies, respite need was a high 60%
for 72 carers also dealing with frequent aggressive behaviour problems

Figure 10.2   Factors associated with respite use: carers of recipients 65+ years

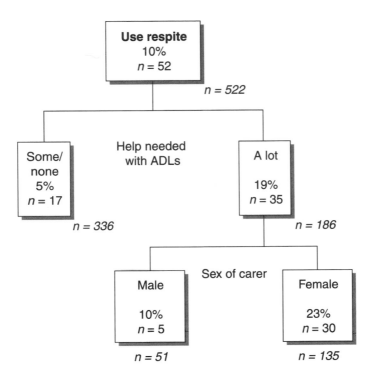

and only 33% for 114 who had no or only infrequent behaviour problems to deal with (Figure 10. 4, p. 150).

As well as questions about formal respite services, carers interviewed at Stage 3 were asked about informal respite provided by family or friends.[34] They were asked whether they had a family member or friend who looked after their relative regularly (daily, weekly, fortnightly/monthly, less often), occasionally, and in emergencies. Carers with regular or occasional support were asked for how long the person was available, either a few hours, all day, overnight, for a few days, for a week or more, or indefinitely. Forty-three per cent had someone looking after the care-recipient regularly, and 48% occasionally. With some overlap between these, 71% of carers had

Figure 10.3   Factors associated with unmet needs: carers of recipients < 65 years

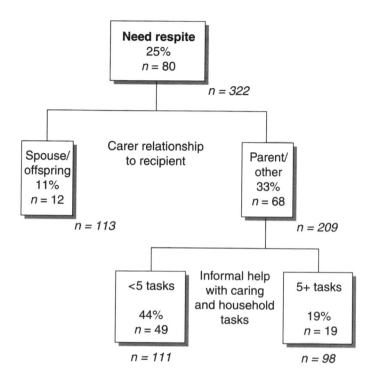

informal respite either regularly or occasionally. A high 82% had someone in emergencies.

Respite care given at home has its problems. According to one parent: 'We have lots of trouble when there are different carers. With lots of people coming into the house all the time it creates problems with the younger child, and he would otherwise go to anybody. During a week we would probably have eight or ten people coming into the house doing different things for the children.'

Figure 10.4   Factors associated with unmet needs: carers of recipients 65+ years

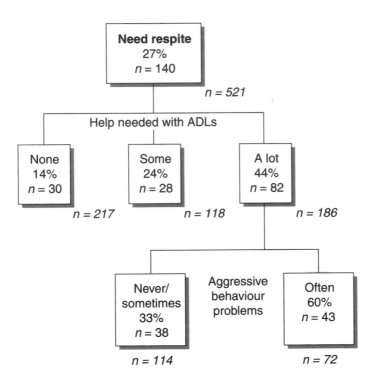

WHAT THE FINDINGS MEAN

Given the emphasis on respite as a crucial service to support carers in their role, it is notable that, consistent with ABS data, only 12% of our community sample had used formal respite in the previous year, and that over two-thirds indicated no need for formal care, suggesting that carers are discriminating in their demand for formal support. This view is supported by the high demands of care typifying users from both carer groups: use predicted by aggressive behaviours and high hours of care for those caring for younger care-recipients and by greater dependency in personal care and mobility for carers of the elderly.

The higher use of respite by carers of people under 65, over half of whom were parents, may suggest greater visibility of this high-intensity group, direct targeting through programs such as Interchange, Specific Home Help and Community Residential Unit short-term care, and perhaps attitudinal differences to service use from care-dyads in the older group. The figure of 15% for the group is almost surprisingly low, given the relatively high usage rates reported in previous studies of similar groups,[35] but it may reflect the paucity of services for younger disabled adults commonly highlighted in local studies.[36] And a somewhat higher 21% of parents had used respite in the previous year.

Importantly, however, a quarter of carers from both age-groups reported an unmet need for formal respite. Indeed these people appeared to be in substantial need. They were more stressed and overloaded than those with no need and were also less likely to have access to regular respite from family and friends. Parent carers, particularly those with less help with household and other tasks, were more likely to express a need in the younger care-recipient group. Among carers of the elderly, high demands predicted unmet need, especially the combination in the care-recipient of high physical dependencies and frequent aggressive behaviour problems.

This suggests the need for services to be responsive to and funded for the carers of highly dependent people of all ages, especially with difficult behaviours which may arise from various conditions (e.g. acquired brain damage, dementia, intellectual disability). Previous local and overseas studies have identified the difficulties such high-need groups have in engaging services,[37] and also obstacles such as the quality and design of programs, the training and reliability of staff, and carers' exhaustion and reluctance in the face of potentially upsetting or unsettling their relative.[38]

Similar barriers were identified by our carers with outstanding respite needs. Although the numbers are small, carers of younger people more often noted the unavailability of suitable programs and delays or difficulties in trying to organise respite as reasons for unmet need (see Table 10.19, p. 304). On the other hand, carers of the elderly were more likely to emphasise their relative's objections to formal respite, perhaps because of expectations of family care later in life, dislike of intrusion and loss of privacy with in-home care or confusion arising from away-from-home respite. But the main barrier to respite care identified by both carer groups was lack of information about services and how to engage them. This reinforces the message of earlier studies of the need to educate carers about respite and for a coordinated approach to inform them about the range of options available in their locality and beyond.[39] The need for information about and the availability of a *range* of respite options is clear from variation in the types used and preferences expressed by carers of people of differing ages.

Carers of the elderly were more likely than carers of children and younger adults to have used and to need respite that provided an extended break from caregiving, half in fact nominating longer respite as a required service. In contrast, carers of younger people were more likely to need overnight and weekend respite, both at home and away from home, perhaps reflecting differences in circumstances as well as the gap in flexible, short-term out-of-hours respite noted elsewhere.[40]

While a sizeable minority of carers needed in-home day respite, very few either needed or used day respite away from home. This low figure for carers of younger people may reflect the 74% attendance rate in educational facilities by our care-recipients who were under 21 years, which provided the carer with incidental respite. More

The decision to seek respite was often quashed by carers' unresolved feelings of guilt.

- A wife caring for her elderly husband: 'When he goes to Day Care he says, "I'm only going because you want me to go". But when he's there he has a ball. I've just got to get rid of that guilt now.'
- The father of a severely-disabled child: 'I didn't take up the respite option for a couple of years due to the guilt feeling. I couldn't take her somewhere and just leave her and walk away.'
- 'You become rather dead inside and the caring can be numbing. I have lost a spontaneity that I used to have. You change as a person, with an altered personality.'
- 'I feel swallowed up in my own despair.'
- 'We can get respite but we don't use it a lot because my son doesn't want to go. He screams and kicks when I take him and I feel guilty.'

puzzling, however, is the low demand among carers of the elderly, given the prevalence of adult day-care centres nationally. The failure to use away-from-home day respite by this group may indicate differences in understanding and definition of respite by carers, service providers and researchers. For example, while day-centre programs are designed to provide relief and recreation for the carer, as well as stimulus and social support for the care-recipient, some carers may see the benefits they give the care-recipient but not the opportunity for respite for themselves. Also, whether carers see day care as providing them with *respite* may depend on how they use this time release. For example, carers of the aged who use the free time to work may not see the recuperative value of the respite period. Several researchers have shown the diversity of activities that carers undertake while respite is provided, including paid work, household and other chores, activities associated with the care-recipient, attending to medical and other personal matters, as well as visiting friends, pursuing hobbies, holidays, and sleep and rest.[41] In general, respite time is seldom used for rest and relaxation.

Our findings indicate that respite programs, diverse in type, length and frequency,[42] are necessary to address such varying needs. Current services appear to be used judiciously, with nearly three-quarters of carers relying exclusively on informal respite care and a further 18% using formal services to supplement it. There is every indication that current respite service use is greater among carers with high-intensity needs and that those expressing unmet

Carers agreed that more flexibility is needed in respite-care arrangements. At present formal support is rarely available after hours, during the night, and at weekends, the most demanding times for carers: 'Things happen at the weekends and you don't know how to handle them.' Some asked that 'a volunteer come on the weekend', while others wanted 'someone to take over at night time'. Some asked that emergency services be made available for these times, suggesting a phone number be provided for caregivers to ring for help or advice. Often parents' needs were greatest in emergency situations such as illness of the carer or the dependent child. The lack of flexibility in the respite services rendered them useless on these occasions.

need are appropriate candidates under existing respite guidelines. That current users are more likely to express a need for more respite may be confirmation that respite care is being directed to the people who need it and that it does in fact benefit them.

Importantly however, over half of the Stage 2 carers reporting an unmet need for respite had not used formal services before. This points up the need to inform carers better about available services, and to devise programs that will address their needs. Given the confusion regarding the meaning and terminology of 'respite' (types of services and intended purposes) and the proliferation of organisations providing respite care, it seems essential to educate carers, care-recipients and those making referrals about respite and the available options.

SUPPORT GROUPS, TRAINING AND COUNSELLING

As well as respite care, support programs of three distinct kinds have been devised specifically for carers:

- peer-led support groups
- professionally led training groups
- counselling/psychotherapy.

These programs have a variety of aims:

- reduction of carers' isolation
- mobilisation of resources and supports to help the carer
- enhanced knowledge about ageing or specific disabilities and illnesses
- improving the carer's management of behavioural or other problems associated with the disability
- increasing problem-solving and coping skills
- addressing the emotional and relationship problems that can arise in caregiving.[43]

The ultimate goals are to enhance carers' physical and emotional well-being and to reduce their burden,[44] and in some cases to delay or reduce the care-recipient's admission to residential care.[45]

While carers report great satisfaction with the support they received through many of these programs,[46] it is not clear that programs have achieved their stated aims; the findings are equivocal. In their early work with dementia carers, for example, Zarit and colleagues (1987) concluded that counselling had no effect in reducing carer burden (relative to control group effects), although a re-analysis by Whitlatch and colleagues (1991) indicated that burden was significantly reduced and maintained over time. Sutcliffe and Larner (1988) reported that short-term therapy significantly reduced carers' depression and distress but had no effect on their burden or their knowledge about dementia. Similarly, with carers of mentally-ill adults, MacCarthy and colleagues (1989) found no significant improvement in burden, knowledge of the illness or sense of control by therapy participants over the control group, although enhanced coping strategies and relationship with the care-recipient were evident. Individual counselling for carers of the frail elderly was found by Toseland and Smith (1990) to reduce psychiatric morbidity, enhance well-being and perceived competence in caregiving, but it made no difference to the carers' formal and informal supports or reported burden.

Research investigating the benefits for carers of education and support groups has shown equally mixed results. Several studies have demonstrated benefits in terms of reductions in carer burden, stress, depression and anxiety.[47] On the contrary, other studies have reported no significant effects on these factors.[48]

Nonetheless, education and support programs are often found to have an impact on mediators of carer stress and well-being. For example, improved knowledge of the condition,[49] carers' competence and coping,[50] social support[51] and increased use of services[52] are commonly reported outcomes.

Most of these and other carer support programs reported in the literature focus on a limited number of caregiving situations and disability types, in particular dementia, mental illness, and the frail elderly. With a few notable exceptions they are located outside Australia. But the past decade has seen a growth in support groups and training programs for carers throughout Victoria, under the auspices of disability-specific organisations and consumer groups, hospitals and community health centres, local government and, more recently, the Carers Association of Victoria (CAV 1995). While many of these focus on the three main conditions reported in the literature, many also cover illnesses or disabilities such as cancer, acquired brain

Many carers said they had 'gained a lot' from their involvement with the support group, largely because of the shared experiences of participants, 'because we have all been through it—you can relate to one another on the same level, and that helps an awful lot'. Some felt that after having a 'good old whinge' with other carers they would feel 'some of the load lift off'. Even so, some carers indicated that 'it took a long time' before they felt ready to get in touch with the support group, again illustrating difficulties in acknowledging stress and the need for help.

injury, Parkinson's disease, arthritis, developmental delay and congenital disability, or are generic in nature. To date there is little information on the extent to which carers generally have used these supports or derived benefits from their participation.

WHAT WE FOUND

COUNSELLING AND TRAINING

All carers were asked whether they had ever participated in a training course on caregiving, and whether they had received counselling about their relative's condition or their caregiving role. Satisfaction with these services was measured on a five-point scale from 'very satisfied' to 'very dissatisfied'. Reasons for dissatisfaction were recorded.

Use and need of services Of the full sample of 976 carers, 167 (17%) had received counselling, while 104 (11%) had done a training course. There was significant overlap in the use of these two services, with those having had counselling being more likely than others to have also done a training course, and vice versa. As with formal respite care, neither the carer's sex nor marital status made any difference to the use of counselling and training. But use of counselling services did vary with the carer's relationship to the recipient, the ages of carer and recipient, and living arrangements (Table 10.21, p. 305). Those who had received counselling were more likely to be parent carers, to be younger, to be caring for someone under 21, and to have their relative living with them. These effects are all consistent with this group being parent carers. Participation in counselling was also significantly related to mental disability in the care-recipient. Unlike counselling and other community services, involvement in a training course was not affected by the carer's relationship to the recipient or the recipient's age. There was, however, a significant carer-age effect, with younger carers again being more likely than others to have done a training program. Participation in training was not significantly related to the severity or type of the recipient's disability.

Carers' well-being Carers who had taken part in a training course reported greater positive affect than others, but there were no differences in negative affect or life satisfaction (Table 10.22, p. 305). On the contrary, those who had had counselling reported significantly higher negative affect and overload and significantly lower life satisfaction and social support than those who had not. This may reflect the high stress and intensity often experienced by parent carers, the group most likely to seek and receive counselling.

Satisfaction with counselling and training All carers who had had counselling or training were asked to report their satisfaction with the service they had used. Only 4% were dissatisfied with a training course, while a larger 10% were dissatisfied with counselling. As for other services reported elsewhere in this section, these figures represent only a small proportion of the full sample of carers.

The main reason for dissatisfaction with counselling was the feeling that it had been of no benefit, some carers reporting that it actually worsened the situation by increasing tension in the family and decreasing the family's sense of hope. A handful of carers also complained about the 'insensitive and condescending' manner of the counsellor. The few carers dissatisfied with a training course said that the information had not been relevant.

Need for counselling and training Given the relatively low proportion of carers who had ever received counselling or training, the 615 continuing carers in the Stage 2 survey were asked whether they needed either of these if they had not received this kind of help in the past year. Where carers identified an unmet need, they were asked why they had not received counselling or training. Again, the proportion of carers who had received one or the other in the past twelve months was fairly low, and as with respite and other community services, most reported no need for either type of support (Table 10.23, p. 306). A small minority did mention an unmet need for counselling (10%) and training (13%).

Unmet need varied according to a number of factors concerning the carer and care-recipient. Carers reporting an unmet need for training were more likely to be younger (under 35), have higher education (completed Year 12 schooling), and to be of NES background (Table 10.24, p. 306). Similarly, those dealing with serious aggressive and cognitive behavioural problems in their relative and those reporting higher overload, greater negative affect and lower life satisfaction and social support more frequently identified a need for training (Table 10.25, p. 307). Furthermore, carers reporting lower well-being and facing more difficult behaviours were also more likely to express an unmet need for counselling. Consistent with the association with behavioural problems, carers looking after a person with both physical and mental disability and those providing more help with instrumental activities of daily living were more likely than others to need counselling. Conversely, male carers and those with a less central relationship to the care-recipient ('other carers') were less likely to say they needed counselling.

The need for counselling and training was not related to other socio-demographic factors (carer marital or work status, geographic location, care-recipient age, sex and living arrangements), to the care-recipient's need for help with personal care/mobility and its provision, or the hours or duration of care provided by carers. The main reasons carers gave for not receiving the counselling and training they needed were consistent across both services (Table 10.26, p. 307). The most common were: not yet enquired; lack of information; time and other pressures.

MEMBERSHIP OF SUPPORT GROUPS AND ORGANISATIONS

At Stage 1, 8% of carers reported that they were a member of a carer support group, such as the Alzheimer's Society. Membership varied according to the carers' relationship, with 20% of parent carers belonging to a support group in contrast to only 9% of spouse carers and 3% of adult offspring. The low rate overall, however, was very important given the reliance of much previous research on recruitment from support groups and organisations. Feedback from carers suggested that it would be useful in our Stage 2 interviews to enquire about past as well as current membership and to broaden our notion of 'carer support group' to capture more fully the range of involvement likely with this type of formal support. As such, 621 continuing carers in Stage 2 were asked additional questions about their involvement with 'support groups or *organisations*' (omitting the specification 'carer'). Eighteen per cent of these carers reported that they were currently a member of a support group or organisation, and a further 19% had previous contact with such a body, while 63% had never been involved. Of 106 current members, 65% had not reported belonging to a carer support group at Stage 1, nor had the vast majority (92%) of carers with prior involvement (Table 10.27, p. 307).

Involvement was related to various characteristics of the care situation (Table 10.28, p. 308). As in Stage 1, parent carers were more likely to be involved, especially compared with offspring carers; two-thirds reported either current or past contact with a support group or organisation. Consistent with this, carers of younger people, particularly those under 21, and those caring for males reported greater involvement. Furthermore, co-resident carers and those giving full-time care, particularly compared with those caring less than ten hours a week, were more likely to report current membership.

The nature of the disability was also associated with membership, carers looking after someone with a mainly mental disability reporting greater involvement. Consistent with this, current members were more likely to report difficult behaviours in their relative, particularly aggressive behaviours and those related to cognitive impairment (Table 10.29, p. 308). The level of the care-recipients' need for assistance with personal care and mobility and instrumental activities of daily living, and the amount of help carers gave with these tasks, were also related to membership patterns, with current members reporting highest demands. In keeping with this, carers who were current members reported highest overload and lower life satisfaction, with past members being less negatively affected. Consistently, past members reported higher positive affect compared with carers who had never been involved with support organisations.

Involvement was not, however, related to carers' age, sex or marital status, their education level, ethnicity, geographic location or number of years spent caregiving. Neither was membership linked to carers' degree of negative affect or their perceived level of social support.

Type of support group or organisation   Overall, 199 different groups and organisations were nominated by carers with either past or current involvement. Nine were excluded because they represented broad service-group membership (such as Lions and Probus clubs), or work-related or volunteer involvement with no connection to the personal needs of carer or care-recipient.

Only ten carers identified more than one group, most nominating a single organisation, together spanning a variety of conditions and localities. A quarter of the groups nominated were general support or carer groups run by local councils, churches, community health centres, and the Carers Association of Victoria. Most were disability-specific organisations that provided support to carers as well as the care-recipient; for example, a number were support groups attached to the particular special school or day program the recipient attended.

The largest category (38%) comprised organisations concerned mainly with intellectual and/or psychiatric disability, which is consistent with the association between membership and disability type noted above. The most commonly identified organisations within this category were the Down's Syndrome Association, the Alzheimer's Association and the Autistic Children and Adults Association. Organisations relating to mainly physical disabilities accounted for 14% of those identified, the Spastic Society being the only one mentioned more than twice. A smaller 6% were supports offered through sensory disability organisations, such as the Royal Victorian Institute for the Blind and Parents of Hearing Impaired Children. Involvement with organisations concerned with long-term or chronic health problems accounted for the remaining 17% of identified support groups; in particular the Arthritis Foundation, the Parkinson's Disease Association and Diabetes Australia were commonly mentioned.

Type of involvement by the carer   Carers were asked to describe the type of involvement they had (currently or in the past) with the support group or organisation they had nominated. Receipt of the organisation's newsletter was the most often cited contact, although over a third attended support group meetings and a quarter social events (Table 10.30, p. 309). A sizeable minority reported more focused support through education sessions, telephone support and counselling. Specific information about the recipient's condition, treatment options and available services was an important part of their involvement for a smaller number of carers. Of contact in the 'other' category, carers nominated their involvement in running the organisation, such as being committee members and fundraising, and activities directed to the recipient, such as classes or service advocacy. The 86 carers who reported ever attending support group meetings (37% of those 'involved'), represent 14% of Stage 2 carers, and constitute the group most closely resembling support group participants as described in the intervention literature.

Satisfaction with help received and reasons for discontinued membership Carers were asked how satisfied they were with their nominated support group or organisation. Almost half (49%) were very satisfied, while 36% were satisfied. A further 6% were not sure, leaving only a small 9% overall who were dissatisfied or very dissatisfied. Given this high satisfaction rate, the reasons given by 114 carers who no longer had involvement in a support group were of interest. The main reason given has been coded *post hoc* into six categories (Table 10.31, p. 309).

Over a third gave reasons associated with the perceived usefulness of support groups or their satisfaction with a particular organisation. This ranged from positive statements in which the support was no longer needed or relevant, to a minority who were critical of the support they had received. A fifth had withdrawn because of pressures of time and competing commitments (such as work, caregiving responsibilities, family) or other changes in their circumstances (moving locality and deteriorating health). Difficulties in access (such as timing and distance) or changes in the support organisation itself (e.g. closing, moving, shift in focus) also accounted for a sizeable number of discontinuations. Other carers more generally said they had lost interest or let their membership lapse, with a further small group saying they kept up their involvement as they felt the need or just kept informal social contact outside the group. A further group said they had stopped being involved because of factors relating to the recipient, in particular stopping attendance at a specific program (e.g. special school or day program) or changes in the recipient's attitude towards the organisation.

WHAT THE FINDINGS MEAN

Our results indicate that, consistent with other formal services, only a minority of all carers have ever used these services, which aim to

> Several carers felt that the support group discussions had provided useful information about the symptoms of dementia:
>
> - 'They helped me understand that she's not just doing it to spite me.'
> - 'I treat everything lightly rather than as drama now—there's no drama any more. I want things to sail smoothly.'

give carers information, support and increased well-being: a low 11% used training courses, 17% counselling, and although current carer membership of support groups was 8%, involvement at some time in support *organisations* was higher at 37%.

There was considerable overlap in the use of these three services, suggesting that they are reaching a specific cohort of carers. In particular, carers who had taken part in counselling and support groups were 'high-intensity' carers—more likely to be parents looking after co-resident younger people, with mainly mental disabilities. Although an overlap existed with carers who had attended training courses, these were less distinguishable as a group from non-participants apart from being younger, a finding consistent with training programs in other health promotion areas.

Carers who had had counselling or were current members of support groups typically expressed greater overload and lower life satisfaction and, in the case of counselling, more negative affect and lower social support. This may suggest that such services are used by people whose emotional well-being is most at risk, though without information about their emotional state beforehand, the benefits or otherwise of participation cannot be known. However, consistent with programs reviewed in the literature, carers expressed great satisfaction with all three services. And carers with previous involvement in support groups also revealed greater positive affect and life satisfaction and less overload than other carers, which may suggest they had derived some benefit.

The considerable distress in carers who expressed a need for counselling and training, tells us that these services are relevant. Consistently for both services, regardless of age or relationship, those in need had higher negative affect, overload, and lower life satisfaction and social support, and commonly dealt with more frequent problem behaviours. The distress arising from dealing with difficult behaviours (often associated with mental impairment) suggests the importance of knowledge, behavioural management and coping strategies as emphasised in the literature, as well as other approaches that may relieve carers' distress and mobilise supports.

The greater participation by parent carers in support groups and counselling may partly reflect their more specific engagement with service systems, for example the more definite start to caregiving with the birth of a disabled child. There are early intervention systems that assess educational and support needs and provide information, referral or, indeed, the relevant program (training, counselling, support group). In contrast, spouses and offspring caring for someone with, for example, gradually deteriorating cognitive impairment and other physical conditions, attended by the local doctor, may have much greater difficulty in knowing about and accessing relevant educational and emotional supports.

In contrast to more traditional services provided through home care and disability services, appropriate counselling, carer education programs and support groups are less visible in the community and local resource directories, perhaps because of their less permanent status and the diversity of public and private service providers. To a certain extent the information bases held by peak bodies such as the Carers Association, the Disabled Persons Information Bureau, the Action Group for Disabled Children and other disease/disability-specific consumer organisations meet this need, but they themselves may not always be known or referred to by health and other professionals. Given the range of information and services that carers reported receiving from support groups and organisations, it is particularly desirable to direct information about their role to service providers and carers generally, thereby increasing information and support pathways. To achieve this, however, comprehensive and updated resource listings would need to be maintained and publicised, preferably at central and regional levels.

However, given the limited nature of our examination of counselling, training and support-group programs, much is still unknown about the relative merits of generic or disability-specific services and where best to locate them for access by carers. We also need to explore further how carers see these as potential supports, especially in contrast to more practical services and informal peer networks which may also provide incidental emotional support and advice. And considering the inconsistent findings from overseas research, existing programs require more comprehensive evaluation to find out the benefits or otherwise that carers gain from participation in these three types of supports.

INFORMATION FOR CARERS: NEEDS AND PREFERENCES

Several studies have emphasised the importance of information for family carers: in particular, information about the care-recipient's condition, and about services and organisations available to assist caregivers in their role. In this section, data from Stages 1 and 3 of the VCP survey are used to explore how carers *receive* and *like to receive* information about:

- the care-recipient's condition
- services and organisations that could assist them.

Carers in Stage 1 were asked who or what was their *main source* of information on their relative's condition and on relevant services and organisations. Carers in Stage 3 were asked who or what they considered to be the *best source* of information and what they considered to be the *best format* for it. Of course, comprising as it does those who have been caregiving at least two years, the Stage 3 sample is no longer representative of all family carers.

WHAT WE FOUND

MAIN AND PREFERRED SOURCES OF INFORMATION

On the *care-recipient's condition*, over half of the carers reported that the general practitioner (GP) had been their main source of information, with medical specialists and allied health professionals next (Table 10.32, p. 309). The other formal sources, namely support organisations and government agencies, were less commonly nominated. Fewer carers nominated informal sources (family and friends, the media and the care-recipient) as their main source. Very few had received no information. Just over half the sample reported the GP

Several carers complained that they had not been informed adequately about the caregiving role.

- One man caring for his wife said: 'Carers are never told what is going to happen to them when they start. The doctors will tell you what is going to happen to your patient. "Your loved one has got Alzheimer's disease, this is what's going to happen." Nobody says to you, "But do you know what is going to happen to *you?*" '
- Another endorsed the view that 'the stress and strain you are going to be under, what it is going to do to you and to your family life, you have got no idea at all. You stumble into it yourself and by fits and starts try to control it. Nobody warns you.'

as their *preferred* source, with medical specialists next. Far fewer preferred allied health professionals and support groups, and government agencies were preferred by only a few. Informal sources were seldom preferred.

While medical professionals were the main source of information on the care-recipient's condition, information sources on *services and organisations* were more varied. GPs, allied health professionals and government agencies, all formal sources, were variously the main information source for approximately a quarter of carers; medical specialists were less often reported as the main source. Again informal sources were less commonly nominated as the main source. A relatively high 19% had received no information at all. Government agencies were the preferred source of a relatively high number, with the GP, support organisations and allied health professionals next.

The GP was clearly the preferred source for information about the care-recipient's condition and, together with government agencies, one of the preferred sources for information about services and organisations (Table 10.32, p. 309). Carers who nominated the GP as a preferred source and those who did not were compared in terms of their characteristics (age, sex, education and qualifications, geographic location, country of birth, income), care-recipient characteristics (age, sex, nature of disability, ADL dependencies) and situational characteristics (relationship between carer and recipient, living arrangements, hours of care provided, years of care provided, reliance on informal support, use of formal respite, and use of community care services).

Those who nominated the GP as a preferred source of information about the care-recipient's condition were more likely to be older carers (over 65), spouse carers, and those caring for people over 60 (Table 10.33, p. 310). Conversely, parent carers, younger carers, those caring for people under 21, and those caring for people with mental disability only were the least likely to prefer the GP for information about the condition. The groups did not differ on the carer, recipient or situational characteristics listed above. There were no differences in the characteristics of those who nominated the GP as a preferred source of information about services and organisations and those who did not.

After GPs, medical specialists were the next preferred source for information about the *care-recipient's condition* (Table 10.34, p. 311). Those who nominated medical specialists were more likely to be co-resident parents under 35 providing 30–100 hours of care a week, and to be caring for males under 21. Offspring carers, those caring for people over 80 and those providing less than ten hours care a week were the least likely to prefer medical specialists. The groups did not differ on other carer, recipient or situational characteristics.

Government agencies were the preferred source of information about *services and organisations* (Table 10.35, p. 312). Those who nominated government agencies here were more likely to be caring for someone living alone, to have some tertiary qualifications, to live in the city rather than the country, and to have used community care services in the past twelve months. The groups did not differ on the other characteristics.

Table 10.36 (p. 312) shows that the preferred format for information about both the *care-recipient's condition* and *services and organisations* was verbal/personal communication, with pamphlets next. The clear majority of carers who preferred getting information by word of mouth were compared with those who did not, on all carer, care-recipient and situational characteristics. There were no differences between the two groups on any variable, for information about either the condition or services and organisations.

Other variables, however, did show up. Those who nominated pamphlets as their next preferred format for information on the *care-recipient's condition* were more likely to be younger carers (35–49), parents, and those caring for males under 21 and/or those with mental disability. Carers over 65 and those caring for people over 80 were the least likely to prefer pamphlets (Table 10.37, p. 313). But they did not differ on other carer, care-recipient or situational characteristics. No differences showed up between those who nominated pamphlets for information about *services and organisations* and those who did not.

WHAT INFORMATION WAS NEEDED

Carers were asked what information would be most helpful to them; their responses covered all their information needs. The first two of their responses were coded, but as fewer than 4% mentioned more than one type, only the first mentioned was included in the analysis presented in Table 10.38 (p. 314). Information on services, including respite, was the most commonly nominated (25% of carers); fewer wanted information on the care-recipient's condition (16%) and on carers' coping and well-being (14%). All other kinds of information were needed by fewer than 5% of carers. Almost half (45%) wanted no particular information.

We compared four broad categories: 84 carers wanting information on services, 53 wanting information on the care-recipient's condition, 47 wanting information about their own well-being and coping, and 151 wanting no information. Parent carers were most likely to want information about their child's condition and less likely to want no information. Consistently, those caring for younger people were more likely to want information about the condition. Spouse and 'other' carers, on the other hand, were more likely to want no information, while 'other' carers were least likely to want information about the condition (Table 10.38, p. 314). Carers with higher school

Information about the disease itself was also regarded as useful in helping caregivers understand their relative's symptoms. One woman explained how seeing a film about dementia helped her understand her husband's behaviour: 'It really helped me more than anything else, because I realise he can't help what he's doing, he's not just doing this just to be difficult.'

167

education and/or tertiary qualifications were more likely than others to want information about services, as were metropolitan carers more so than rural carers. The type of information needed was not related to the other carer, care-recipient or situational characteristics.

WHAT THE FINDINGS MEAN

Information about their relative's condition can enable carers to deal more effectively with symptoms and behaviour problems and be more positive about their own role in the treatment process. Information about services can enable carers to get practical and emotional support other than that provided by family and friends. Although there are variations in how carers receive and like to receive information and about the sort of information they need, clearly most prefer information given in a personal or verbal way. It is not surprising, then, that our evaluation of the Carer Support Kit (Chapter 12) suggested that carers' use of written information is limited—overall, only 23% of 103 carers offered the kit, read or used any part of it. Since our evaluation, the kit has been made available through a variety of outlets, including post offices, pharmacies, Department of Social Security offices, and politicians' electorate offices and can be given to carers in the context of personal verbal support and advice.

Two other closely related findings with major implications for carer support are lack of information being the most frequently cited reason for not receiving needed services, and the most frequently consulted source of information being the carer's GP. GPs, and indeed other medical and health professionals, then, not only need to be aware of the potentially deleterious effects that sustained caring for a frail aged or disabled person can have on the carer, but also to have comprehensive and up-to-date information on community services that could ease this load in order to make appropriate referrals. These needs were addressed in our GP/pharmacist intervention (Chapter 12).

11

RESIDENTIAL CARE
AND PLACEMENT

Recent decades have seen a substantial policy shift in the balance of care provided between nursing homes, hostels and community care under the Aged Care Reform Strategy (Mid-Term Review 1991), with admission to residential care becoming more controlled to prevent premature and unnecessary admission. There has also been an emphasis on community care of younger people (adults and children) with disabilities; integration and deinstitutionalisation policies apply in all disability sectors providing intellectual, sensory, physical and psychiatric services.[1]

While these policies do address the rights and quality of life of people with disabilities, even where family carers are available, serious impairment and the innate stresses of caregiving may mean that residential placement becomes inevitable. The longitudinal nature of our study enabled us to profile carers with a relative already in residential care and take a prospective view of the factors affecting residential placement.

PREDICTORS OF RESIDENTIAL PLACEMENT

Previous studies have identified significant factors in the decision to use residential care. Factors associated with the *care-recipient* (older age,[2] cognitive impairment[3] and physical and instrumental dependencies[4]) have been commonly identified as reasons for institutional placement. Specific problems associated with disability (wandering, forgetfulness and incontinence[5]) have been isolated as key predictors.

In terms of the *carer*, offspring carers[6] and carers not living with the recipient[7] are more likely than others to place their relatives in care, whereas spouse carers are less likely.[8] Other significant factors are stress or burden,[9] being in paid work,[10] or having time constraints due to work.[11] Importantly, a carer's attitude towards nursing-home care and expressed desire to use institutional care are also associated with subsequent residential placement.[12]

Finally, several researchers have also found that *use of more formal services* and paid help increased the odds of institutional placement.[13] Conversely, a high use of informal support networks has been identified as a factor lessening the likelihood of residential placement.[14]

Several longitudinal studies have examined the rate of residential placement, again mainly among carers of the elderly or those with dementia. For example, Colerick and George (1986) found that 22% of 209 community-based dementia patients were institutionalised over a twelve-month study period, but their study was restricted to carers in contact with a family support program. Lieberman and Kramer (1991) reported the same rate of 22% residential placement over one year among their sample of 321 dementia carers; again, however, the sample was non-representative, being selected through several Alzheimer support centres. Tsuji and colleagues (1995) reported a rate of 25% residential placement in a period of almost six years, but was restricted to those previously using community-based home-care services. We would stress that without involving a representative sample of community-based care-dyads such as that in our study, these reported rates of institutional placement are not comparable or meaningful for the population as a whole.

Two American longitudinal studies have assessed residential placement using a representative sample of community-based carers and/or elderly dependants. Using a stratified population sample of community-based disabled elderly (over 70), Jette and colleagues (1995) found that 94 of 586 (16%) had moved into a nursing home within four or five years. A rate of almost 16% nursing-home placement over *two* years was reported by Kasper and Shore (1994), who used data from the 1982 and 1984 National Long Term Care surveys.

Almost all these previous studies have examined residential placement among carers of the elderly, and particularly among dementia carers. The VCP, however, includes all ages and disability groups, and thus allows examination of residential placement in a broad context of all family caregiving.

Carers contemplating residential placement for their relative have great difficulty in letting go. Some never really do let go, still maintaining a regular and significant role in caring for their relative in residential care. On the advice of medical professionals and because of his own ill health, a man who had been caring for his wife at home for many years 'sort of relented' in agreeing to seek nursing-home care for her, at first for brief periods and later permanently. 'I only agreed because I was able to get her out every day if I wished.'

This chapter outlines the extent of use of residential care among carers in the VCP Stage 1 survey. Carers using residential care, those considering using it, and those not considering it are compared in terms of care-recipient and carer characteristics, the nature and severity of the recipient's disability, the amount and nature of care provided, and carers' attitudes to their caregiving role, providing a profile of users and potential users. The incidence of residential placement during the fifteen months from the Stage 1 to the Stage 2 interview is also examined. In order to identify factors associated with residential placement, carers whose relative moved into residential care are compared with those whose relative remained in the community in terms of carer and care-recipient characteristics and, at Stage 1, the nature and severity of the care-recipient's disability, the amount and nature of care provided, use of services, carers' attitudes to their caregiving role, and carers' well-being.

WHAT WE FOUND

USE OF AND ATTITUDES TO RESIDENTIAL CARE

All carers in the Stage 1 survey were asked where their care-recipient lived. For those using residential facilities, carers' satisfaction was measured on a five-point scale from 'very satisfied' to 'very dissatisfied'; reasons for dissatisfaction were recorded. Those not using it were asked whether they had considered residential care and whether they saw it as a good option. Reasons for not using it were also recorded.

Of the full sample of 976 carers, 114 (12%) were caring for a relative or friend living in residential accommodation, including hostel, nursing home, community residential unit, or other supported accommodation. Generally the person lived in residential care seven days a week (11%), the remaining few using it for four or five days a week (1%); these carers were combined for analysis. A further 213 (22%) were considering using residential care and the remaining 629 (66%) were not considering it. Those using residential care, those considering using it, and those not considering it were compared in terms of carer and care-recipient characteristics, the amount and nature of care provided, and carers' attitudes to the caregiving role, providing a profile of users and potential users.

Carer and care-recipient characteristics Compared with spouse and parent carers, adult offspring and 'other' carers were more likely to be using or considering residential care. Indeed, most parent and spouse carers had not considered using it. Carers under 35 and those caring for people under 21 or for males (reflecting a high proportion of parent carers) were also less likely than others to have considered residential care, whereas those caring for people over 80 or for females (reflecting a high proportion of offspring carers) were more likely than other groups to be using it (Table 11.1, p. 315). There were no differences in terms of carer sex, work status, or marital status.

Importantly, those not considering residential care were more likely than others to report financial difficulty (75% of this group reported difficulty in meeting living costs, cf. 63% of remaining carers). Consistently, those using or considering residential care were more likely to own their own home (75% of users and 66% of those considering it, own their home, cf. 54% of those not considering residential care) and to have tertiary qualifications (27% of users and 25% of those considering it, had tertiary qualifications, cf. only 15% of those not considering residential care).[15]

The severity of the care-recipient's disability was also associated with residential care: those whose relative had only minor disability were least likely to have considered it, while those whose relative had a moderate or severe level of both mental and physical disability were more likely to be using it (Table 11.1). In terms of care-recipients' behaviour problems, those considering residential care reported more frequent aggressive, depressive and cognitive behaviours than those not considering it (Table 11.2, p. 316). Those

172

using residential care similarly reported more frequent depressive and cognitive behaviours than those not considering it, and in turn reported more frequent cognitive behaviours than those considering it. In terms of care-recipient dependencies, those using or considering residential care needed more help with physical and instrumental activities than those who had not considered it.

Amount and nature of care Those providing less than ten hours a week were *ipso facto* more likely to be using a residential facility, whereas those caring for more than 100 hours a week were the least likely to have even considered using one (Table 11.1). In terms of the amount of help the carer provided, carers considering residential care were providing more help with instrumental activities than were those not considering it while, not surprisingly, those using residential care were providing the least help with physical activities (Table 11.2). There were no differences between the three groups in terms of the number of years of care that had been provided.

Three scales measured carers' **attitudes to their caregiving role.** Carers considering residential care reported more anger and resentment than did those not doing so, and more resentment than those using it. On the other hand, those not considering residential care reported more satisfaction in their caregiving role than those either using or considering it (Table 11.2).

Those carers whose relatives were in residential care were asked how satisfied they were with the service received. Of the 114 carers, 88% were satisfied, while 10% were dissatisfied. This represents only a handful of the full sample of carers. Their reasons for dissatisfaction were mainly to do with the inadequate care provided because of limited staff.

Of the 213 considering residential care, over half (57%) saw it as a good option. There were no differences between those who saw it thus and those who did not in terms of carer sex, age, marital status, care-recipient age, sex, or nature of disability, the carer-recipient relationship, or the hours or duration of care.

All those carers who had considered residential care were asked why they were not currently using it. As shown in Table 11.3 (p. 316), concern that their care-recipient would not like it was the main deterrent for almost half those who had considered residential care. About a third of carers felt it was not necessary at the time.

INCIDENCE OF RESIDENTIAL PLACEMENT: CHANGES IN LIVING ARRANGEMENTS OVER A YEAR OF CAREGIVING

Of community-based carers from Stage 1 (that is, excluding those caring for someone in residential care), 568 were reinterviewed at Stage 2. Of these, 44 (8%) had since moved their relative into residential care: 23 self-identified as 'still the main carer', while 21 said that they were 'no longer the main carer'. Of 346 care-recipients aged over 60, 39 (11%) had been placed in care. Over half (56%) of the carers reported that their relative had gone into residential care because of a deterioration in health, 17% because of deterioration in their own health, 10% because of changes in their family circumstances, and 17% for other reasons. Regardless of the identified carer status, those who had moved their relative into residential care in the period since the initial interview are combined for the present analyses. They are compared with continuing community-based carers in terms of carer and care-recipient characteristics, the amount and nature of care provided at Stage 1, and the use of community services at Stage 1.

Carer and care-recipient characteristics Adult offspring carers were more likely than others to have had their relative moved into residential care, a substantial 13% having done so. Parent carers were the least likely (1%). Consistently, care-recipients who had moved into residential care were most likely to be in the older age-groups, and to have lived either alone or with someone other than the carer (Table 11.4, p. 317). There were no differences in terms of carer age, sex, marital or work status, education, financial difficulty or home ownership, or care-recipient sex. Not surprisingly, those whose relative had since moved into residential care were more likely than others to have considered this at the time of the Stage 1 interview.

Those who had moved into residential care most likely had both mental and physical disability of at least a moderate degree at Stage 1, and were highly unlikely to have had only mild or only physical disability (Table 11.4). They were also more likely to have had both depressive and cognitive behaviour problems at Stage 1, though they did not differ in aggressive behaviours. They had greater functional dependencies at Stage 1 than those who remained in community-based care (Table 11.5, p. 318).

174

There was no difference on the basis of the *hours of care* provided at Stage 1, or on the amount of *physical and instrumental help* provided by the carer at Stage 1. But the difference in duration of care almost reached statistical significance: those who had been caring less than a year were the most likely to have had their relative placed in residential care, whereas those caring six years or more were the least likely (Table 11.4).

While the two groups did not differ in the anger or resentment they felt at their caregiving role, they did differ in role *satisfaction:* compared with those who remained community carers, those whose relative had since moved into residential care had at Stage 1 reported significantly less satisfaction.

Use of regular community services at Stage 1 clearly distinguished the two groups. Those whose relative had since moved into residential care were more likely than others to have been using general home help, specific home help, community nursing, and transport services at Stage 1, and they were more likely than others to have reported an unmet need for meal services (Table 11.6, p. 318). There was no difference in terms of home maintenance. Similarly, those whose relative had moved into residential care were more likely to have been using respite care at Stage 1, and more often indicated that they wanted more respite. There were no differences in terms of whether informal support was available at Stage 1.

Measures of *carer well-being* did not distinguish the two groups. Carers whose relative had since moved into residential care did not differ from others in terms of reported overload, life satisfaction, positive affect, negative affect or perceived social support at Stage 1.

CARERS' COMMENTS ON THEIR REACTIONS
TO RESIDENTIAL PLACEMENT

Carers were given the opportunity to comment on how it had been for them since their relative moved into residential care. These open comments were coded *post hoc* into three categories:

- positive reactions
- mixed reactions
- predominantly negative reactions.

Over half (59%) of the carers commented on positive changes for themselves or their family since placement. In particular they reported a sense of relief, a decrease in the stress, pressures and family tensions associated with their former caregiving. Some commented on regaining their independence and former lifestyle, or improved family time. A few noted their positive adjustment to new roles and being alone, or their feeling comfortable and confident with the quality of residential care provided.

- 'It's been a bloody relief. We have an hour and a half together in an evening, which is a lot better than before when I was always running around after her.'
- 'It's been a lot easier. I'm able to spend more time with my family and it's not such a strain.'
- 'Very free and very good. I have a lot more freedom and independence.'
- 'The first month was horrific, but once she was in the nursing home I felt comfortable with the home and the care.'

For about a quarter (22%), however, the personal benefits they derived were balanced by feelings of loss, difficulties with the recipient in the initial phase, concerns about the quality of care received or disruption to the newly settled placement because of the continuing deterioration of their relative's health and need for more intensive care.

- 'It's been much more relaxed. I feel like I've put my family back together again as it was rapidly falling apart. But I'm not happy with the care he's gone into. The food's poor, he's lonely and there's not much to do. I worry about his state of mind in a place like that. It puts a bit of strain on me.'
- 'Initially it was good because she got the care she needed, and now, moving into a 24-hour centre, which she needs, is not easy to do.'
- 'It's been pretty up and down, but it's reassuring to know her meals are prepared and she's no longer on her own.'

A smaller group (18%) of carers solely focused on the struggle they were having in adjusting to the placement or their discontent with the quality of care.

- 'Very difficult still, looking after the house physically, financially and mentally.'

- 'She is on a holding basis in the home, waiting to get a place. I've been lonely since then. She wasn't much company in a way due to her illness, but the place is empty without her. We'd been a long time together, just had our 48th anniversary. I cry a bit and it hurts.'
- 'I went back working and intend to get my parents back when the pressure on me is reduced. At the residence, restrictions are unnecessarily imposed on their activities; their independence is taken away and the personal attention is not sufficient.'

Thus while a majority of carers were positive about the impact of placement on their lives, for others difficulties in adjusting to their new status and ongoing issues or concerns about the recipient's care created new stresses.

PREDICTORS OF RESIDENTIAL PLACEMENT OVER FIFTEEN MONTHS OF CAREGIVING

In order to identify significant factors from the Stage 1 interview that made residential placement likely by Stage 2, we looked first at carer-related factors (being an offspring, being a parent, co-residency, role satisfaction, months caregiving, considered residential placement); second at care-recipient factors (age, ADL and IADL dependency, depressive and cognitive behaviour problems, levels of physical and intellectual disability); and third at service-related factors (use of general home help, specific home help, community nursing, meal services, transport and respite care, and unmet need for respite). Not being a parent and having considered residential placement were the best carer-related predictors of residential placement; being elderly and more mentally disabled were the best care-recipient predictors; and using community nursing and not getting needed respite care were the best service-related predictors. Taking all these into consideration, we found the overall best predictors were:

- use of community nursing
- more mentally disabled
- having considered residential care
- less satisfaction in the caregiving role.[16]

Some carers were concerned about the standards of care in residential settings, believing that some nursing homes and hospitals 'do not cater for the different levels of dementia' or were 'seriously understaffed and under pressure'.

- Some worried that there was no adequate substitute for their own care: 'You worry about who will give that same love and care if you can no longer do it.'
- An elderly man caring for his wife said: 'I would hate her to be in there. A lot of the people, they can't talk, they just sit there, they can't do anything. My wife loves to have a talk. So I'm going to keep her home as long as I possibly can.'

Some carers were further burdened by their relative's earlier request that 'you never put me in a nursing home'. These worries weighed against the choice of institutional care:

- 'It's more of a load when they are in than when they are at home.'
- 'Nursing-home care would become more of a burden on me than keeping him at home.'

WHAT THE FINDINGS MEAN

Of the full sample of 976 carers who participated in the initial interview, 12% were caring for a relative living in residential care. Of 568 community-based carers from Stage 1, 8% overall moved their relative into residential care in the fifteen-month period to the second interview, while a higher 11% was found for recipients over 60. Although not directly comparable in terms of sample and study period, two studies which have involved a representative sample provide some comparison. In their two-year follow-up, Kasper and Shore (1994) reported a rate of 16% institutional placement among over-65s, somewhat comparable given the longer study period. However, Jette and colleagues (1995) also reported 16% placement over a longer four- to five-year period for their sample of over-70s.

Overall, four factors were associated with *use or consideration of residential care* at the time of the initial survey:

- the *carer–recipient relationship*, with offspring and 'other' carers more likely than parent or spouse carers to use or consider using residential care
- the *care-recipient disability*, with those caring for more severely disabled and/or older relatives and those with more frequent behaviour problems and greater physical dependencies more often using or considering it
- *socio-economic factors*, with home-owners, more highly educated carers, and financially secure carers more likely to use or consider residential care
- *emotional factors*, with carers expressing more anger and resentment with their role and less satisfaction more likely to consider residential care.

In terms of *movement into residential care* during the fifteen-month study period, again four key factors were identified:

- the centrality of the relationship between carer and care-recipient
- the severity of the care-recipient's disability
- the use of services
- having considered using residential care.

Specifically, those with a less central relationship (offspring carers, non-resident carers, those caring for a shorter duration, and those reporting lower satisfaction) were more likely to have moved the care-recipient into residential care during the study period. Where the care-recipient had more severe disability, more frequent behaviour problems, and higher ADL needs, residential placement was also more likely. Those using community services (community nursing, home help, transport and respite) were more likely to have moved into residential care. And finally, carers who had considered residential care were more likely than others to pursue this avenue later. Indeed, use of community nursing, high mental disability in the care-recipient, the carer having considered residential care, and low satisfaction in the caregiving role were the key predictors of residential placement during the fifteen months.

Previous studies have similarly emphasised the importance of the centrality or closeness of the carer–recipient relationship,[17] cognitive impairment in the care-recipient,[18] and use of community-based formal services.[19] While no previous studies have measured consideration of residential care, one has identified 'desire to institutionalise' as a predictor of subsequent movement into residential care.[20] Both variables indicate that having considered residential care as a possibility for the future is associated with actual residential placement.

In terms of the centrality of the relationship, it has been suggested earlier that co-residency rather than kinship ties is the important factor in predicting residential placement.[21] In our findings, both offspring carers and non-resident carers were more likely than others to use residential care. But neither of these variables emerged as a significant *predictor* of residential placement. Instead, low satisfaction with the caregiving role was a significant predictor of residential placement, accounting for the variance of both relationship and co-residency. This suggests that, regardless of the kinship tie or the living arrangements, *residential placement is more likely among carers less positively involved in their caregiving*. In a similar vein, Orbell and Gillies (1993) in their general population study identified the degree of satisfaction as the single most powerful predictor of a carer's desire to relinquish their caregiving role.

Contrary to findings from previous studies, various factors indicating high involvement in caregiving tasks and carer burnout were not associated with movement into residential care. Specifically, carers providing many hours of care and/or a great deal of hands-on care were no more likely to place their relative in care than were carers providing few hours and little such care. Moreover, carers' stress and well-being were not associated with residential placement, again in contrast to previous reports.[22] Given the generic nature of our sample (including care-recipients of all ages and disability levels), in addition to the range of residential facilities covered in our analysis, differences may be expected. For example, parent and young spouse carers, the most highly stressed subgroups in our sample (see Chapter 6), may be less inclined to seek residential care whatever the emotional costs, by virtue of the centrality of their relationship to the recipient and/or the scarcity of appropriate residential services. Thus for the general carer population our findings suggest that there are more important determinants of residential placement than carer stress or burnout.

Finally, an important finding emerges from these results: even after moving their relative into residential care, over half the carers nonetheless identify as 'having the main responsibility in caring' as defined in our screening question for the VCP interview. This view of continued responsibility concurs with other studies of carers who have placed their relatives in residential care.[23] It suggests that carers may need acknowledgment of this ongoing role through creative involvement in the life of the residential facility and in the continued care of their relative. In some instances, especially where ongoing carer stress is high, they may need additional support, for example counselling or support groups, to manage issues associated with the transition to residential care, such as those noted by our carers.[24]

Such recognition and support would help carers' coping with new stresses, such as feelings of guilt inherent in the decision, the shock of a nursing-home atmosphere with many highly-impaired residents, tensions with formal caregiving staff, and economic demands. Additionally, help with feelings of grief, loss and loneliness associated with changes in the carer–recipient relationship, and generally rebuilding their lives may be important for some carers.[25] Importantly, however, such attention to carers' adjustment needs requires recognition at a broad funding and policy level to ensure commitment and resources at the community or service level.[26]

12

Health promotion strategies

Parallel to our survey research, we explored various interventions to promote the well-being of carers and their relatives. The longitudinal nature of our study allowed us first to identify carers' needs, second to devise strategies to meet those needs, and third to implement and test the effectiveness of those strategies with sub-samples of our survey participants. Each of the strategies has a generic, public health focus and uses existing service systems. That interventions could be tested with a random selection of Victoria's caregivers was a strong aspect of the design of the VCP.

The main aims of our interventions were:

- to identify what intervention strategies are most likely to improve the well-being of caregivers or groups of caregivers
- to facilitate the development and introduction of measures promoting the well-being of caregivers
- to evaluate each measure introduced.

In order to identify the strategies we used several sources of information:

- consultation with service providers, support groups, researchers and planners
- a review of policy related to caregivers and service provision
- literature relating to local and overseas interventions
- an analysis of ABS survey data on carers of people with disability
- results from our exploratory interviews and the 1992 pilot survey.

The VCP with its diverse range of study participants was in a good position to identify the 'common' needs of carers and to conceptualise interventions accordingly. This enables the consideration of broader policy options for carers and future recommendations about appropriate services for all carers, rather than those from a particular disability group. Previous studies, as pointed out already, have chosen caregivers according to the disabling condition of the recipient, with the assumption that carers of people with a specific condition have needs in common and are linked by the problems specific to that illness or disability. While the condition can be a useful starting point, there are other important aspects of caregivers' lives that may be much more important, for example life-stage, other family commitments, whether resident or non-resident, the relationship between carer and recipient, and so on. And it is important to recognise that categorising disability is often problematic: findings from our study present a huge range of conditions, and in a large proportion of these there was no specific primary disability but rather multiple, often age-related, problems. It is also true that similar symptoms, dependencies and behaviour problems can result from quite different conditions. For example, there are similarities between Alzheimer's disease, alcohol-related brain damage, traumatic brain injury, and some psychiatric conditions.

Given the broad pragmatic aims of the intervention study, the size and nature of sampling, and the generic focus of the VCP as a whole, we wanted to use interventions that could be implemented feasibly on a large scale and within the existing system.

Various services are currently available to carers throughout Victoria, provided by local councils, specific disability support groups, and voluntary organisations. But from our own research and others' we know that few carers are receiving support from formal sources in their caregiving role (see Chapter 10), and for various reasons the effectiveness of the available services has for the most part not been assessed. There was little point in the VCP devising interventions that already existed in the community, even if not widely used or evaluated, and that would have no future beyond the life and resources of the VCP. We therefore collaborated with existing service providers in devising and implementing interventions that would use existing resources and make it more likely that effective interventions had some mechanism for continuing.

THE RANGE OF INTERVENTIONS

Interventions were designed on the basis of:

- carers' needs, which were identified empirically and through research literature
- consultations and collaboration with service providers and support organisations
- practical considerations such as time, resources and geographic location.

In framing interventions to address needs, it was useful to consider previous strategy evaluations, the expressed needs of carers, and the factors identified as crucial to the caregiver role. The choice about becoming a carer is often severely limited by the pre-existing relationship between carer and cared for. But choice, even within circumstantial constraints, has been shown to empower people and positively affect their health and well-being. It was decided therefore that the VCP interventions be framed to allow carers maximum choice by:

- providing information about caregiving and relevant services
- facilitating links to services.
- liberating and supporting carers to address their own needs.

Carer Support Kit Throughout Victoria one in ten randomly selected carers were allocated to the Carer Support Kit intervention. The kit was developed by the then Commonwealth Department of Health, Housing and Community Services and launched in the months preceding our Stage 1 interview.

GP and pharmacist link to services The population of identified carers in the Western metropolitan region of Melbourne were allocated to the GP/pharmacist intervention. Carers living in half of the local government areas (again clustered by geographic proximity) were allocated to the GP intervention and those in the other half to the pharmacist.

Home-based assessment Carers in the Eastern and Northern metropolitan areas were allocated to the Home-based Assessment intervention. This intervention was planned and implemented in collaboration with local aged care assessment teams.

The population of carers identified in the Southern region (excluding those selected for the Support Kit intervention) formed the control group for all interventions.

UPTAKE AND USE OF THE CARER SUPPORT KIT

As an example of information that is accepted by some carers and appears to have some benefit, we conducted a study of the Carer Support Kit (CSK). Developed in consultation with carers, it comprises:

- fact sheets relating to home safety, respite care, self-care and financial help
- information about specific disabilities
- a directory of services
- an emergency care plan
- a 'medi-list' for recording medications
- a relaxation tape
- a tape of discussions with carers.

At the time our evaluation was made, kits were distributed through the Carers Association in each state of Australia. Carers could request a kit either by telephoning the Carers Association in their state or by completing and mailing a request leaflet.

Little is known about the use or effect of written information for family carers, or about the best way to disseminate information packages.[1] Smith and Birchwood (1987) found that carers receiving mailed educational material reported the same significant decrease in stress and burden as did carers participating in a series of professionally-led educational sessions. In contrast, Sutcliffe and Larner (1988) found that carers receiving and discussing information sheets showed an increase in knowledge but no change in levels of distress. Both studies were limited by their small and non-representative samples.

With its longitudinal design and large, representative sample, the VCP provided an ideal opportunity for evaluation of the CSK. The VCP team has published a study on the uptake and use of the kit by a random sample of carers interviewed for Stage 1.[2] Its aims were:

- to compare the demographic and health characteristics of
  (a) carers requesting and not requesting the kit
  (b) carers using and not using the kit
- to evaluate carers' perceptions of the usefulness of the kit.

From the full sample of 976 carers who participated in the Stage 1 interview, a random sample of 103 carers was offered the Carer

Support leaflet, which describes the kit and tells people how to get it from the Carers Association. There were no significant differences between carers who were offered the leaflet and the remainder of the full sample. Every tenth carer interviewed in Stage 1 was asked if they had heard about the CSK and if they would like to receive the leaflet. Those who had been sent the leaflet were interviewed three months after their Stage 1 interview to see what use they had made of it.[3]

WHAT WE FOUND

Of the sample of 103 carers, 28 (27%) did not want the leaflet sent and 75 (73%) accepted the leaflet offer. Thirty-six of these 75 had asked the Carers Association to send the kit. Most of the remainder said they had not wanted the kit or had been too busy to send for it. Five reported no need for the kit because their relative had since died or gone into residential care. By the time of the follow-up interview, twelve (33%) had not read any parts of the kit. Half of these said they had been dealing with a crisis at the time, or had themselves been too ill or busy to read it. The other half said they had felt no need to do so. The remaining 24 carers (66% of those who received the kit and 23% of the eligible sample of 103) had read or used all or part of it. There were no significant differences in sex, age, marital status, education level, geographic location or relation-ship to recipient between those who had initially applied for the kit and those who had not, but there was a trend for spouses to be more likely than other carers both to request and to use it.

Those who had applied for the kit had more overload and less life satisfaction than those who had not, but those who had applied for it *but not used it* reported higher anxiety, depression and more health problems than both those who had used the kit and those who had not applied for it. Those who had applied for the kit were more likely to use medication, and were more likely to rate their own health as either fair or poor compared with those who had not applied. Those who had applied for it but not used it were signifi-cantly more likely to report major health problems in the past twelve months.

Those who had applied for the kit reported using more formal services: general and specific home help, community nursing, meals services, home maintenance, home modifications, transport, training programs, counselling and respite services.

At the follow-up interview, all 24 carers rated the kit as well presented, easy to understand, and encouraging. Most also rated it as relevant to their needs and informative. A few thought it irrelevant and uninformative. Most were satisfied overall; several mentioned having passed the kit on to carer friends who had also found it very useful. Carers rated the usefulness of each component and nominated the 'most useful' component (Table 12.1, p. 319).

Nine of the 24 carers reported that the kit 'reinforced things I already knew' rather than giving new information. Others had gained knowledge about available services, their relatives' condition, their need for respite, safety in the home, and the extent of family caring in the community. Some had learned new ways of coping with the stresses of caring. Half the carers reported having taken some action suggested in the kit, such as having planned or implemented home modifications, completed the emergency care card or medi-list, discussed home safety issues with the family, contacted services listed in the directory, contacted a solicitor, taken more time for self-care and relaxation, or instigated an assessment through the local aged care assessment team. Again, those who had not taken specific action emphasised the value of having the information at hand to refer to when necessary.

Ten of the 24 carers offered suggestions on other information which would have been helpful. Most wanted more information about specific services, including facilities available in nursing-home care, services to improve coping, support groups, after-hours support services for carers, assessment services, physiotherapy and activities for children with physical disabilities, special government-subsidised accommodation, linkage services, interpreter services, veterans' affairs and various helpful tips. Specific fact sheets for sight and hearing loss were also listed as potentially helpful.

WHAT THE FINDINGS MEAN

Evaluation of the efficacy of the kit was problematic because of the low uptake rate and subsequent small sample size, but some useful indications did emerge. Those who applied for the kit were more stressed, and reported lower life satisfaction and poorer health than those who did not want the leaflet or did not apply for the kit, confirming that the kit had reached a group in need. It was therefore recommended that the kit be disseminated in more community outlets in addition to the Carers Associations: it has since been made available through post offices, pharmacies, DSS and electoral offices.

Those who had received the kit *but not used it* also reported higher anxiety, depression and more health problems than other carers. Where the relative's condition or the carer's own health had deteriorated, it is likely that the carer considered the information as less immediately relevant: being in crisis, it was too late for the information to be used preventively. This finding was consistent with previous observations that educational sessions are of greater use to carers in the early phases of illness,[4] and emphasises the need for the CSK to be disseminated widely and to be readily available to carers not just when they reach a crisis point.

While adequately motivated to *apply* for the kit, some carers felt no need to read it: they either believed the information would not benefit them or felt incapable of using it. Particularly for those feeling depressed or overloaded, it is probably easier to find the motivation to ask for the kit than it is to actually sit down and read it once it arrives. And it may be that the opportunity to have telephone contact with someone from the Carers Association was also a motive for applying for the kit, at least for some of these carers. Unfortunately, the method of application—telephone or mail—was not recorded during the evaluation interview, so this explanation remained speculative.

Carers clearly needed more opportunities to use the kit in a context of interpersonal contact and discussion. Several interviewed carers commented that they felt 'less alone' after listening to the tape of carers' stories. It was therefore recommended that the kit be disseminated in more community outlets such as community health centres, carer and disability support organisations in addition to the Carers Association.

Our findings suggested, then, that the CSK gave new information or reassurance to those who used it. Provision of the kit in the context of group discussions with carers would no doubt increase the accessibility, potency and, therefore, the use of this information, particularly if made available to carers *before* they reach a crisis point.

THE ROLE OF GENERAL PRACTITIONERS AND PHARMACISTS IN LINKING CARERS WITH COMMUNITY SERVICES[5]

Despite their potential benefits, community services are not widely used by family carers. This is due, to a large extent, to carers' lack of awareness of what is available and how to access it. Indeed, in the VCP survey the most common reason carers reported for *not* receiving a needed service was lack of information (see Chapter 10). Clearly, mechanisms for effectively informing carers about service availability and access have not been found.

The question is who is to give this information. General practitioners and pharmacists are well placed to reach a high proportion of carers: Australia's GPs are consulted by over 80% of the general population and by 90% of the elderly in any year, while pharmacists give an estimated 17 million consultations.[6] With this regular contact with patients and customers and, in many cases, the concomitant knowledge of caregivers' responsibilities and needs, GPs and pharmacists can provide a much-needed link with community support services. The VCP survey found that GPs were the most commonly nominated source of information about relevant services and organisations.

But GPs' and pharmacists' knowledge of available services is limited (see Brodaty et al. 1994). In order to provide an effective link between carers and services, they need information about local services and the resources to help them disseminate it. With this in view, the VCP produced tear-off pads with lists of services available to carers in the Western region of Melbourne and delivered them with an accompanying poster to GPs and pharmacists. We conducted a five-month trial of GPs' and pharmacists' use of the resources, and assessed changes in their attitudes and reported practices regarding discussion with caregivers. The information in this section has been given in more detail in Murphy, Nankervis et al. (1997).

Listed services included general and specific home help, home-delivered meals, centre-based meals, home modifications and maintenance, interchange, day care, home nursing, respite care, home and centre-based paramedical services, transport, information, carer support and training, assessment, monitoring, recreation, and friendly visiting.

RECRUITING AND VISITING GPs AND PHARMACISTS

With the endorsement of the Western and Westgate Divisions of General Practice and the Pharmacists Society of Australia (Victorian Branch), GPs and pharmacists were visited by six trained facilitators (second-year medical students) who explained the materials and conducted the pre-trial interview. In initiating discussion with carers, GPs and pharmacists were to ask carers if they were receiving any help in caregiving, give them a tear-off list of services, highlighting any which seemed particularly relevant, and encourage them to make enquiries. Each GP and pharmacist received pads with a list of services specific to their suburb and also one of ethnic services. Three months after the visit, the facilitator telephoned participating professionals to reinforce the strategy and to check supplies of materials. Additional pads and posters were mailed where necessary. A second interview took place five months after the first.

Both interviews assessed GPs' and pharmacists' perceptions of the numbers of carers seen weekly and the impact of caring on carers' health, their self-rated knowledge of community services and frequency of discussion with carers about services, and their attitudes to the rewards and difficulties of working with family carers.[7]

WHAT WE FOUND

PRE-TRIAL RESULTS

Two hundred and twenty-seven GPs and 81 pharmacists were given the materials and interviewed; 7% of GPs and 6% of pharmacists approached refused to be interviewed. Most of the GPs were male and most were in group practice. In years of experience 51% had ten years or less, 29% 11–20 years and 21% over twenty years. Similarly, pharmacists were mostly male but had had longer experience.

Before the intervention, GPs reported greater knowledge of services than did pharmacists: 34% of GPs as opposed to only 11% of pharmacists reported a 'good or excellent' knowledge of what was available for carers. A large 60% of pharmacists and a small 19% of GPs reported a 'very poor' or 'poor' knowledge. Those remaining reported a 'limited but adequate' knowledge. GPs also reported more frequent discussion with carers than pharmacists: 48% said they discussed caregiving 'often or always', compared with 35% of pharmacists. A substantial 23% of pharmacists reported that they 'rarely' discussed caregiving, compared with only 10% of GPs. GPs were also more likely to report that they discussed carer services 'often or always' in these discussions (39% cf. 7%). A large 68% of pharmacists reported that they 'rarely' discussed services with carers, compared with only 16% of GPs. The two groups differed only a little when asked who started discussion, most reporting that it was started equally often by the carer or the professional.

Despite less knowledge of services and less likelihood of discussing issues with carers, pharmacists saw more carers each week than GPs did and were more likely to report that caregiving had an impact on the carers' health and well-being: over half the pharmacists saw more than ten carers a week, compared with only 14% of GPs; and about twice the proportion of pharmacists as GPs saw caregiving as having 'a large impact' on carers' health and well-being. Not surprisingly, for GPs and pharmacists combined, those reporting greater knowledge of services were more likely than others to also report greater frequency of discussion with carers before the trial about caregiving generally and services specifically.

POST-TRIAL RESULTS

One hundred and nine GPs and 58 pharmacists were interviewed after the trial; 29 GPs and eight pharmacists refused this second interview. Again, they were predominantly male, and most of the GPs were in group practice. Demographically, those who dropped out did not differ significantly from those who remained, and the second sample did not differ significantly from the first. Each GP and pharmacist had distributed from none to 90 locality-specific lists and up to 50 ethnic services lists. The low and concentrated use of ethnic services lists was largely due to the clustering of non-English-speaking carers in particular practices and pharmacies. There was no difference in distribution between GPs and pharmacists, although there was a trend for higher distribution by pharmacists for the local lists.

The locality-specific tear-off pad was rated 'useful' or 'very useful' by 67% of GPs and 76% of pharmacists. The ethnic services pad was rated as 'useful' or 'very useful' by 46% GPs and 35% pharmacists. A high 81% of GPs and 83% of pharmacists rated the pads as 'easy' or 'very easy' to incorporate into their usual consulting style.

Participants were asked to which community services they had most often referred carers during the trial period. HACC services, including home help, meals, home maintenance and transport, were the most commonly recommended. Royal District Nursing, aged care assessment teams and Linkages were commonly mentioned by GPs. Both groups sometimes referred carers to day or respite care, para-medical services, support groups and other services.

There was a significant increase in pharmacists' reported knowl-edge of carer services: while only 12% reported 'good' or 'excellent' knowledge before the trial, a relatively large 49% reported this afterwards, and reports of 'poor' or 'very poor' knowledge decreased markedly from 50% to 5%. GPs' knowledge of services increased a little, with reports of 'poor' or 'very poor' knowledge dropping from 17% to 6%. While before the trial GPs reported higher knowledge than did pharmacists, there was no difference between the two in self-rated knowledge of services afterwards.

There was also a significant increase in pharmacists' reported frequency of discussions with carers: while only 9% 'often' or 'always' discussed services with carers before the trial, 21% did so after it. Consistently, the proportion who 'rarely' discussed services decreased from 64% to 37%. GPs also increased in their discussion, though not significantly: the proportion who 'often' or 'always' discussed services increased from 32% to 39%, while the proportion who 'rarely' dis-cussed services decreased from 18% to 14%. But though pharmacists had more discussion with carers during the trial period they still discussed services less often than GPs. There were no differences on any of the post-trial variables on the basis of sex, type of practice, or years of experience.

Supporting their validity, self-reports of knowledge of services and frequency of discussion were both found to be associated with the number of service lists distributed: compared with those who had distributed no lists, twice the proportion of those who had distributed over ten lists reported good/excellent knowledge of and often/always discussing services in consultations with carers.

The participants spoke of an increased awareness of local carer services and the available range, and also of the difficulties and strain of caregiving, the ageing of the population and the need for care-giving to be given a higher profile. Several said they now had greater confidence in initiating discussion with carers and dealing with any problems that arose. Pharmacists in particular expressed their appreciation of the opportunity to improve their knowledge of local community services and to be provided with written materials to distribute.

Participants noted the following difficulties in working with carers, in order of commonness:

- carers' reluctance to accept help outside the family
- professionals' frustration at being unable to help
- dealing with stress
- working within time constraints
- the inadequacy of services
- helping with decisions on residential placement
- the lack of remuneration in counselling work.

There were also rewards:

- their effectiveness in reducing carers' stress
- establishing a bond with families
- delaying or avoiding residential placement
- carers' gratitude
- improved professional reputation.

WHAT THE FINDINGS MEAN

GPs showed a fairly high involvement with carers before the trial and a modest increase in their knowledge of services and frequency of discussions with carers. Pharmacists were very receptive to the present strategy and saw information exchange for carers as part of their role. The improvement in knowledge of services and frequency of discussion with carers highlights their potential for working with carers once they are given the resources to do so. Pharmacists reportedly saw more carers than GPs and were more likely to acknowledge the impact of caregiving on health.

In the light of Sanson-Fisher and Cockburn's (1993:83) comment that 'it is unrealistic to expect a practitioner to make a substantial change in behaviour over a relatively short time', our results are particularly encouraging, even with the limitations we found it necessary to impose. The high response rate and the observed receptivity indicate that despite the difficulties they encounter, many GPs and pharmacists are willing to learn more about caregiving issues and local service networks. Undoubtedly, this

The dilemma for general practitioners and other medical professionals concerns the amount of information to provide, the timing and the approach: overloading patients and carers with information, or giving information insensitively can have equally negative effects. The responsibility of medical professionals and the vulnerability of carers is highlighted in the comments of one man caring for his wife: 'A social worker said to me the other week, "In about six to eighteen months' time you won't be in this situation", and I didn't dare ask him what he meant. I'm just trying to cope with everything, and . . . I *know* it, but when you actually have someone *telling* you that, someone who you consider knows what they are talking about, that's frightening. I nearly broke down there and then.'

Others praised general practitioners for their support in providing information about services. One man whose wife had a terminal and debilitating illness remarked: 'As soon as a diagnosis was made the doctor said, "Now I want you to join the relevant society". He was the most caring doctor. He looked after me.'

low-intensity strategy has merely touched the tip of the iceberg in helping health professionals in their information exchange with carers. Nonetheless, our approach and findings provide an example of what can be done.

HOME-BASED ASSESSMENT

There is some evidence that receiving formal support, for example, respite care, education, self-help carer groups and other home-based supports have positive effects for both carers and their relatives.[8] Despite this, formal services are typically engaged only when informal supports are unavailable or a crisis is reached.[9] One goal of the health promotion component of the VCP is thus to enhance caregivers' choice, health and well-being through a more *timely* provision of information or linkage to services. We set out to test whether a non-crisis *comprehensive* assessment of the carer's situation would provide these things. To do this we adapted the existing home-based assessment procedure carried out by aged care assessment teams (ACATs).

The purpose of preventive home-based assessment is typically to identify needs and promote attitudes, behaviours and services that enhance the health of relatively healthy older people. Studies of this procedure have usually focused on the care-recipient;[10] our intervention extends the home-based preventive strategy to include the caregiver. Our specific objectives were to identify the extent and pattern of unmet need for formal community services by carers and recipients, and, where need was identified, to facilitate earlier access to community supports by providing information and referral. Findings on these matters are referred to only briefly here; a fuller description of the assessment and the method used have been published in Nankervis and colleagues (1997). The present focus is on the response to the visit and its effectiveness in promoting carers' well-being and longer-term service use.

The intervention consisted of a single outreach visit to care-dyads. A staff member of a regional ACAT conducted a standard home-based assessment accompanied by a specially trained member of our research team. ACATs were chosen for their holistic, multi-disciplinary approach and their capacity to assess people from a range of age and disability cohorts. Their skill in assessing people with multiple or undefined needs, their capacity to work in cooperation with medical and other professionals, as well as their extensive local knowledge, further matched our requirements.

The Northern and Eastern Metropolitan and South-West (Rural) health regions were selected for the intervention. All 186 Stage 1 carers whose relative was over 25 years and not in residential care were invited by letter to participate. They were typically married, middle-aged women looking after parents or spouses. Sixty-seven (53%) agreed, with those declining giving privacy, temporary circumstances (e.g. holidays, ill health), and the care-recipient's refusal or improvement as the main reasons. Care-dyads taking part did not differ from those declining or ineligible in socio-demographic characteristics, carers' reported health status and well-being, recipients' dependency levels, the amount of assistance provided by the carer or the supports available to them.

IMPLEMENTING THE HOME VISIT

Eight ACAT services collaborated with the VCP over six months in 1994. The ACATs organised the actual visit and followed their usual allocation procedures; staff from one of six disciplines (nursing, social work, occupational therapy, geriatric medicine, physiotherapy or psychiatric care) thereby attended. Visits lasted 60–90 minutes, with the ACAT staff member taking the lead in assessment and formulating with the care-dyad an agreed action plan for referral to community services or for independent family follow-up.

Within the ACAT assessment, information is routinely collected about client health and treatment, cognitive or behavioural problems, independence in physical and instrumental activities, community and family supports. The researcher also rated the client's level of depression, the amount of assistance provided by the carer with everyday activities and the level of informal support provided by family members to the carer. Other data relating to carer health and the dyads' socio-demographic characteristics were available from the Stage 1 survey.

EVALUATING THE VISIT

Evaluation proceeded in two stages: first, participating carers were interviewed two months after the visit. A different researcher from the home visit administered a brief questionnaire which explored care-dyads' emotional reactions to the visit and carers' opinions about the visit's convenience, length and relevance, follow-through on the action plan, and satisfaction with both service links and the intervention as a whole. Second, the effectiveness of the intervention was evaluated in terms of carers' health and well-being. Sixty-one carers (91%) who took part in the home visit were reinterviewed at Stage 2. The 52 who identified themselves as still the main carer were compared with a control group of carers drawn from the Southern metropolitan region. This group comprised 68 carers who would have met the initial home assessment criteria and who were still caring at the main Stage 2 interview. The two groups did not differ significantly at Stage 1 except in the greater impairment of the recipient. The comparison included assessment of differential changes between participating carers and the control group on seven measures of health and well-being collected during the Stages 1 and 2 interviews.

Comparative use of health and community services by both groups was also included.

WHAT WE FOUND

WHO THE CARERS WERE

Most of the care-recipients had multiple conditions or illnesses, mainly arthritis (42%), musculoskeletal disorders (31%), heart disease (25%), gastro/urinogenital problems (19%), Parkinson's and other diseases of the central nervous system (18%), and respiratory conditions (16%). Almost half were rated by the ACAT as having two or more moderate/severe impairments from six functional areas. Most were reasonably self-sufficient in physical activities of daily living, but two-thirds were dependent in four or more instrumental activities, particularly shopping, preparing meals, transport, housekeeping and managing finances.

In over three-quarters of the assessments at least one unmet need for formal services was identified on which ACAT staff would make a referral to community services, a secondary assessment, or more detailed specific resource information. The most common recommendations were for respite care, aids and paramedical services (Table 12.2, p. 319).

The follow-up interview established that 72% of care-dyads visited had been linked to a new service by the ACATs and that of all the recommended services half had been used *and* found useful by the carer in the two months since assessment. Links to services had not been made because of changes in the carer's or recipient's circumstances, the recipient's refusal or lack of interest, or a failure to (re)contact by either the ACAT or the service provider. Referrals were of no use in the few cases where the recipient subsequently refused to use the service or where there were difficulties in using it such as stringent eligibility criteria, waiting lists or unavailability for specific client groups.

THE BENEFITS OF THE ASSESSMENT AND ITS SEQUEL

Carers were overwhelmingly positive in their rating of the assessment visit. They found the assessment thorough (91%), informative (88%) and relevant to their needs (77%). A high 93% also reported that everything they had expected to be discussed had been covered, although 19% had later thought of other things that could have been raised, such as general issues of financial assistance or social activities. Carers also overwhelmingly agreed that the visit was relaxed (97%) and convenient (95%); very few thought it too long or intrusive or involved too many people. A large majority said that the visit made them feel listened to (98%), reassured (88%), more positive (78%) and less alone (74%). A small number had felt upset, embarrassed or confused.

Carers reported an overall positive but more mixed range of emotional responses to the visit by their relative. Many said they believed the care-recipient had felt listened to (85%), reassured (60%), more positive (57%), and less alone (47%). But 25% had been confused by the visit, 13% upset and 13% embarrassed at the time. Even where specific negative reactions were reported for the recipient, a number of carers qualified their responses. For example, several commented these reactions were unavoidable or not too problematic given the nature of the condition or the reality of the issues to be tackled.

- 'Mother felt indignant about being assessed. She didn't think she should be. It wasn't how they handled it but how she took it. She really liked them, but what was discussed was a little too near the truth.'
- 'He did get upset and tearful as it's hard to talk about how things were for him. He doesn't like speaking about his own problems.'

The assessment served as a trigger for new discussion about caring with other family members or service providers; 10% of carers reported that their doctor had commented positively on the visit, and 26% that family members or friends had been interested and encouraging. A woman caring for a parent suffering from a stroke, memory problems and arthritis revealed the impact the visit had for the whole family.

- 'I phoned my sister and copied bits of paper for her. She found it helpful and passed it on to our other sister. Now we can share the responsibility better.'

Three-quarters of carers rated the assessment and subsequent events as generally helpful or very helpful. Male carers, interestingly enough, were more likely than females to rate the visit as 'very helpful'. In particular, carers valued the benefits they derived from using the services—improved morale, comprehensive information about services, and help to access them.

- 'We both have much more peace of mind and feel more content with the caring situation.'
- 'It absolved me of my guilt feelings. I feel very much reassured.'
- 'The visit was helpful because we'd never thought of getting her a hearing aid. The volunteer visitor is very helpful. It's changed her mood; she's much happier now.'
- 'People should be made aware of all the services that are available. The hospital told me about some, but I had no idea of the range that was out there or how to access them.'
- 'I'm very grateful that the visit came at that time. When the appointment was made no help was required, but that changed after the visit with mother being admitted to hospital. It all became relevant and there's going to be a stage soon of looking for alternative accommodation.'
- 'I felt I was connected to a system that would address my needs and my mother's, now and in the future.'

In contrast to the generally positive rating were eleven carers who had expected but not found the visit helpful. 'I knew it all already' was a typical response.

- 'There was some useful information but nothing that revolutionised our lives. It brought home that a lot of support is designed for the care of older people. Not much is offered for younger people, particularly respite.'
- A mother of an intellectually-disabled young adult requiring respite commented: 'It wasn't helpful, [but] it's a lot to do with me. I didn't learn anything and I'm continuing on as before.' Despite this, she later passed on the ACAT contact name to two other sole parents of disabled young adults and referred three more to the Carers Association.
- Three carers were frustrated and distressed that promised services did not eventuate, especially because of waiting lists for particular client groups: '[The visit] didn't help me to care for Mum. I really needed hands-on help then and there, not months later on.'

EFFECT ON CARERS' HEALTH AND WELL-BEING

When interviewed at Stage 2 of the main survey, carers in our assessment were not significantly different from the control group, nor as a group different from their Stage 1 status, on any measure (the self-health-rating, experience of major health problems in the past year and use of medication). Overall, 65% participant carers reported being in good or excellent health, although 48% acknowledged serious health problems in the past year and 59% currently used medications. Similarly, differential change between the participant carers and the control group following the intervention was not evident on any of the individual measures of well-being: overload, life satisfaction, positive and negative affect, satisfaction in caregiving or feelings of social support. As a measure of change in more objective carer burden (potentially relieved by the intervention), there was no differential change from Stage 1 between participant and control carers in the proportion of assistance provided with their relative's personal care, mobility and instrumental dependencies.

EFFECT ON USE OF SERVICES

Participant care-dyads had undertaken more home modifications in the past year than the comparison group (44% cf. 12%), obtained more personal aids (52% cf. 28%), and overall consulted more medical/health professionals. This last difference was largely accounted for by contact with social workers (37% cf. 12%) and occupational therapists (31% cf. 9%) and represented a significant increase in the contact with these professions by participant dyads over Stage 1.[11]

There was no differential change in the total number of respite and regular community services used overall or in the use of any specific service. Participating carers were, however, more likely at Stage 2 to desire more respite than the comparison group (54% cf. 17%), although this difference perhaps reflected the higher pre-existing need in the participant group, there being no significant increase in their rate of expressed need (54% cf. 38% at the Stage 1 interview). The reasons given by a small number for not receiving desired respite were the care-recipient's negative feelings, cost, waiting lists and lack of suitable services in the area.

Overall, almost half (45%) of participant dyads reported no unmet need for respite or community services, while a further 22%

identified one needed service. Of the 65 services required, over half were new needs that had not been identified either during the home assessment or by the carer in the Stage 1 interview. Of the 27 previously identified needs, over half were for respite care, further indicating this to be the single most difficult service for carers to access.

WHAT THE FINDINGS MEAN

The outreach assessment identified considerable unmet need for formal supports, even with a reasonably independent mixed-age recipient group, and facilitated linkage to a variety of supports for the carer and care-recipient. These findings extend reports elsewhere of the value of an unsolicited home assessment in identifying unrecognised risks or needs, particularly non-medical ones, among a relatively healthy older population.[12] Moreover, they resemble assessment outcomes in the recent review of Victorian ACATs, in which approximately three-quarters of clients surveyed reported practical benefits.[13]

Roughly similar proportions of carers in the ACAT review and the VCP study said that the assessment had been helpful. Importantly however, while the direct benefits of new supports were nominated as the most helpful impact by a fifth of carers, it is particularly noteworthy that a majority nominated other factors, in particular enhanced morale and reassurance, and confidence to access future supports through more comprehensive information and a known entry point to the service system. While such benefits were also evident in the ACAT review, their greater emphasis in our study may reflect the early non-crisis nature of our intervention assessment.

Our carers' appreciation of knowing the 'what, where and how' of engaging community supports and the subsequent use made of this knowledge by a number of participants is consistent with our Stage 1 findings, which highlighted lack of information as a major barrier to service use (Chapter 10). The importance of such centralised information about services and eligibility has been noted in case management studies,[14] as well as in the ACAT review. Moreover, the relationship formed through the contact with such a key service appeared to have ongoing preventive value, with 84% of carers saying they would recontact the ACAT in the future if a need arose and 8% having already done so for new needs.

The long-term effectiveness of the intervention, however, seems less evident: carer health and well-being were not significantly enhanced by the assessment or the supports subsequently implemented. A number of factors may have accounted for this outcome. The current intervention was of relatively low intensity, for example, in frequency of contact, and only a minority of the supports implemented were of the regular service type, such as home care.

Given the ongoing demands and constraints of caring, broad measures of carer well-being may not be sensitive to the specific carer benefits such as reassurance, information and confidence identified in our follow-up interviews. As Silliman and colleagues (1993) showed, the carer's overall perception of their caregiving experience was predictive of later emotional health. Enhanced choice and mastery of the situation, arising from a review assessment which gives information and support, may be one important part in the complex web of factors which contribute to carers' access to effective formal and informal support and to their personal well-being. Regular planned review of carer and recipient needs may have even greater power to achieve these goals.

From a practice and policy perspective, this study suggests that there are modest yet real and ongoing benefits for carers from a comprehensive non-crisis review of their caregiving situation. Conducted in the home environment, by a respected professional, an assessment can affirm carers in their role, provide accurate and specific information that will enhance their management of their relative or their choice of and access to a range of community supports. Our study indicates that service linkage is more effective where assessment staff instigate necessary referrals and recontact to ensure their successful implementation.

The often changing nature of care needs, evident in our study, suggests that carers should be encouraged to make contact again at any time and that reviews should be routinely conducted every six or twelve months. Not only would this monitor needs and sustain carers in their role, but by establishing a trusted relationship with one key person (or service) potentially address family barriers to the timely use of services. Where reluctance or conflict exist, time and sensitivity are required to address family feelings, attitudes, and perceptions of services.

It is debatable where in the health care or service provision network such an assessment and review procedure should be located and which professionals should be involved. Ideally, such a relationship should build on naturally existing and ongoing ones, such as with the family doctor, treating hospital or local community service, all of these models having been trialled with the elderly in the reported literature.

Further research of such alternative strategies would be essential to identify the relative value of each approach, especially for particular care-dyad groups since previous research has concentrated on aged care.

On a broader scale, such individual strategies need to be complemented by changes in the service sector and community attitudes if carers and their relatives are to have real choice and confidence in formal services. On the one hand, for carers to be receptive to earlier linkage to services, formal services may need to be seen as an entitlement which complements and supports family care, rather than a 'welfare' provision indicating failure, loss of control and the 'end of the road'. Educational materials and community campaigns would be desirable to create a climate where carers, relatives and other key professionals understand and value the assistance of formal supports. On the other, such changes in community perception would be undermined without changes to the availability and accessibility of some services and to the complex systems within which they are located.

13

A SURVEY OF CAREGIVER COUNSELLING

Evaluation of several counselling programs in Australia and overseas indicates that individual, family and group counselling may be helpful in reducing carers' burden, depression and distress, and in dealing with other difficulties arising from the caregiving role.[1] But few carers in our study used counselling services: only 17% reported having ever received counselling on their relative's condition or their own needs. At Stage 2, only 12% of carers had received counselling in the past year, although 10% said they needed or wanted counselling.

The literature on counselling for carers indicates a considerable diversity of conceptual approaches:

- eclectic psychotherapy
- brief psychodynamic therapy
- family therapy, specifically insight-oriented and behavioural approaches
- problem, cognitive behavioural therapy
- crisis intervention.[2]

The modes of delivery, both here and overseas, are equally diverse:

- telephone counselling
- home-based counselling
- individual carer counselling
- family counselling
- group counselling for carers and family groups.[3]

There are also variations in the duration of programs and the training level of counsellors. But importantly, there is no agreement on which model is effective or preferable, and for whom,[4] so it is an open question how programs for Victorian carers could best be developed.

Given this diversity in the published literature and the low uptake of counselling by our carers, we felt we needed to explore what direct emotional support was available to carers through counselling. The study of service providers reported in this chapter was additional to the longitudinal VCP survey of carers. In 1995 we surveyed 47 representative organisations in the health and disability sectors. Our aims were to identify:

- the problems carers present to counselling services
- the approaches currently adopted in counselling
- the context in which counselling is delivered.

Together these aims contribute to our longer-term goal of exploring whether a generic counselling model is relevant, given the diversity of caregiving situations and organisational contexts. We adopted a definition of counselling that allowed us to distinguish it from self-help groups with no designated trained facilitator, educational groups delivered in a didactic rather than an interactive manner, and advice or support given in conjunction with practical or other health services. While there may be overlap in goals and techniques, we believe that conceptually counselling has distinct properties.

The study consisted of a two-phase survey of organisations selected to represent a range of disabilities and organisational structures. The initial phase was a face-to-face interview on site with representatives of ten organisations, followed by an extensive guided telephone interview with a further 37 organisations. In all, 62 counsellors and service managers were interviewed. The interview schedule explored four main domains:

- the carer client group (characteristics, presenting needs, triggers to seeking assistance)
- the conceptualisation of the counselling service (aims and approaches)
- the practicalities of counselling (e.g. referral, service accessibility, form and length of counselling, counsellor qualifications, and training provided through the organisation)
- evaluation and changes to the counselling program.

The services surveyed included self-help organisations, non-government services and organisations, foundations/peak bodies and medical services such as public hospitals and clinics. The majority (70%) had a statewide focus, the exceptions mainly being hospitals with a regional catchment. They dealt with physical, mental, sensory and psychiatric disabilities. In most organisations the counselling program was one of a range of activities or services such as health, educational, accommodation and recreational programs for the disabled person; information, support and recreation for their carers or other family members; training of professionals and community education; advocacy, research and fundraising.

WHAT WE FOUND

CARERS AND THEIR NEEDS

The age of clients targeted by the organisations was diverse, 38% of services dealing with all ages, 30% predominantly adults, 17% children/adolescents and 15% mainly the elderly. Counsellors thus encountered the full spectrum of carers: men and women caring for adult or elderly spouses, adult offspring caring for ageing parents, and parents (mainly mothers) caring for disabled children.

Five circumstances typically prompted carers to approach the counselling service:

- being at a *critical point of engagement* with the wider service systems: namely the time of diagnosis; admission or discharge from hospital or rehabilitation unit; a transition or breakdown in existing supportive formal services
- *deterioration* in the relative's condition or behaviour or arrival at a new life-stage (e.g. adolescence) which calls for alteration to the existing care situation
- *exhaustion* or other changes in the carer's situation (e.g. ill health, other commitments) some time after taking on the caregiving role
- other *crises in family life* (e.g. death, loss of job, accommodation disruptions)
- *coincidental alerting* about the counselling service, either through publicity or through informal networks.

The problems carers bring to counselling form the basis and rationale of the program provided, ideally affecting its design, counselling approach and evaluation. Not surprisingly, issues carers sought help with typically reflected the circumstances triggering contact with the program. Their needs, as reported by counsellors, have been broadly divided into five categories common to all services, albeit expressed and highlighted somewhat differently from service to service. The following list outlines the main categories and subsets of problem areas, reflecting a shift from the practical to the personal, rather than frequency or importance. A fuller description and discussion of these needs is reported in Nankervis and colleagues (1997).

1 **Need for information and formal supports**
- *Information and education:* confusion due to lack of or conflicting information about the condition, its prognosis and treatment options; paucity of information about and access to formal services (e.g. respite, home and residential care); problems with communicating effectively with health professionals and others.
- *Assistance with practical matters and service provision:* help required with financial matters, benefits, compensation, employment, legal issues and accommodation. More complex problems regarding family conflict over service use; the lack of services, their suitability, associated costs, means of access; engagement with multiple service systems and associated feelings of intrusion and powerlessness; changes in service provision and philosophy.

2 **Carer role: choice and change**
- *Choice and responsibility for caring:* feelings and decisions about taking on the caregiving role; anticipating and/or dealing with changing care needs of relative or existing service provision; managing multiple special care responsibilities; relinquishment of primary care; expectations of others about caregiving including agency and cultural pressures.
- *Role changes:* difficulties in fulfilling other broader roles in family life (e.g. breadwinner, parenting, financial management); adjusting to different lifestyle.

3 **Carer coping and adjustment**
- *Coping with the relative's behaviour:* problems in coping with changes in the relative's personality or behaviour (e.g. denial of disability and non-compliance with treatment, risk-taking, sexual activity, depression and apathy, aggression and disorientation or wandering); confusion about the validity of their own emotional response and relative contribution of the disability to difficulties experienced.
- *Carer health and well-being:* problems of carer exhaustion, fatigue and stress; time and emotional dilemmas in balancing competing responsibilities and/or meeting their own needs; physical health issues and felt lack of priority.

4 **Carer emotional issues**
- *Grief and loss:* feelings of grief about the relative's disability or illness; about loss of previous family lifestyle; recurrent grief in a child's failing to meet 'normal' milestones; anticipatory grief, including near-death episodes; and grief on role relinquishment or bereavement.
- *Guilt* associated with perceived causation of the disability/illness; for wish/action to relinquish caregiving role; for needing additional support or desiring to meet own needs.
- *Anxiety* about capacity to provide care and/or continuation of services; about recurrence of illness/episodes and relative's deteriorating health; about their own health status; about future care when they personally can no longer manage or they die; about facing life after their caregiving ends.
- *Anger* felt towards family and friends for their lack of support; towards the care-recipient for their attitude or difficult behaviours; towards doctors and others in the service system; more generalised anger over the disability/illness.

5 **Relationships**
- *Family-related issues:* problems due to revival of or increase in prior family conflict; wider family intrusion or criticism; balancing competing family needs or commitments; communication within the family; impact on children in the family; impact on sexual and marital relationships, including differential acceptance of condition; decisions on who will provide primary care in the future.

- *Social relationships of carer and care-recipient:* loneliness and isolation of both parties; disruption to the carer's personal life; rebuilding relationships on role relinquishment; concerns about the disabled child's identity and future social relationships.
- *Wider social/cultural:* alienation and reclusiveness arising from stigma or shame attached to the disability or disease.

Each category includes related issues, combining problems experienced by carers at different points in their caregiving and specific family life-stage. The classification includes here-and-now realities (i.e. carers' social and environment needs) rather than purely clinical ones, indicating the diverse emotional and practical difficulties faced and their interaction in ordinary life. This is shown, for example, in the prominence of needs relating to disability information and formal services that go beyond pure 'information-giving', both issues reflecting the complexity of personal and service system interactions.

The ramifications of caregiving on the family system is likewise emphasised, with 80% of services reporting this as a common problem, whether the impact is on the carer's nuclear family (especially spouse and children) or on relationships with other family members. Emotional difficulties assumed varied forms of distress, at times masked by other issues and often interacting with other problems. As a group, however, they were consistently reported across the different sectors.

Difficulties commonly viewed as associated with the carer role, such as fatigue, stress and the dilemmas of balancing competing demands, featured consistently, as did carers' need to talk through decisions on current or future needs. A problem of more frequent concern across sectors was carers' need for help in dealing with their relative's difficult behaviours or personality changes—aggression, depression, disorientation, non-compliance with treatments or other risk-taking behaviours. A final issue, not often discussed in carer literature, was the difficulties carers faced with other role shifts (financial management, income provider, parenting) and other lifestyle changes.

Given these needs, how were organisations placed in responding to them?

CHARACTERISTICS OF COUNSELLING PROGRAMS

Focus on the carer Organisations varied considerably in size, complexity, and overall focus on carers relative to the care-recipient. One in three provided other services that directly helped carers, such as self-help support groups, advocacy, supportive friendly visiting, information sessions and the like, which were not included in this study. The extent to which counselling was complementary to or separate from other services also varied. In approximately half the counselling programs the carer was considered a secondary client and in a number of cases could only access the counselling service with their ill or disabled relative's permission. Where the carer was viewed as an equal client, the orientation was generally towards supporting better care rather than addressing carers' needs in their own right.

Staff qualifications Overwhelmingly, the counselling service was provided by professional staff, either exclusively or in combination with trained lay people. Only one service operated solely with peer counsellors. Professionals came mainly from disciplines such as social work or psychology, as well as from backgrounds in health or teaching. A third of programs were staffed by a mix of these professionals, providing flexibility and specialisation.

Attendance Most counselling sessions were attended by the carer alone; in two-thirds of programs the care-recipient attended also, and in half, other family members. There appeared to be little emphasis on children in the family or on adult siblings who potentially shared the caregiving and decision-making.

Format Most organisations provided both face-to-face and telephone counselling. Face-to-face counselling, either individually or in groups, was the chief method in two out of three services, usually at a service centre. About a third of programs offered visits to the family's home, which were the chief means of contact in six services. Although several counsellors had the flexibility to do home visits according to carers' circumstances, an equal number commented on the constraints of time, distance and funding in providing this desirable service.

Telephone counselling was the dominant method in sixteen programs, notably those not associated with a range of other direct care services, such as foundations and consumer advocacy services. Others saw it as the most feasible way to service rural carers or to reach those unable to travel because of care commitments, transport diffi-culties or other factors. While more time-efficient than home visits, a number of participants commented on costs and lack of funding for telephone counselling to rural areas.

Modality Counselling was provided in a variety of modalities, almost a third of services offering group as well as individual sessions. But *group counselling* was the core program in only three instances which were directed exclusively to carers, as indeed were two-thirds of the groups described. Group counselling mainly involved time-limited psycho-educational programs averaging six sessions, although a number of open-ended therapeutic/supportive groups were also reported, usually monthly. Sessions were typically one and a half to three hours, longer sessions occurring at times in conjunction with recreational components or a more intensive educational focus.

Short-term *individual counselling* predominated in all services, the range varying from single interviews, through brief intensive work, to periodic contact averaging five sessions. Where prolonged coun-selling was required, almost half the services referred to other local or more specialist services. A minority of programs worked to a prescribed session length, although most counsellors spent between 30 and 90 minutes with clients. Services that provided home-based counselling reported longer sessions, especially for country visits or those involving a number of family members.

Referrals Multiple pathways were used to contact counselling services. Referrals were most often reported from other mainstream and specialist services in the community (over half), self-referrals (42%) and informal networks (44%). Media publicity (31%) and internal referrals (29%) also featured as a referral source in larger organisations, while written materials such as pamphlets were less often cited (20%). In a few cases participants noted the organisation's reluctance to promote itself more widely because of limited resources and already heavy demand.

Access For most programs, access to counsellors in terms of waiting periods and direct cost was good. About two-thirds of services pro-vided same-day contact by virtue of their counselling line, duty system or policy of immediate phone contact before scheduling a counselling appointment. About one in four had a wait of up to a week, with only four organisations specifying longer waiting times.

In all but one instance counselling was provided free, although several counsellors noted costs associated with getting counselling (e.g. transport, respite care) or carer services provided by the organisation (e.g. membership, informational resources and equipment, and training/recreation programs for the care-recipient).

Carers from a non-English-speaking (NES) background For these carers access to counselling was more complex and varied. While several organisations commented that they made no provision for and had little contact with NES background carers, two-thirds attempted to use either a centralised interpreter service or the Telephone Interpreter Service when the need arose. A fifth, mainly large public hospitals, relied mostly on in-house interpreters and, apart from four ethno-specific services, only three other organisations employed any bilingual staff. A considerable proportion of counsellors (17%) used English-speaking relatives or family friends in working with carers, some through preference, others from necessity.

The effectiveness and ethics of using informal interpreters was discussed by participants, who found themselves facing problems of limited professional interpreters in the required language or region, the prohibitive costs of private services and the need for immediate help. Other counsellors noted the variability of professional interpreting standards, the lack of counsellors' skills in using interpreters, and their more fundamental belief that counselling could not be effectively conducted through the medium of an interpreter. Many referred to a bilingual professional or ethnic agency. Written materials about the service or the disabling condition were available in community languages in only ten organisations.

A number of counsellors also raised issues of cultural sensitivity and complexities in counselling NESB carers. The most frequently mentioned was cultural variation in the knowledge about and meaning given to the illness or disability (e.g. permanence, causation, stigma) and the 'sick' role subsequently attributed to that person. These and other cultural factors were seen to influence the carer's communication with the care-recipient and other family members, their view of appropriate treatments, and their acceptance/undertaking of suggested plans or treatments.

Counsellors saw in NESB families a greater obligation regarding family care, which they thought affected the designation of who would become the primary carer, the carer's choice in adopting the role, what supports were deemed appropriate to the situation, and, in particular, a greater resistance to formal help. While several counsellors commented on the positive implications of these factors, others noted the significant burden placed on female relatives and the ensuing sense of guilt and failure in acknowledging difficulties with the role or a desire to relinquish care.

Further barriers in helping ethnic carers obtain formal supports included a lack of ethno-specific services (e.g. respite, residential care); limited culturally appropriate mainstream services; poor understanding by carers of the various health, disability and education systems; little information and insensitive communication on the part of the services; carers' suspicion of bureaucracies, and concerns about privacy and confidentiality. Indeed, such feelings and values (e.g. stigma, confidentiality) could equally work against carers' involvement with the counsellor. Several participants also noted the lack of cultural relevance of counselling to some ethnic communities, a mismatch in expectations of the counsellor's role, and a need to modify usual counselling practices in work with ethnic carers.

While most of these concerns are common to other carers, counsellors believed that for many NESB groups these were heightened issues, requiring a different awareness and intervention by the counsellor. Some reported using ethno-specific organisations to help.

COUNSELLING APPROACHES

Most counselling programs had several aims, although few had written aims applying specifically to carers. Five broad counselling goals were identified.

- To empower carers to decide on and take appropriate action.
- To enhance carers' adjustment to and coping with caregiving
  - Help carers adapt to change
  - Improve carers' management of the car
  - Reduce carer stress and increase well-
- To help carers resolve practical issues
  - Deal with practical issues
  - Access, use or mobilise resources
  - Cope with the service system.
- To provide support to carers (emotio
- To promote family well-being and a

213

For organisations that dealt primarily with the needs of the disabled or ill person, the last aim focused on creating an optimal care environment for that client. It thereby included balancing the needs of the care-recipient, the carer and other family members (such as children), enhancing communication and adaptive family relationships, and bolstering family or carer 'survival'.

Many counsellors noted that before the survey their organisation had given no specific thought to their *counselling approach* with carers. Four programs, however, had been particularly devised for carers,[5] and three other organisations were addressing the issue.

The four programs for carers had been developed in response to the paucity of services which support carers and address their emotional and psychological needs. The Highfields Centre model, at first directed to carers of the elderly and later extended to parent carers, has 'a three-tiered approach to developing personal coping skills and social supports, through awareness and a problem-solving orientation'.[6] This model is based on a blend of the phenomenological-psychodynamic and cognitive-behavioural approaches, with an understanding of caregiving pressures, loss and grief, family dynamics, communication and conflict-resolution skills, community resource use, stress management and relaxation.[7] While this generic psycho-educational model usually operates as a set small-group program, the approach is also used in individual and family counselling.

In contrast, the 'Family Sensitive Practice' model developed by the Bouverie Family Therapy Centre responded to the long-term needs of carers of adults with acquired brain damage, schizophrenia and intellectual disability.[8] This counselling model is grounded on systems theory (family and broader systems) and a four-stage post-trauma adjustment model. The approach emphasises family empowerment, flexibility to address multiple needs within the family and over time, and is 'holistic in relation to affect, behaviour and cognition . . . in order to support families effectively at a number of levels'.[9]

The counselling services of the Alzheimer's Association of Victoria is mainly an eclectic approach based on a systemic/contextual ...ework which uses the following theoretical orientations: family ...s (structural, systemic and strategic); grief/loss and adjust-...opmental/life cycle; role theory; feminist; social learning (labelling); and cognitive-behavioural approaches (problem-solving and stress management).

The interactive psycho-educational group model of the Schizophrenia Fellowship aims to empower family members to become active carers rather than passive stakeholders in the mental health system. The model is based on a self-help philosophy and underpinned by fourteen principles for coping with schizophrenia (Alexander 1993). It comprises an eight-session course covering information about schizophrenia, associated behaviours and treatment options; carers' isolation, loss and grief; feelings of guilt and distress; problem-solving and stress management approaches; communication and relationships within the family and with the person with schizophrenia; caregiving tasks, help required and understanding professionals. These themes are expanded in two subsequent stages of the model.

Most counsellors, however, described their own or their program's approach as 'eclectic', drawing unsystematically on multiple familiar approaches. Considering the specifically designed programs and the components of more eclectic ones, it was possible to identify eight common counselling approaches:

- basic client-centred counselling
- cognitive behavioural approaches
- interactive psycho-educational approaches
- family therapy approaches: systems, structural, strategic, narrative, solution-focused
- ecological systems approaches
- grief counselling
- crisis intervention
- existential/psychodynamic approaches.

And a further three conceptual frameworks cited as valuable in working with carers:

- role theory
- life cycle theory
- feminist theory.

IMPEDIMENTS TO COUNSELLING CARERS

Counsellors identified certain difficulties in providing effective counselling to carers.

- Matters concerning the management and mission of the organisation, including definition of the target group, view of counselling, policy on length of client contact, funding cuts.
- Reduced staff hours and morale, loss of expertise, multiple role expectations of counsellors, role strain and staff burnout.
- Difficulties in the operation of programs: client access because of geographic location, operating hours, physical constraints (transport, appearance of site), knowledge of the service; limited privacy and poor amenity; lack of complementary resources (respite care).
- Procedural constraints such as inadequate supervision, screening and case allocation procedures. At a case-practice level, difficulties over confidentiality, conflicting carer/recipient opinions, and locating a workable counselling model to engage/deal with multiple demands.
- Clients' perceptions of counselling and the counsellor's role, readiness for counselling, negative attitude to the organisation, limited self-identification as 'carer' and valuing of own needs.
- Inadequate counselling resources in the community; confusion and/or conflicting strategies because of engagement with multiple organisations; limited and changing community services to support the care-dyad.

Participants identified several options within their organisations or program to address these difficulties, including:

- debate on and clarification of carers' needs and their place as a primary client group
- a commitment to counselling as a valuable service by management
- better articulation/marketing of the counselling service to carers and referral agencies
- earlier engagement with carers and a focus on prevention rather than crisis work
- more follow-up and longer-term work
- the greater use of educational resources and groups in working with carers
- greater flexibility in operating hours
- a need for outreach and improved cultural sensitivity to NESB carers
- program evaluation.

WHAT THE FINDINGS MEAN

The 47 organisations surveyed presented a realistic and challenging view of public counselling resources available for carers in the Victorian community. On the one hand, counsellors reported an awareness and richness of carer needs beyond that typically articulated in the counselling research literature.[10] In particular, we noted the breadth and complexity of carers' environmental and social needs, additional to and interactive with personal and emotional problems. In part, these differences may be accounted for by variations in target group and service position between our sample and programs reported in the literature. Past research has generally focused on counselling specific carer groups. In contrast, counsellors in this survey worked with numerous carers across the whole range of disabilities, chronic and terminal illnesses, relationship groups and life-stages, and they were placed at key points in naturally existing service pathways, thus maximising their exposure to carers at different points in their caregiving career. This enabled us to compile a comprehensive classification of carer needs that will undoubtedly prove useful in counsellor training and program planning.

In general, carers had reasonably good access to available counselling services in terms of costs, referral and waiting time. Problems with access related mainly to rural carers, those with transport difficulties, NESB carers, and carers' 'secondary' client status. These issues warrant further attention and flexible responses if carers are to make the best use of existing services.

Counsellors appeared to value the empowerment of carers and were important resources for carers in dealing with medical, rehabilitative, educational, HACC, residential and legal services. Importantly, counselling covered a mix of therapeutic and practical assistance which broadly matched the range of environmental and affective needs identified. Most services offered brief face-to-face counselling by professional counsellors, although the counselling offered was generally far less structured in its goals, theoretical approach, modality and duration than published programs.[11]

Essentially, most counselling programs reported in the caregiving literature emphasise a *psycho-educational model*, combining cognitive-behavioural approaches with various degrees of carer education and support. Underpinning this model is the view that carers' appraisal of available support and of their own coping critically affects their level of stress.[12] The model therefore focuses on the carer's acquisition of information and skills. Three types of information are typically included:

- on ageing or the relevant specific disability, its likely course and associated behavioural or personality changes in the care-recipient, medication and treatment options
- on typical caregiver feelings, adjustments and experiences, including stress, isolation and the reactions of other family members
- on available community services, health and other systems, and how to deal effectively with them.[13]

While *cognitive-behavioural approaches* to carers' problems were commonly reported in our survey, their application appeared less formalised as 'carer skills training' than programs described in the literature. Those typically include problem-solving strategies, communication, conflict resolution and assertiveness skills.[14]

Surveyed counsellors made less reference to *behavioural approaches* often described in the literature to reduce carer depression and stress, in particular teaching relaxation skills, stress management, time management and pleasant activity management.[15] Similarly, apart from organisations primarily dealing with children with disabilities, few services in our study included behavioural strategies for carers' management of difficult behaviours. The literature spans mental illness, dementia and the frail elderly, and in most situations training is incorporated within a *behavioural family therapy approach* with individuals or with small family groups.

A similarity between our survey and published studies was the use of *supportive counselling approaches* based on a model of active listening, encouragement and respect which promotes the expression and validation of carers' feelings and experiences. This approach aims to help carers deal with emotional isolation and negative feelings, to increase confidence, and to identify and support personal and familial strengths.

Almost half of the counsellors surveyed (typically those from medical or service organisations) incorporated family therapy approaches in their work with carers, in particular systemic and brief therapies, as well as a broad understanding of family dynamics and life-stages.

The emphasis placed on family concepts and approaches by our counsellors would appear to meet criticism of overseas carer counselling programs.[16] And this emphasis seems highly appropriate to the numerous problems presented by carers about taking on the caregiving role and their families' ongoing adjustment to the needs of a seriously ill or disabled relative, a point recognised by Power's (1988) generic model. Local counsellors' use of crisis intervention concepts, grief and adjustment models and a fundamental ecological/contextual approach we believe also merits further attention. These approaches address aspects of the affective and environmental difficulties for which carers seek help and which are largely ignored in documented programs.

In a workshop held with participants after the completion of the survey, counsellors generally supported the development of counselling principles and initiatives in training and professional development. Nevertheless, they reiterated the importance of change in contextual factors before counselling programs for carers can advance. Workshop participants highlighted a number of issues that warrant further debate:

- the organisation's view of carers as clients and possible conflict of interest with care-recipient needs and interests;
- the organisation's role in the wider health/disability network and how the concept of 'counselling' fits with that;
- the priority and resources allocated to counselling and professional development given the increasing and competing demands on workers' time;
- the marketing of 'counselling' so as to overcome negative community attitudes and perceptions; and
- more broadly achieving a heightened community awareness of carers and their needs.

These challenges indicate the need for ongoing collaboration and dialogue between carers, researchers, funders and the many organisations in the field with whom carers interact.

PART IV

*I*MPLICATIONS

14

KEY FINDINGS AND
POLICY IMPLICATIONS

It is a mistake to view caregiving as *typified* by burden, by negative effects on carers' physical, emotional, social and financial well-being. About four out of five are content with their life as a whole, its personal, emotional and financial aspects, and the amount of freedom and independence they have. Most feel supported by family and friends and most get a great deal of satisfaction caring for their relative or friend. Only a minority feel angry and resentful. Nevertheless, it is true that *as a group* they report poorer health, more anxiety and depression, more overload and social isolation than those with usual family reponsibilities. Particularly affected are parents, young carers generally, and those caring for a person with a mental disability and associated behaviour problems. Caregiving therefore presents a distinct area of need.

The aim of this chapter is thus to draw together a number of the policy and practice implications of the VCP research and health promotion activities. In so doing, we have used a number of underlying principles for providing services. These include the desirability of:

- a *positive regard for caregivers* and the social role they fill
- attributing to caregivers a specific, *independent client status* alongside the care-recipient, because of the stresses and needs that arise from their caregiving role;
- a *preventive approach* to providing information and engaging formal and informal supports

- caregiver policies, information and services that are *appropriate and relevant* to the care-dyad's life-stage, disability and culture
- *flexibility in services* for caregivers because of the diversity of circumstances and the changing nature of their needs over time.
- a *multiple and comprehensive range of supports* that will enhance caregivers' well-being
- a *co-ordinated approach* to the provision of information and supports, both geographically and in the individual case
- *regular review* of the needs of caregiver (and care-recipient) from a holistic perspective
- *data-based planning* of caregiver policies and services
- the recognition that carers and those they care for have many *needs in common* with other frail, aged and disabled people who do *not* have carers.

KEY FINDINGS

THE DIVERSITY OF CARERS AND CARE-RECIPIENTS

- The most striking aspect of the findings was the diversity of carers and caregiving roles. Most carers were women. The main groups were adult offspring, spouses and parents.
- The length of time carers had been providing care ranged from one month to 50 years. Most parents had been caring more than five years.
- Adult offspring were more likely than others to be working and hence balancing multiple roles.
- Spouses and parents were more likely to have a higher-intensity caregiving role in terms of hours of care, co-residency, and amount of personal care provided.
- Care-recipients ranged in age from one to 98 years, but almost half were 75 or over, and one in five was under 30.
- Women predominated in the elderly care-recipients as they tend to live longer than men, whereas males predominated in the younger age-groups as they are more prone to congenital conditions and traumatic injury.
- Care-recipients suffered from a very large range of congenital, degenerative and traumatic conditions.

- Most had multiple disabilities, dependencies and behaviour problems. Few had minor disabilities only, one in five had predominantly mental disabilities, one in four mainly physical impairments, and almost half were impaired both mentally and physically.
- Carers were found in 5.3% of Victorian households. The prevalence of NESB carers matched that in the Victorian population.

THE IMPACTS OF CAREGIVING ON CARERS' HEALTH AND WELL-BEING

- Carers, *as a group*, reported poorer health and well-being than non-carers. Yet most expressed satisfaction with their life and with the support and recognition they got from family and friends.
- Compared with *men*, *women* tended to be less satisfied with their lives; to feel more overloaded, angry, anxious and depressed; and to report more conflict in the family and more behaviour problems in their relative.
- Parents and spouses tended to be more positively involved in caregiving than adult offspring and to report more closeness in the family. On the other hand, parents and adult offspring were generally younger than spouses and tended to report more overload and more conflict in the family.
- More parents than spouses or adult offspring were caring for those with predominantly mental disabilities and associated behaviour problems, which was more stressful than caring for a person who was physically disabled only.
- Stress was associated in carers with their younger age, living with the care-recipient, being single, being unemployed, and caring for a person with mental disabilities and associated behaviour problems.
- Health and well-being were similar in NESB and Anglo carers, and in those living in different geographic locations.

IMPACTS ON EMPLOYMENT AND FINANCES

- Almost half of the carers of workforce age who were not in paid employment had given up work or were unable to work because of caregiving. Mainly affected were co-resident carers, women, parents and young spouses, and those caring for a person with mental disabilities.

- Most employed carers reported some adverse effects of caregiving on their work, and over half saw work as a welcome relief. Mainly affected were women, parents, young carers, and those caring for a person with both mental and physical disabilities.
- Well-being was highest in carers who were employed with no adverse effects and lowest in those excluded from the workforce and in workers experiencing conflict between work and caregiving.
- Difficulty in meeting living costs was experienced by one in four carers, particularly parents, co-resident carers, the young and those prevented from working.
- Financial difficulties were associated with poorer well-being.

Assistance from family and friends

- Most carers had help from family and friends, particularly social and recreational support rather than help with personal care.
- Larger support networks were associated with better well-being. Women, parents, adult offspring and those caring for young recipients got the most help.
- More help from their spouses was wanted by one in five carers—particularly mothers, young carers, part-time workers and those dealing with a lot of aggressive and cognitive behaviour problems.
- More help from other family and friends was wanted by one in three, particularly adult offspring, middle-aged carers, and those dealing with care-recipients with depressive behaviour problems and more severe disability.

Support from community services

- Only a minority of carers was getting regular support from any one community service. Use of services was more common in adult offspring, older carers, and female care-recipients living alone who had higher personal-care dependency and more severe disability.
- Use of services was less common in NESB carers and the need for some services was higher.
- Use of services was not related to carer stress.

- Unmet need for services was higher among carers who were more overloaded and dealing with more frequent behaviour problems and more severe disability and dependency.
- Most common reasons for unmet need were lack of awareness and care-recipients' reluctance, and only 8% belonged to a support organisation, but just about everyone had seen their GP and most reported help from family and friends.
- Few carers had used respite in the previous twelve months. Unmet need was reported by one in four carers, particularly the more distressed.
- Few carers, but more parents, had ever had counselling or done a training course or been a member of a support organisation. Unmet need for counselling or training was reported by one in ten carers, particularly distressed carers dealing with more behaviour problems and mental disability.
- Participation in counselling and support groups was associated with poorer well-being in carers, and with higher mental disability, dependency and behaviour problems in care-recipients.
- The main and preferred sources of information about the care-recipient's condition were GPs and medical specialists. The main and preferred sources of information about services were GPs, allied health professionals and government agencies.
- Carers prefer to get information from verbal or personal communication.

STRATEGIES TO SUPPORT CARERS

Five central domains have been identified for policy application:

1. Information and education
2. Mobilising informal support
3. Formal services
4. Financial provisions
5. Employment.

Given the heterogeneous nature of the carer population, strategies across these domains can be considered as ranging from those applying to carers and others through to those applying only to select groups of carers. In particular, strategies such as needs assessment, home and community services, counselling and training, and so on, apply to a substantial minority of carers, but not to all.

1. INFORMATION AND EDUCATION

COMMUNITY EDUCATION

As detailed in Chapters 2 and 3, there is enormous diversity in characteristics and circumstances among the carers identified in one in twenty households. Education is required about who is a family carer, about the prevalence, diversity and normative nature of caregiving, about the diversity of carer experiences and carers' need for support. Since carers are most commonly women (Chapter 2), and women carers are generally more stressed than men (Chapter 7), community education would be valuable in raising awareness and debate about gender expectations regarding caregiving, so that caregiving and its impacts are more equally shared between the sexes. This broad approach would reach main and anticipatory carers, their families and other potential sources of informal support, such as neighbours, friends and fellow employees. Strategies adopted by carers' associations and resource centres (funded by the Federal Government) and mass media (e.g. the publicity given to Carers Week) could be complemented by other initiatives from the relevant government departments and professional bodies.

CARER INFORMATION

The provision of information to all carers is vitally important to their own understanding of their role and the available supports. There is a need for better information about their relative's illness or disability, its likely course, medications and treatment options, what this may mean in terms of changes in their relative and the type of care they will require (Chapter 10). Information about the feelings and experiences of other carers in similar circumstances and how they have coped can also benefit carers in reducing the emotional isolation of their experience, as evidenced in carers' positive response to the tape of carers' stories in the Carer Support Kit (Chapter 12). Most importantly, however, carers require appropriately timed and tailored information about formal supports available in the community: mainstream and home and community care services, allied health (rehabilitative) and recreational programs for their relative, respite care, carer support groups, financial entitlements and subsidies for services and equipment, transport and legal assistance, residential options, counselling and training programs, as well as aids and equipment for their relative or the home. Carers' non-engagement of needed services and modest uptake of financial benefits seems related largely to lack of awareness of these available supports (Chapters 8 and 10).

Such information needs to be in plain language (rather than sophisticated medical or service provider terminology), easily available from an identifiable point in the health-care system and preferably given in the context of a personal discussion which can be tailored to carers' own circumstances. Particular attention needs to be given to the requirements of community language groups, as noted in Chapter 4. The Carers Association of Victoria has outlined 'Principles to underpin the provision of information' (Bowman 1994), which emphasise the importance of personal contact, the timing of information, the use of existing infrastructure and networks, the resourcing of service providers, and the use of multiple strategies and media. The VCP evaluation of the CSK similarly highlights the importance of personal contact and appropriately timed information, which needs to be provided before carers reach a crisis point, when needs begin to emerge and particular help becomes relevant. The VCP survey questions on carers' information preferences (Chapter 10) highlight GPs and government agencies as preferred sources, and personal contact, with written back-up in the form of pamphlets, as their preferred format for information.

EDUCATION OF HEALTH AND WELFARE PROFESSIONALS

Although GPs and other health professionals are a relatively well used source of information, both about disability/illness and services and organisations, lack of timely and accurate information is the most common reason for carers' failure to engage the services they need. There is a clear call for strategies that raise the general awareness of health and welfare professionals about carers and their needs. In fact, the VCP strategy involving GPs and pharmacists (Chapter 12) shows the feasibility of using existing service networks, and the value of resourcing health professionals such as GPs and pharmacists. Undergraduate or postgraduate education of GPs, medical specialists, pharmacists, nurses, social workers, psychologists, counsellors, occupational therapists, gerontologists and the like, prepares them for future work with carers. Core class presentations could be supplemented by specific units and electives such as occurred during the project. Additionally, questions about whether a person is or has been a carer in patient case histories and agency assessments would facilitate identification of primary carers and exploration of their needs.

Local doctors, pharmacists, allied health professionals and social service providers play a central part in acknowledging, informing and supporting carers (see Chapters 10 and 12). Strategies that resource and support their role should also be addressed. In particular, they may need education on carers' experiences and needs, including vulnerable carer groups and the value to carers of a specific diagnosis, as discussed in Chapter 6 in relation to dementia; on the importance of repeated discussion, early referral and a coordinated non-intrusive approach to care for the care-dyad; and on relevant updated information about available financial entitlements, formal services and key entry-points. As the VCP intervention showed, GPs and pharmacists improve in knowledge of services and frequency of discussion with carers when provided with information about local services. Opportunities for peer discussions could facilitate resolution of problems encountered and enhanced commitment to carer strategies. Ideally, professionals need to be backed up by organisational or professional policies that endorse this key role and by financial remuneration for the time taken in discussion with carers, referral networks and peers.

TRAINING SERVICE PROVIDERS AND HEALTH PROFESSIONALS

Professionals and other service staff may be offered training appropriate to understanding and working with the level of needs they encounter. Respite, home and community care staff, whether employed by public, private or voluntary organisations, require special skills if, as well as providing a practical service, they are to respond adequately to the need of carers and recipients for emotional support. Given the greater care dependency, mental disability and behavioural problems revealed in carers reporting unmet service needs, educational strategies that improve the knowledge and competence of staff working with these situations appear highly desirable. Development and greater participation in accredited courses and in-service training should be encouraged and resourced by employing bodies and responsible government departments.

Given the prevalence of ethnic care-dyads in the community (Chapter 4), and the special difficulties these groups face in using community services, training in cultural sensitivity and in the use of interpreters should be encouraged and provided for all mainstream service staff.

Service coordinators, ACAT staff and other professionals who make referrals may also require training in approaches that resolve reluctance or conflict between carer and recipient or other family members regarding formal and informal supports. Health professionals and peer caregivers responsible for providing counselling, carer training programs and support groups may require specific training in how to run such programs and in the typical needs of the carers entering them. Clearly universities or peak bodies could play a part here by providing accredited courses or relevant in-service training.

2. MOBILISING SUPPORT FROM FAMILY, FRIENDS AND OTHER CARERS

FAMILY AND FRIENDS

While most carers have at least some informal help, few have more than two available helpers, and a substantial minority identify a need for greater assistance from partners and other family members (Chapter 10). Moreover, informal support appears to provide an emotional buffer for carers: those with more helpers report higher life satisfaction, positive affect and perceived social support, and less resentment and anger in their caregiving role. Health professionals are and should be active in mobilising family networks or linking carers to other informal supports (e.g. self-help groups). The inclusion of other family members in individual discussions (telephone or face-to-face) or family case conferences would inform them better of the care-recipient's illness/disability and care requirements and provide an opportunity to discuss and commit themselves to sharing the responsibilities.

SUPPORT GROUPS AND ORGANISATIONS

For some carers, involvement with a support group or organisation appears another valued source of support (Chapter 10). Support organisations are most used by those caring for relatives with demanding and complex needs, and by carers experiencing high stress and low life satisfaction. While membership was often time-limited or intermittent, carers used these peer resources to fill various needs: information, social contact, education and support-group membership, to name the most commonly cited activities. This suggests that health professionals and service providers need to encourage stressed or isolated carers to contact relevant support organisations, whether based on locality or disability. Strategies and resources are therefore required to inform potential referrers better of the benefits of membership (CAV 1996) and of existing support group networks, as well as to develop/maintain central databases to this effect.

Specific disability organisations (e.g. the Anti-Cancer Council, the Alzheimer's Association, the Arthritis Foundation) and services such as Community Health have set up a wide range of self-help groups, peer-support telephone link-ups and individual buddy systems. The Carers Association of Victoria has also recently committed itself to the development of a statewide support-group network for carers (CAV 1996). The diversity of support programs, while not systematically evaluated, allows for some carer choice in the type of informal support preferred, but requires resourcing (financial and personnel) to be used to best advantage.

3. MOBILISING HEALTH AND COMMUNITY SERVICES

The range of caregiving situations, diversity of impacts and changing nature of carer needs mean that *policies and practices that acknowledge and explore carer needs are important* wherever carers are encountered, be they patients in their own right or accompanying a care-recipient. Thus care planning by local doctors, medical specialists, hospital discharge teams, rehabilitation and disability organisations, ACATs, community nurses, home-care coordinators, and so forth, should be systematic in their inclusion and consideration of carers' needs. The boost to morale and validation of their experiences that carers reported from discussing their situation, as evidenced generally in the survey responses and in particular in the home-based assessment study (Chapter 12), suggests that for many carers this recognition may be important in strengthening their own resources. Follow-up or a regular review of the care-dyad's needs would consolidate coping capacities or facilitate earlier referral for formal supports.

ASSESSING NEEDS

While half the carers surveyed used at least one formal community support, rarely did they use more than two, indicating a sparing use of community resources by carers (see Chapter 10). At any time over two-thirds of carers reported not needing each specific service. But a sizeable minority reported unmet needs for services, mostly because of lack of information or the care-recipient's reluctance to use a service. Carers with unmet needs were more overloaded and dealt with more frequent behaviour problems and more severe disability than other carers. Moreover our home-based assessment study suggests that supports in addition to those nominated by carers (such as aids, rehabilitation and social activities) may be beneficial and that considerable change in service needs occurs over time. These findings indicate the desirability of strategies that promote a continuing and *more comprehensive assessment of care-dyads' needs* and that provide follow-up on service referrals.

This practice could, over time, ensure that relevant information is provided, concerns about engaging formal services are addressed, and supports are coordinated before crises arise. Various strategy options regarding this assessment role could be resourced and evaluated, for example a specialised nurse or social worker attached to general practice areas, a role for ACATs that is wider than aged care, and an extension of existing home-care assessments or case-planning practices in the disability sector to include carers.

HELPING THE CARER IN THE HOME AND IN THE COMMUNITY

The use of home and community care services was relatively low among care-dyads. Carers identifying unmet need most often saw lack of information and their relative's attitude as the main barriers to desired HACC services, not the availability, affordability or quality of existing services (Chapter 10). This suggests that GPs, health professionals and service providers need to be more responsive to these carers' needs and active in informing and assisting them to engage available supports.

The fact that unmet need was associated with significantly greater carer stress and care-recipient dependency/difficult behaviours suggests that greater attention to carer health and well-being is required by home-care staff in planning services. While there was no indication that care-dyads with unmet needs had been excluded by the care-recipient's degree of dependency or behavioural problems, the provision of adequate care to this group requires staff who are skilled and comfortable with this degree of care-recipient need.

Our findings suggest that over a third of carers might request at least one new community service if they were better informed and/or comfortable in applying for available HACC services. Demand would rise most steeply for home maintenance, general home help and transport services, suggesting the need for greater resource allocation in these areas. Since NESB carers expressed greater need for general home help and transport services, provision for their specific language and cultural needs could be considered.

Similarly, an increase in day-care places or different alternative care options would help carers wanting to find work or increase their hours while still caring (Chapter 8). Constraints around the regular availability of day care, difficulties in organising the care-recipient before work hours and the affordability of regular care are among the issues that need to be addressed.

RESPITE CARE

While few carers had used formal respite care in the previous year, this was the area of greatest unmet service need. Twice as many wanted formal respite, either for the first time or to supplement their existing use. Carers with unmet needs here were more emotionally taxed than those not identifying a need (Chapter 10). Among carers of the under-65s, parent carers and those with less informal assistance were in greatest need, while difficult behaviours on the care-recipient's part also made for much unmet need. For carers of the over-65s, difficult behaviours and needing a lot of help with personal care were the factors indicating unmet need. Those assessing and allocating respite resources should take particular note of these factors in addition to other traditional indicators of need. The respite and day-care initiatives announced by the State Government for carers of people with serious illness, acquired brain injury and challenging behaviours are pertinent to the needs of these carers.

Carers need different types of respite services: carers of the under-65s identified a need for short-term overnight and/or weekend respite, either at home or elsewhere, whereas carers of the elderly more often needed longer respite. Further, carers of younger people more often reported that the kind of service they needed was unavailable, suggesting a need for greater diversity and flexibility in existing services. The creation of a flexible respite funding pool for carers of children and disabled adults under the recent State Government carer strategy is a recognition of this.

Care-recipients' dislike for formal respite was a barrier for carers of the elderly. This calls for different strategies: practices which support carers in dealing with their feelings about potential upsets over respite and with difficult behaviours that may ensue; discussion and support by a trusted professional or friend of the care-recipient to lessen their resistance to formal respite; the gradual introduction of respite with the capacity to overlap or build on known and familiar services (personnel, locations). The new regional carer support workers for carers of the elderly and those with dementia, and resources to increase respite options, may partly address this issue.

Lack of knowledge was the most common reason for unmet respite needs, again indicating a need for better information (Chapter 10). While the general service information strategies proposed earlier may partly address some barriers (terminology, respite options, entry points), desirable strategies might coordinate information on respite (services, vacancies) and access at a regional, municipal or individual level. In this context the 1997 national strategy for regional respite centres was timely.

COUNSELLING THE CARER

In addition to the support and information offered carers by doctors, health professionals and providers of community services, more specialised support in the form of counselling or training was used by a minority of carers, particularly parents (Chapter 10). Our general findings on family tensions, carers' difficulties in coping with problem behaviours, their feelings about caregiving (Chapter 3) and overall well-being (Chapter 7) suggest a group of carers who may benefit from these programs. Indeed, for both counselling and training, approximately one in ten carers identified an unmet need, particularly parents and offspring, indicating the need to target distressed carers more accurately.

Carers requiring counselling reported significantly worse emotional well-being and difficult circumstances, namely frequent behavioural difficulties and care-recipients with severe mental and physical disabilities (Chapter 10). This and the problems typically presented by carers in counselling (Chapter 13) suggest that counselling programs should specifically aim to help carers with relationship and emotional issues, coping with the role's demands, and managing difficult behaviours. In addition, a family approach to working with carers may be valuable in securing family support—especially where tensions exist—and in helping with decision-making, particularly relinquishing care.

Given the diversity of caregiving situations and of medical and other services used by carers, it is appropriate that counselling resources are located at various points in the aged care, health and disability service systems to optimise early access and meet the range of carers' preferences on sources of support. Additional resources may be required to improve these services, and further exploration is needed of the best design for accessible counselling programs: for example, integrated into existing service provision by hospitals and disability organisations, identifiable carer/family counselling services that span a geographic or specific disability catchment, or provided privately through community-based counsellors and therapists.

Most likely to report a need for training were carers of young people and those from a NES background. The main barriers to program access for carers indicating a need for training were lack of information and not getting around to it. This suggests the need for greater promotion of existing programs, especially at key referral sources, encouragement with actually getting in touch with services, and, in some cases, providing alternative care for the dependent relative to allow the carer to attend. A desirable core program provides *information* on the relevant disability/illness, its management and expected changes in the care-recipient's health and behaviour over time; and *education* in problem-solving approaches, effective coping strategies and self-care measures.

SPECIALIST SERVICES

A small minority of care-dyads may require more flexible or specialist assistance with complex circumstances than is possible through the services and resources discussed so far. This may arise from the severe nature of the care-recipient's disability (especially where mental impairment exists through psychiatric illness, acquired brain damage or severe intellectual disability), from family circumstances (for example, multiple care responsibilities, ethnicity, employment commitments) or geographic location.

Where there is a desire to continue caregiving in the community, specialist equipment or specialised services such as respite, day-care programs, evening care or intensive counselling support may be required, and/or funding to purchase specifically tailored care packages. Such packages have been available in the aged-care sector through the federally-funded Community Options Program and the Commonwealth Aged Care Packages. The continued funding of these and other age-related programs is desirable.

Similarly, packages are available to some care-dyads through work or traffic accident compensation coverage. Limited information from the VCP's home-based assessment study (Chapter 12) and counselling survey (Chapter 13), however, suggests some restrictions in these schemes' coverage of carers' needs (as distinct from victims), especially in the non-medical realm. The adequacy of support to highly stressed carers under existing guidelines appears to warrant further consideration.

During our consultations with carers, a small number of parent carers and others looking after younger adults asked that packages similar to those available in the aged-care sector be provided in situations of complex disability or chronic illness. They argued that this would facilitate better coordination of services, greater flexibility and care-dyad choice regarding formal supports. Such initiatives appear appropriate given the significant levels of distress identified among many parents and other high-intensity carers of younger people in our survey (Chapters 6 and 7) and their lower use of traditional HACC services (Chapter 10). The extension of the Victorian 'Making a Difference' program to children and adults with multiple severe disabilities and the introduction of similar packages for people with complex illnesses are most relevant and welcome initiatives.

RESIDENTIAL SERVICES

Despite the availability of support from formal and informal sources, for a minority of carers residential placement of their relative becomes the best option because of changes in their own or the care-recipient's health, or other family circumstances (Chapter 11). The 8%

incidence rate of placement between Stages 1 and 2 of the VCP survey provides a valuable guide for planners. Of course the incidence is a significantly higher 12% for care-recipients aged 80 or more and is negligible for younger care-recipients.

Not surprisingly, prior consideration was predictive of actual placement. As the eventuality approaches, discussing residential options and issues commonly associated with the transition may help carers and their relatives in resolving conflicts and making the decision. In addition to care-recipient age and objective need (mental disability and high dependency), factors indicative of low caregiving centrality (non-residency, offspring or more distant kin relationship and low satisfaction in caregiving) were associated with the consideration of residential care and actual placement. The significant improvement in physical well-being of spouse carers in particular who relinquished care (Chapter 9) suggests that those caring under great stress should be targeted for support in considering residential placement of their partner. While spouse carers are understandably more reluctant than other kinship groups (except parents) to place their relative, several studies have shown that use of community services may ease the transition. Indeed, use of community nursing, a service more commonly used by spouse and older carers, often preceded residential placement (Chapter 11).

Importantly, an eighth of our initial sample self-identified as primary carers despite their relative being in residential care, and half of those placing their relative in the next fifteen months continued to identify similarly. This indicates the desirability of strategies that acknowledge and incorporate these carers in the life of the residential service and in the ongoing care of their relative: participation in meals and social activities; open communication, newsletters or relatives' groups; and opportunities to contribute to service planning. For some carers, where the transition phase is difficult, provision of personal support or counselling, either from residential care staff or allied service, may also be desirable.

4. FINANCIAL PROVISIONS

TAXATION AND INSURANCE COVERAGE

Our results indicate that although many care-dyads are covered by pensioner subsidies, private health coverage or accident insurance, a significant minority of carers are adversely affected by the costs of providing care and in general have difficulty in meeting everyday living costs (Chapter 8). There are suggestions that some care requirements are extremely expensive compared to the available benefits, that they involve frustrating delays to procure through these avenues, or that they are not covered by insurance schedules or subsidy guidelines. This indicates the need for a broadening of items covered, the level or duration of coverage under federal guidelines, and/or the deductibility of endorsed items for taxation purposes. Preferred strategies should be guided by a more detailed study of the extent and nature of expenses incurred by carers across the spectrum of disabilities, family stages and caregiving phases.

FINANCIAL ENTITLEMENTS AND SUPPORT

Compared with non-carers of workforce age, carer households had significantly lower incomes. Of carers overall, over a quarter experienced difficulties in meeting daily living costs because of the financial impacts of caregiving (Chapter 8). Parents and those (mainly women) carers excluded from the workforce because of their caregiving were identifiably worse off here. Given the valuable social role they fill in caring for a dependent relative and the likely long-term effects of financial difficulties on their own and their family members' life opportunities, our findings suggest that these groups should be eligible for better financial support.

Overall, relatively few carers received Federal Government entitlements relating to caregiving (Carers' Pension, Domiciliary Nursing Care Benefit and the Child Disability Allowance), most reporting that they knew little of these benefits or saw themselves as ineligible. This suggests the need for a closer examination of eligibility entitlements and the circumstances of those carers identifiably most in need of financial assistance.

A preliminary analysis undertaken for the Federal Department of Health and Family Services (VCP 1996) suggests that almost two-thirds of carers seemingly eligible for the CP were not receiving it, as were two in five seemingly eligible for the CDA. In both cases those missing out were younger co-resident carers, who were most likely to be in the group experiencing greatest financial difficulties. This supports the view that lack of information is a major barrier to financial entitlements and indicates the need for strategies that enhance eligible carers' knowledge about such entitlements and promote them as a positive recognition of carers' contribution. In this regard, GPs, health professionals and service providers need to provide information to carers who appear either to meet the respective eligibility criteria or to be struggling financially.

The preliminary analysis for the Federal Government suggested that a majority of carers 'excluded' from the workforce because of caregiving were not eligible for the CP or the DNCB, although this was less so for the CDA. These 'ineligible' carers were again mainly younger carers providing over 30 hours weekly care to relatives with high dependency and supervision needs. As such, the discrepancy between eligibility criteria for entitlements and carers' perceptions of the need to quit or remain out of work requires further study, and potential adjustment to existing criteria. A detailed account is presented in VCP (1996).

In addition, closer examination is required of the circumstances of carers experiencing greatest financial strains than is possible from the VCP data. Even with maximum uptake of benefits and adjusted eligibility criteria, the amounts payable vis-à-vis expenses and income loss may be inadequate, especially for the two allowances. Increases in benefit payments or other measures to assist carers struggling financially may need to be considered.

Other strategies to increase income through maintaining or re-entering employment are addressed under employment initiatives. But the need for financial assistance for alternative day care was noted by 42% of VCP carers who wished to return to work or increase their hours while caregiving (Chapter 8), and it is likely that some may also require financial assistance with job training or other expenses associated with recommencing work.

5. EMPLOYMENT AND INDUSTRIAL RELATIONS INITIATIVES

As discussed in Chapter 8, some carers had to give up their job or felt unable to work because of their caregiving commitment. And of those working, many experienced at least one adverse effect of caregiving on their employment. Despite this, carers often saw work as a source of relief, and the majority of workforce age were either working or wanting to resume employment either while caregiving or after their caregiving ceased. Industrial policies which maximise job flexibility would benefit carers (along with other employee groups, such as parents) by reducing the conflict between the demands of paid work and caregiving. Flexibility in the hours worked, the pace and location of work, the accumulation of time-in-lieu, the availability of personal telephone calls, and flexible leave arrangements (including hourly leave) would assist carers. Similarly, better job-sharing arrangements and part-time work may help carers to remain in or return to the paid workforce, as well as spreading the caregiving load between family members. Education and discussion with employer groups, unions and industrial relations officials is required to promote carers as another group who need more flexible work conditions. Additionally, the extension or introduction of employment-based health promotion programs (such as stress management, assertiveness training, communication skills and physical exercise) would enhance carers' health and well-being.

CARER-SPECIFIC EMPLOYMENT INITIATIVES

In addition to changes in universal employment conditions, VCP findings suggest that carer-specific initiatives may be called for. As reported in Chapter 8, in addition to flexible work conditions many saw alternative care arrangements (and smaller numbers financial assistance for alternative care) as important in enabling them to resume or maintain their employment. The provision of five days per annum carer leave under some federal public service awards could be extended to other public and private sectors: the cost would be fairly small as only a few employees would be claiming specific carer leave at any one time. The value of large organisations (public and private) providing employment-based carer information and referral programs could also be usefully explored as strategies to enhance productivity and help carers to manage their role more effectively. Subsidies for community care costs could be similarly explored for their impact on work patterns and job retention.

EMPLOYMENT RETRAINING

Existing provision of retraining for (ex)carers wishing to return to the workforce appears limited alongside the proportion and characteristics of VCP carers expressing a need for retraining to re-enter or increase employment (Chapter 8). Our findings suggest the need for new strategies to assist carers identifying training requirements, especially those with lower educational qualifications or who have been out of the workforce five years or more. At present cost-neutral retraining is only available through the JET scheme to recipients of the Carers' Pension—a small minority of carers who, as a group, least resemble carers preferring to increase their workforce participation (i.e. parent carers and others looking after younger, male care-recipients). Provision of a carer retraining allowance, subsidy of approved courses via the trainer or carer and other options could be explored alongside the need to broaden carer access to fully-subsidised courses under existing federal programs.

This book has provided an overview of informal caregiving in a Western community. It is a reflection of a social phenomenon at the turn of the century. The implications of our findings are multiple and are variously applicable to individual carers, groups of carers, and countries around the world. We have given thought to what they mean in terms of policy and service development and in the use of resources in our society. We hope that others working in the field and those who are caregivers will find this a useful building block.

ENDNOTES

INTRODUCTION

1 Schofield et al. 1996.
2 Schofield et al. 1996.
3 Schulz et al. 1990; Schulz et al. 1995; Taylor et al. 1996.
4 Herrman, Singh, Schofield, Burgess, Lewis & Scotton 1993.
5 Herrman, Schofield, Murphy & Singh 1994; Schofield & Herrman 1993.
6 Bozic et al. 1993a.
7 Bozic et al. 1993b.
8 Schofield & Herrman 1993; Herrman, Schofield, Murphy & Singh 1994.
9 Frey 1983; Groves 1990; Fenig et al. 1993.
10 Horton & Duncan 1978.
11 James 1992.

1 WHAT DO WE MEAN BY A FAMILY CAREGIVER?

1 Baldock & Ungerson 1991; Graham 1991.
2 'The International Classification of Impairments, Disabilities and Handicaps definition for disability is as follows: "In the context of health experience, a disability is any restriction or lack (resulting from an impairment) of ability to perform an activity in the manner or within the range considered normal for a human being"' (ABS 1993:52).
3 Pruchno & Potashnik 1989; Beckman 1991; Orbell & Gillies 1993a.
4 Atkin 1992.
5 Roberts 1986; Birkel 1987; Hicks 1988; Lewis & Meredith 1988; Barusch 1988; Braun & Nichaus 1990; McCallum & Gelfand 1990; Jutras & Veilleux 1991.
6 Baldock & Ungerson 1991.
7 Respectively, Ozanne 1990, Leibrich 1992, and Thornicroft & Bebbington 1989.

8 Hagemann-White 1984; Lewis & Meredith 1988; McCallum & Gelfand 1990; de Vaus 1994. See also Dalley 1988.

2 A PROFILE OF CARERS AND CARE-RECIPIENTS

1 Some of the material of this chapter was published in Schofield, Herrman et al. (1997).
2 Figure from the 1991 Census.

3 PHYSICAL AND EMOTIONAL ASPECTS OF CAREGIVING

1 Hoenig & Hamilton 1966; Hoenig 1968.
2 χ^2 values were: 6.9, p = .008 for satisfaction; 9.95, p = .001 for worry; 00.45, p = .0007 for grief; 8.30, p = .004 for anger; 8.13, p = .004 for guilt.
3 Role satisfaction significantly correlated with recipient accomplishments 0.37, confidence 0.35, reassurance 0.28 and loss 0.28. Anger significantly correlated with embarrassment 0.47, frustration 0.47, guilt 0.43, lost opportunities 0.39, lost friends 0.40 and time spent caring 0.38. Responses to the items listed in Table 3.17 were factor-analysed, forming three caring-role scales respectively characterised as *satisfaction*, that is, a positive emotional response to the role and the recipient; *resentment* about the negative effects of caring on the carer's life; and *anger*, a negative emotional response to the recipient including guilt and embarrassment. For economy of presentation and enhanced reliability, in subsequent chapters, these scales have been used in analyses rather than responses to the separate items. Schofield, Murphy et al. 1997 present details of the factor analysis.
4 Responses to items assessing changes in the family environment in Table 3.21 were factor-analysed and formed two scales named *closeness* and *conflict*. In subsequent chapters these scales have been used rather than responses to the separate family environment items.
5 χ^2 values were 22.86, p < .0000 for tension; and 8.89, p = .01 for resentment.
6 Haley, Brown & Levine 1987.

4 A COMPARISON BETWEEN ANGLO AND NON-ANGLO CARE-DYADS

1 See Hartley 1995; BIPR 1994.
2 Kendig & McCallum 1986.
3 Schofield 1995.
4 Alcorso & Schofield 1991; Rowland 1991; McCallum & Gelfand 1990.
5 E.g. offspring (McCallum & Gelfand 1990).
6 E.g. Vietnamese (Thomas & Balnaves 1993).
7 Ngo 1994.
8 The chi squared test was used to compare the demographic profiles of NESB and Anglo-Australian dyads; the nature of the care-recipient's disability, care needs and amount of care provided by the carer; carers' self-rated physical health;

support provided by relatives and friends; services used and needed by care-dyads, and sources of information about services. A one-way ANOVA was used to assess differences between groups in carers' emotional well-being, care-recipients' behaviour problems and severity of disability, overall amount of help provided by carers in activities of daily living, and number of services used. For all but socio-demographic characteristics, statistical analysis of difference between groups is restricted to those who participated in the extended interview.

9   χ^2 values were 8.5, $p < .05$ for organising appointments; 23.9, $p < .0001$ for communicating; and 14.9, $p < .001$ for financial support.

10 $\chi^2 = 4.4$, $p < .05$.

11 Alcorso & Schofield 1991; Schofield 1995.

12 Rowland 1991:65.

13 McCallum & Gelfand 1990; NSW Women's Health 1993; Fischer 1995.

14 Jutras & Vielleux 1991a; Horowitz 1985.

15 Davis et al. 1996; Westbrook & Legge 1991; McCallum & Gelfand 1990.

16 Bernardi 1993.

17 Rowland 1991:29; Jakubowicz 1989.

18 Bowman 1994.

19 McCallum & Gelfand 1990; NSW Women's Health 1993; Barnett & Cricelli 1990; Legge & Westbrook 1991; Whelan 1986. The exception is one comparative study of Italian and Anglo-Australian carers which found the Italians to be in better health and less strained. Carrafa et al. 1997.

20 E.g. the Victorian Ethnic Home & Community Care Policy (H&CS 1993).

21 Szwarc 1988; McCallum & Gelfand 1990; NSW Women's Health 1993; Plunkett & Quine 1996.

22 H&CS 1995.

23 NSW Women's Health 1993; Davis et al. 1996.

24 Fischer 1995; McCallum & Gelfand 1990; Fitch et al. 1992; Plunkett & Quine 1996.

5 A COMPARISON WITH NON-CARERS

1   Livingston et al. 1995; Schulz et al. 1995; Taylor et al. 1995.

2   A t test was used to assess the age difference between carers and non-carers. The chi squared statistic was used to assess differences between the carer and comparison groups within three age-groups in country of birth, partner and work status, education, post-school qualifications, number of children and responsibility for household tasks. Stepwise (Wald) logistic regression analyses were used to predict: (1) major health problems in the past year (Yes, No); (2) use of medication (Yes, No); and (3) self-rated health (excellent/good or fair/poor). Factors entered into each analysis were age, marital status, work status (employed full-time, part-time or not employed), number of children and carer status. Three-way ANOVAs were used to examine main and interactive effects of carer status (carer, non-carer), age-group (under 40, 40–59, 60 and over) and partner status (partnered, single) on health rating, life satisfaction, positive affect, negative affect, social support, and overload. No significant two-way or three-way

interaction effects were observed except for carer status by age-group interaction on social support.

3 Jutras & Veilleux 1991a; Miller & Cafasso 1992.

4 Respective χ^2 values for partner status were 7.37, $p < .01$ for those under 40 and 8.04, $p < .01$ for 40–59-year-olds; for work status 3.98 for those under 40 and 4.92, $p < .05$ and 13.75, $p < .05$ for 40–59-year-olds; for children under 18, 13.75, $p < .001$ for 40–59-year-olds.

5 A discriminant function analysis distinguishing carers from non-carers correctly classified 71% of cases: canonical correlation = .41, Wilks' Lambda = .83, $p = .0000$.

6 These findings are consistent with those of Baumgarten et al. (1992) and Grafstrom et al. (1992) in dementia caregiving, and Scharlach et al. (1994) in caring for the elderly. In their study of 55-year-olds, however, Taylor et al. (1995) found better health and functioning among carers than among non-carers. They note that their findings cannot be generalised to carers of the young (possibly parents) or elderly. Interestingly, the non-carers in the Taylor et al. sample were more disabled than the carers, and those who stopped caring more disabled than those who continued. Could their non-carer sample have included care-recipients?

7 Sarason et al. (1991) argue that social support has been measured in various ways and it seems that *perceived* support is more critical than *actual* support in determining the buffering effects on caregiver stress.

8 Moen et al. 1994; Scharlach 1994; Scharlach et al. 1991; Scharlach & Boyd 1989.

9 Murphy et al. 1997.

6 THE RELATIVE BURDEN OF PHYSICAL AND MENTAL DISABILITIES

1   Morris et al. 1988.
2   Gilleard 1984; Brodaty & Hadzi-Pavlovic 1990; O'Connor et al. 1990.
3   Baumgarten et al. 1994.
4   Draper et al. 1992.
5   Anderson et al. 1995.
6   Jorm et al. 1993.
7   Cattanach & Tebes 1991.
8   Draper et al. 1992.
9   Gallagher et al. 1989.
10 Rabins et al. 1990.
11 The chi squared statistic was used to assess differences on all categorical variables. One-way ANOVAs were used to assess differences on all continuous variables. *Post hoc* carer group differences were assessed using the Newman-Kuels procedure. Two-way ANOVAs were used to examine the main and interactive effects of carer group and living arrangements on all continuous variables. There were no significant interaction effects. Multiple regression analyses were used to predict: (1) a composite measure of burden (negative affect, overload, life

satisfaction and social support, with scores inverted for the positive dimensions; and (2) carer resentment.

12 Brodaty & Hadzi-Pavlovic 1990; Yeatman et al. 1993.

13 These findings support those of Livingston et al. (1996), also based on a representative sample.

14 Sutcliffe & Larner 1988; Whitlatch et al. 1991.

15 Montgomery & Borgatta 1986.

7 THE EFFECT ON CARERS' WELL-BEING

1 Also in the USA, Harper & Lund (1990) investigated factors associated with caregiver burden in wives, husbands and daughters caring for relatives with dementia living in institutionalised and non-institutionalised settings. In a population-based study in Canada, also focusing on caregiving to the elderly, Jutras & Veilleux (1991a) found that although women provided more assistance to their elderly relatives than did men, the groups were similar on a 'global' measure of burden.

2 Other investigators finding an association between caring for children with disabilities and psychological distress are Breslau & Davis 1986 and Pahl & Quine 1987.

3 The information in this chapter is presented in more detail in Schofield, Murphy, Nankervis et al. 1997.

4 Logistic regression analyses were used to check the extent to which relationship differences in reporting major health problems and use of medication were accounted for by other factors. Carer age (up to 44, 45–59, 60 and over), work status and marital status were entered into each analysis. Work status was the only significant predictor of major health problems (Wald statistic = 8.30, p = .004, Odds ratio = .77), with working carers less likely to report such problems. Age was the only significant predictor of taking medication (Wald statistic = 67.65, p = .0000, Odds ratio = 2.48), with carers 45 and over twice as likely to be using medication as those under 45.

5 On all measures of emotional well-being, social support, family environment, caregiving role, care-recipient disabilities, dependencies and behaviour problems, three-way hierarchical ANOVAs were used to assess the main and interactive effects of carer gender, relationship (adult offspring, parents, partners) and, given the significant age difference between relationship groups, three carer age-groups (0–44, 45–59, 60+). While there were no significant two-way or three-way interaction effects, main effects for sex, relationship and age are presented in tables and discussed.

6 Only fourteen spouses and fifteen parents did not live with their care-recipients.

7 One-way ANOVAs, limited to co-resident carers only, were used to assess the effects of relationship independent of living arrangements.

8 $\chi^2 = 18.4$, $p < .01$.

9 $\chi^2 = 23.1$, $p < .001$.

10 Dwyer & Coward 1992.

11 E.g. in spousal caregiving (Fitting et al. 1986; Barusch & Spaid 1989; Pruchno & Resch 1989; Harper & Lund 1990), in adult offspring caring for parents

(Johnson & Catalano 1983; Horowitz 1985; Montgomery et al. 1985) and in parents caring for children (Romans-Clarkson et al. 1986; Kazak 1987; Beckman 1991).

12 Murphy, Schofield et al. 1997.
13 Mui 1992; Stull et al. 1994.
14 Brody et al. 1987.
15 Finley 1989; Kaye & Applegate 1990.
16 Lawton, Brody & Saperstein 1989.
17 Solomon & Evans 1992; Wolstenholme 1994.

8 THE EFFECTS ON CARERS' EMPLOYMENT AND FINANCES

1 Kingson & O'Grady-LeShane 1993; Beresford 1994; Stommel et al. 1994; ABS 1995.
2 Beresford 1994; Stommel et al. 1994.
3 Kendig 1988; ABS 1991; Brody 1990.
4 Moen et al. 1994; Matthews et al. 1989; Brody & Schoonover 1986.
5 Scharlach & Boyd 1989; Stone & Short 1990; ABS 1995; Chappell 1985.
6 Lechner 1991; Franklin et al. 1994; Wagner & Neal 1994; Stone et al. 1987; ABS 1995; Kinnear & Graycar 1984; Brody et al. 1987.
7 Stone & Short 1990; Jutras & Veilleux 1991a; ABS 1995.
8 Brody et al. 1987; Franklin et al. 1994; Moen et al. 1994. These differential impacts were not evident in Scharlach et al. 1991, a study of employed carers of the elderly.
9 Franklin et al. 1994; Enright 1991; ABS 1995.
10 Brody et al. 1987; Stone & Short 1990; Scharlach et al. 1991; Franklin et al. 1994; Gerstel & Gallagher 1993.
11 Scharlach et al. 1991; Franklin et al. 1994.
12 Kendig 1983; Harper & Lund 1990; Mui 1992; Tennstedt et al. 1992; Doress-Worters 1994.
13 Stoller & Pugliesi 1989.
14 Brody et al. 1987; Scharlach et al. 1991; Gerstel & Gallagher 1993; Murphy, Schofield et al. 1997.
15 $\chi^2 = 14.4$, 2 df, $p < .001$.
16 The differences may be partly explained by the concentration of older carers since rates of employment decrease sharply over the age of 45 (women) and 60 (for men) (Wolcott 1997:83).
17 Moen et al. 1994; Wolcott & Glezer 1995.
18 Brody et al. 1987 Scharlach et al. 1991; Gerstel & Gallagher 1993.
19 Cantor 1983; Scharlach et al. 1991; Moen et al. 1994; Scharlach 1994; Rosenman & Le Broque 1996.
20 Wolcott & Glezer 1995.
21 Bowman 1994; Rosenman & Le Broque 1996.
22 Rosenman et al. 1992.
23 Graham 1987; Stommel et al. 1994.
24 Bowman 1994.

9 THE EFFECTS OF CAREGIVING OVER TIME

1 Three-way repeated ANOVAs were used to assess differential change in measures of well-being (overload, life satisfaction, positive and negative affect social support and family conflict) and self-reported health between Times 1 and 2 and between Times 1 and 3 in carers and those no longer caring. Factors in each analysis were carer status (still carer, no longer carer), relationship group (spouse, adult offspring and parent) and Time (1 and 2, or 1 and 3).

2 A significant main effect for time, F (1,589) = 9.69, p = .002, and a significant time by carer status interaction, F (2,598) = 15.27, p = .000, were observed in the Times 1 to 2 analysis. No significant main or interaction effects were observed in the Times 1 to 3 analysis.

3 No significant main or interaction effects were observed in the Times 1 to 2 analysis. In the Times 1 to 3 analysis a significant carer status by time interaction effect, F (1,413) = 11.60, p = .001, was observed.

4 A significant main effect for time, F (1,598) = 14.48, p = .000, and a significant carer status by time interaction effect, F (1,598) = 4.75, p = .03, were evident in the Times 1 to 2 analysis. No significant effects were observed in the Times 1 to 3 analysis.

5 Main effects for time, F (1,598) = 57.57, p = .000, and carer status, F (1,598) = 7.11, p = .008, and a significant time by carer status interaction effect, F (1,598) = 40.23, p < .001, in the Times 1 to 2 analysis. Similar effects were observed in the Times 1 to 3 analysis.

6 Significant relationship by time, F (1,598) = 10.94, p < .001, and carer status by relationship by time interaction, F (1,598) = 8.99, p < .001, effects were observed. None were evident in the Times 1 to 3 analysis.

7 The Logit model predicting change, from Time 1 to Time 2, in presence of major illness from carer status (still carer, no longer carer) and relationship group fitted well, $\chi^2 = (6) = 3.82$, p = .701, as did the Times 1 to 3 model, $\chi^2 = (6) = 10.36$, p < .110, and a good fit from Times 1 to 3, $\chi^2 = (6) = 4.11$, p = .662. Similar analyses were undertaken to predict differential change in carers and non-carers. Odds ratio: 1.30, 95% ci: 1.02–1.67.

8 Odds ratio: 1.27, 95% ci: 1.01–1.58.

9 Odds ratio: 1.40, 95% ci: .05–1.86.

10 Odds ratio: 1.55, 95% ci: 1.26–1.91.

11 Odds ratio: .80, 95% ci: .66–.97.

12 Odds ratio: 1.62, 95% ci: 1.24–2.11.

13 The Logit model predicting change in presence of major health problems from carer status (carer, non-carer) and age-group (0–44, 45–59, 60+) fitted well, $\chi^2 = (6) = 5.81$, p = .445, as did that predicting medication use, $\chi^2 = (6) = 4.78$, p = .572. Odds ratio: 1.33, 95% ci: 1.05–1.68 (health problems).

14 Odds ratio: .52, 95% ci: .41–.64.

15 For example: Schulz et al. 1988; Baumgarten et al. 1994.

16 Silliman 1993; Haley et al. 1987.

17 Murphy et al. 1997.

10 SUPPORTS FOR THE CARER AND CARE-RECIPIENT

1   Braithwaite 1990; Rosenman 1991.
2   One-way ANOVAs were used to assess the effects of: (1) socio-demographic factors on the number of secondary carers and of secondary activities; (2) size of support network on measures of well-being and caregiving role; (3) type of secondary help on measures of well-being and caregiving role; (4) desired support (Yes/No) on measures of carer well-being and caregiving role, and recipient disabilities, dependencies and behaviour problems.
3   Green 1988; Chappell & Littenhaus 1995a, b.
4   Miller & Furner 1994 also reported socio-demographic influences to be stronger than functional status in determining the size of elderly people's informal networks.
5   These findings support the importance of secondary assistance for the carers' emotional well-being reported by others. See Harper & Lund 1990; Wilson et al. 1990; Seltzer et al. 1991; Lechner 1993.
6   As suggested by Zarit et al. 1986 and Cohen et al. 1994.
7   Noelker & Bass 1989; Edelman & Hughes 1990.
8   See also Bowman 1994.
9   HACC National Guidelines 1989.
10 See HACC 1992; McCallum & Gelfand 1990; Baume et al. 1993; Fine & Thomson 1993; Wolstenholme 1994.
11 See Action 1988; Kendig et al. 1992; Rosenman et al. 1992; Baume et al. 1993; Fine & Thomson 1993; Reynolds et al. 1993.
12 House of Representatives Standing Committee on Community Affairs 1994.
13 Tennstedt et al. 1990 (spouse carers); Chappell 1991; Bass et al. 1992; Penning 1995. The relative weight of predisposing factors, such as residency and relationship characteristics, compared with objective need factors in predicting service use is unclear: the above researchers report conflicting findings on living arrangements, while Kosloski & Montgomery (1994) showed that the relative impact of relationship and need factors depended on the 'discretionary' nature of particular services.
14 Brown et al. 1990; Kirwin & Kaye 1991; Penning 1995.
15 Biegel et al. 1993.
16 Respectively: Penning 1995; Wolinsky & Johnson 1991; Gonyea & Silverstein 1991; Bass et al. 1992; Wolinsky & Johnson 1991; Gonyea & Silverstein 1991.
17 In, respectively: Baume et al. 1993, Action 1988; Baume et al. 1993 and Wolstenholme 1994; Hollingsworth 1990 and Baume et al. 1993; Hollingsworth 1990.
18 See Rosenman 1991; Fine & Thomson 1993; Reynolds et al. 1993.
19 *Predisposing factors* included carer age, sex and marital status, care-recipient age and sex, relationship between carer and recipient, and living arrangements. *Care-recipient need factors* included a 'severity of disability', ADL and IADL dependencies, and the behaviour problems scales. *Carer need factors* were hours spent caring and duration of care, 'carer overload', and perceived social support.
20 χ^2 and p values were 43.93, $p < .00001$ for relationship; 15.50, $p < .0001$ for

sex; 41.05, $p < .00001$ for age; 32.92, $p < .00001$ for care-recipient age; and 19.29, $p < .001$ for living arrangements.

21 Green 1988; Chappell & Littenhaus 1995a, b.
22 Stone et al. 1987; Green 1988; ABS 1993.
23 Bass et al. 1992; Biegel et al. 1993.
24 Biegel et al. 1993; Penning 1995.
25 See Geiser et al. 1988; Montgomery & Borgatta 1989; Adler et al. 1993.
26 Barnett & Cricelli 1990; McVicar & Reynolds 1993; Clarke & Finucane 1995.
27 Szwarc 1988; Hollingsworth 1990; Reynolds et al. 1993; Wolstenholme 1994.
28 Wells et al. 1990; Wilson & Rosenman 1990.
29 Szwarc 1988.
30 Respectively, Cullinan 1993 and Ashby & Moo 1993.
31 Respective means were 1.05 cf. .69 ($F = 63.40$, $p < .0000$) for aggressive behaviours; 1.42 cf. 1.34 ($F = 4.75$, $p < .03$) for need help with physical ADLs; and 1.69 cf. 1.51 ($F = 10.51$, $p < .001$) for provide help with ADLs.
32 Two-way ANOVAs were used to assess the effects of respite need (Yes/No) and care-recipient age-group on all measures of well-being. There were no interactions between care-recipient age-group and respite need for any of the well-being measures. Significant main effects are reported in Table 10.20 (p. 305).
33 CHAID was used to identify major variables associated with increased use of and need for respite. See Magidson 1993.
34 Excluding 54 people looking after someone in residential care, 345 carers are included in the following analyses. Because of the smaller sample size, findings are reported for all carers combined, rather than separately for carers over and under 65 years.
35 61%, Szwarc 1988.
36 Cullinan 1993; McVicar & Reynolds 1993.
37 Ashby & Moo 1993; Biegel et al. 1993; McVicar & Reynolds 1993; Penning 1995.
38 See also Burdz et al. 1988; Zarit 1990; Rosenman et al. 1992.
39 Lawton et al. 1989; Ashby & Moo 1993; McVicar & Reynolds 1993.
40 Ashby & Moo 1993; McVicar & Reynolds 1993.
41 Lawton et al. 1989; Barnett & Cricelli 1990; Rosenman et al. 1992; Adler et al. 1993.
42 As recommended by McVicar & Reynolds 1993.
43 See Zarit et al. 1987; Abramowitz & Coursey 1989; Chiverton & Caine 1989; Greene & Monahan 1989; Kuipers et al. 1989; Piktialis 1990; Smith et al. 1991; Bruce & Schultz 1992; Lippmann et al. 1993; Schultz, Smyrnios, Grbich and Schultz 1993.
44 Greene & Monahan 1987; Zarit et al. 1987; Toseland & Smith 1990.
45 Brodaty & Gresham 1989; Mittelman et al. 1993; Hebert et al. 1995.
46 Haley 1989; MacCarthy et al. 1989; Toseland & Rossiter 1989; Schultz, Schultz, Bruce, Smyrnios, Carey & Carey 1993.
47 Burden: Smith & Birchwood 1987; Montgomery & Borgatta 1989; Whitlatch et al. 1991. Stress: Brodaty & Gresham 1989; Kirkham & Schilling 1989. Depression: Pakenham & Dadds 1987; Mittelman et al. 1995. Anxiety: Abramowitz & Coursey 1989; Schultz, Smyrnios, Grbich & Schultz 1993.

48 Haley et al. 1987; Toseland et al. 1989; Mohide et al. 1990; Schultz, Schultz, Bruce, Smyrnios, Carey & Carey 1993; Brodaty et al. 1994.
49 Kahan et al. 1985; Barrowclough et al. 1987; Chiverton & Caine 1989.
50 Chiverton & Caine 1989; Kirkham & Schilling 1989; Toseland et al. 1989.
51 Moseley et al. 1988; Kirkham & Schilling 1989; Goodman & Pynoos 1990.
52 Abramowitz & Coursey 1989; Gonyea & Silverstein 1991.

11 RESIDENTIAL CARE AND PLACEMENT

1 *Disability Services Act 1986* (Cth); *Disability Services Act 1992* (Vic.).
2 Mittelman et al. 1993.
3 Cohen et al. 1993; Kasper & Shore 1994.
4 Mittelman et al. 1993.
5 See, respectively, Kasper & Shore 1994; Pruchno et al. 1990; Mittelman et al. 1993.
6 Colerick & George 1986; Lieberman & Kramer 1991.
7 Jette et al. 1995; Tsuji et al. 1995.
8 Lund et al. 1987.
9 Colerick & George 1986; Lund et al. 1987; Lieberman & Kramer 1991; Cohen et al. 1993; Jette et al. 1995; Tsuji et al. 1995.
10 Colerick & George 1986.
11 Tsuji et al. 1995.
12 Deimling & Poulshock 1985; Pruchno et al. 1990.
13 Colerick & George 1986; Cohen et al. 1993; Kasper & Shore 1994; Jette et al. 1995.
14 Jette et al. 1995.
15 χ^2 values were 14.65, $p < .01$ for living costs; 27.72, $p < .001$ for own home; and 19.68, $p < .01$ for tertiary qualifications.
16 Four separate discriminant function analyses were used to predict residential placement over 15 months. The first used carer-related predictors; the second, care-recipient predictors; and the third, service-related predictors. The fourth used the significant predictors from the first three analyses. In this final analysis discriminant function coefficients for the significant predictors were 0.43 for used community nursing, 0.39 for mental disability, 0.38 for considered residential care, and 0.37 for caring-role satisfaction. Percentage of cases correctly classified was 77%; canonical correlation 0.37.
17 Colerick & George 1986; Lund et al. 1987; Lieberman & Kramer 1991; Jette et al. 1995; Tsuji et al. 1995.
18 Pruchno et al. 1990; Cohen et al. 1993; Kasper & Shore 1994.
19 Colerick & George 1986; Cohen et al. 1993; Kasper & Shore 1994; Jette et al. 1995.
20 Pruchno et al. 1990.
21 Chappell 1991; Jette et al. 1995.
22 Colerick & George 1986; Lieberman & Kramer 1991; Cohen et al. 1993; Jette et al. 1995; Tsuji et al. 1995. While the longer study period may account for this difference in some cases, sample differences may also play a part. As Tsuji et al. (1995:765) have pointed out, predictors of nursing-home placement 'are

highly dependent upon the nature of the study population', carer stresses being more prominent in studies of more highly disabled care-recipient samples compared with general elderly population samples.

23 Zarit & Whitlatch 1993; Tilse 1994; Gold et al. 1995.

24 See Gilhooly 1987; Ade-Ridder & Kaplan 1993; Zarit & Whitlatch 1993; Tilse 1994; Pfeiffer 1995.

25 Gilhooly 1987; Ade-Ridder & Kaplan 1993; Flemming 1994.

26 Tilse 1994.

12 HEALTH PROMOTION STRATEGIES

1 Studies examining the efficacy of various carer supports have often included 'information provision' as either a control or minimal intervention condition as comparison for a more intense intervention program, presumably on the basis of the relative ineffectiveness of information alone (e.g. Smith & Birchwood 1987; Sutcliffe & Larner 1988; Lawton, Brody & Saperstein 1989).

2 Full details of the CSK are given in Murphy et al. 1995.

3 The chi squared statistic was used to compare the demographic profiles of the Stage 1 sample and the random sample of carers offered the *Carer Support Leaflet*. ANOVAs were used to assess differences on well-being scale scores between carers who used the kit, carers who applied for but did not use the kit, and carers who did not apply for the kit. The chi squared statistic was used to compare these three groups on self-rated physical health, use of medications, major health problems in the past 12 months, and use of community services.

4 Brodaty & Gresham 1989; Haley 1989.

5 The information in this section has been given in more detail in Murphy et al. 1997.

6 ABS 1991, 1992; Jorm & Henderson 1993.

7 The chi squared statistic was used to assess differences between GPs and pharmacists at pre-trial, and differential change for GPs and pharmacists from pre- to post-trial in all variables. The latter comparisons involved only those who participated in both pre- and post-intervention interviews. Where relevant, the Mantel-Haenszel test for linear association was applied.

8 Johnson & Maguire 1989; Schultz & Schultz 1991; Brodaty & Peters 1991; Opie et al. 1992.

9 Montgomery & Borgatta 1989; Opie et al. 1992; Fine & Thomson 1993.

10 See overseas studies such as Hendrickson et al. 1984; Vetter et al. 1984; Carpenter & Demopoulos 1990; Fabacher et al. 1994. Several hospital-based studies have, however, included carers: Brown et al. 1990; Silliman et al. 1990.

11 χ^2 values were 16.2, $p < .0001$ for home modifications; 7.48, $p < .01$ for personal aids; 11.07, $p < .001$ for social workers; 9.48, $p < .01$ for occupational therapists; and 17.8, $p < .0001$ for respite need.

12 Harrison et al. 1985; Ramsdell et al. 1989; Carpenter & Demopoulos 1990; Fabacher et al. 1994.

13 Elton & Associates 1995:67.

14 MaloneBeach et al. 1992.

13 A SURVEY OF CAREGIVER COUNSELLING

1 Sutcliffe & Larner 1988; Kirkham & Schilling 1989; Mohide et al. 1990; Toseland & Smith 1990; Whitlatch et al. 1991; Schultz, Smyrnios, Grbich & Schultz 1993; Gallagher-Thompson & Steffen 1994.

2 See, respectively: Baum & Gallagher 1985; Rose & Del Maestro 1990; Zarit et al. 1987, Goldstein & Miklowitz 1994; Mohide et al. 1990, Toseland et al. 1995; Pinkston & Linsk 1984, Gallagher et al. 1989, Singer 1993, Bland 1994.

3 See, respectively: Skipwith 1994; Sutcliffe & Larner 1988, Bloch et al. 1995; Toseland & Smith 1990, Gallagher-Thompson & Steffen 1994; Zarit et al. 1987, Mittelman et al. 1993; Haley et al. 1987, Kirkham & Schilling 1989, Bland 1994; MacCarthy et al. 1989, MacFarlane 1994.

4 Gallagher et al. 1989; Zarit 1990.

5 Highfields Centre (Cynthia & Noel Schultz) model: Caring for Family Caregivers and Caring for Parent Caregivers; The Schizophrenia Fellowship (Ken Alexander) model; The Alzheimer's Association; The Bouverie Clinic ABI program (Perlesz and colleagues): Family Sensitive Practice.

6 Schultz, Schultz, Bruce, Smyrnios, Carey and Carey (1993):207.

7 Schultz, Smyrnios, Grbich and Schultz 1993:9.

8 Furlong et al. 1991; Perlesz et al. 1992.

9 Perlesz 1992:147.

10 MacCarthy et al. 1989; Smith et al. 1991; Mittelman et al. 1993; Gallagher-Thompson & Steffen 1994; Bloch et al. 1995.

11 Zarit et al. 1987; Bloch et al. 1995; Toseland et al. 1995.

12 Zarit & Zarit 1982; Gallagher et al. 1989.

13 Haley et al. 1987; Zarit et al. 1987; Sutcliffe & Larner 1988; MacCarthy et al. 1989.

14 Toseland et al. 1989; Bentley 1990; Mohide et al. 1990; Toseland et al. 1995.

15 Baum & Gallagher 1985; Haley et al. 1987; Gallagher et al. 1989; Singer 1993.

16 Richardson et al. 1994 argue that greater attention is needed to life-cycle concepts and family systems approaches. See also Sanborn & Bould 1991 and Power 1988.

APPENDIX II

1 Mossey & Shapira 1982; Idler, Kasl & Lemke 1990; McCallum et al. 1991.

2 The modified Barthel Index of ADLs (Fortinsky, Granger & Seltzer 1981), the Lawton and Brody IADL Scale (Lawton & Brody 1969), and the Folstein Mini Mental State Examination (Spencer & Folstein 1986). The Depression Scale from the Abbreviated Canberra Interview for the Elderly (Social Psychiatry Research Unit 1993), and an adapted version of the sensory scale used in the Mannheim study of the elderly (Cooper, Bickel & Schaufele 1992) were also included for the purposes of this study.

TABLES

Table 0.1   Summary of measures relating to carers and non-carers

Measures relating to	Domain	Scale
Caregiver and non-caregiver	Emotional well-being and physical health	Life satisfaction Positive affect Negative affect Social support Overload Health rating
Caregiver	Family environment	Closeness Conflict
	Caregiving role	Satisfaction Resentment Anger
	Care-recipient	Disability
	Help needed by recipient	Personal ADL Instrumental ADL
	Help provided by carer	Personal ADL Instrumental ADL
	Behaviour problems	Aggressive Depressive Forgetfulness/confusion

Table 2.1 Characteristics of carers (*N* = 976)

	%
Sex	
Female	78
Male	22
Age	
15–29	6
30–44	29
45–59	37
60–74	23
75 and over	5
Marital status	
Married	77
Living with a partner	2
Neither	21
Employment status	
Full-time	24
Part-time	15
Not in paid employment	62
Relationship of carer to care-recipient	
Adult offspring	39
Partner	23
Parent	20
Other relative or friend	17

Table 2.2 Living arrangements of care-recipients (*N* = 976)

	%
Lives with carer	61
Lives alone	19
In residential care	12
Lives with other	8

Table 2.3 Sex and age of care-recipients (*N* = 976)

	%
Sex	
Female	58
Male	42
Age	
0–14	12
15–29	7
30–44	5
45–59	8
60–74	20
75+	48

Table 2.4 Degree of disability in care-recipients (N = 976)

	Severe %	Moderate %	Minor %	None %
Physical/mobility problems	33	24	7	36
Sensory loss	20	25	15	40
Long-term health problems	20	19	9	52
Coordination difficulties	19	18	9	54
Intellectual impairment	15	23	13	49
Problems communicating	14	18	7	61
Psychiatric/emotional problems	12	17	12	59

Table 2.5 Care-recipient behaviour (N = 917–955)[a]

	Often %	Sometimes %	Rarely %	Never %
Repeats questions or stories	34	25	5	36
Becomes listless and fatigued	29	37	7	20
Cannot concentrate/easily sidetracked	28	26	10	40
Is cranky or easily irritated	24	36	12	30
Is forgetful and confused	24	32	6	33
Seeks attention	21	26	5	48
Is hyperactive or restless	16	21	15	57
Gets depressed	15	36	10	34
Is uncooperative	14	25	13	52
Is fearful and afraid	13	29	8	48
Has very changeable moods	13	23	8	56
Is withdrawn and hardly ever speaks	13	23	7	56
Keeps you up at night	10	16	8	67
Is suspicious or accusing	8	16	10	68
Is aggressive	7	20	4	63
Is physically violent	3	6	7	89
Endangers him/herself	3	9	3	81
Doesn't know who you are	3	3	4	92
Injures or abuses him/herself	2	5	5	89
Wanders and gets lost	2	5	7	88
Shows inappropriate sexual behaviour	1	2	7	20

Note: [a] Carers of recipients aged under 3 years were not asked about behaviour problems.

Table 2.6 Care-dyads using community services

	% Yes
Regular services (N = 864–870)	
Transport	24
General home help	24
Specific home help	13
Community nursing service	14
Home maintenance	7
Meals on wheels	7
Home modifications	32
Respite care in past 12 months (N = 961)	12
Other services (N = 975)	
Counselling or therapy	17
Training course for carers	11

Table 2.7 Sex and age distribution of carers: VCP primary and ABS 'principal' carers

	VCP primary carers %	ABS 'principal' carers %
Carer sex		
Female	78	67
Male	22	33
Carer age		
15–24	3	4
25–34	9	12
35–44	23	22
45–54	26	24
55–64	21	17
65–74	13	13
75+	5	7

Table 2.8 Comparison of UK General Household Survey 'main carers' with VCP sample: percentage distributions

	VCP (N = 976) %	GHS (N = 2374) %
Carer sex		
Female	78	65
Male	22	35
Carer age		
16–29	6	7
30–44	29	25
45–64	47	47
65+	18	20
Carer marital status		
Partnered	79	76
Non-partnered	21	23
Carer age: men		
16–29	8	8
30–44	26	23
45–64	39	46
65+	27	24
Carer age: women		
16–29	6	7
30–44	30	27
45–64	49	48
65+	16	18
Family type		
No partner no children	16	13
Married couple no children	31	37
Married couple and children	45	41
Sole parent	8	10
Care-recipient sex		
Female	58	70
Male	42	30
Care-recipient age		
<16	13	3
16–44	12	7
45–64	12	13
65–74	16	23
75–84	29	38

Table 3.1 Living arrangements: differences according to carer relationship and age

	Total (N = 976)	Relationship to recipient[a]				Carer age[b]			
		Offspring %	Spouse %	Parent %	Other %	< 35 %	35–49 %	50–64 %	65+ %
With carer	61	37	94	93	34	78	54	54	77
Alone	19	34	0	2	31	12	23	25	6
With other	8	13	0	1	17	7	12	7	3
Residential	12	15	6	4	19	3	11	14	14

Notes: a $x^2 = 339.88, p < .00001$
b $x^2 = 74.50, p < .00001$

Table 3.2 Duration of care: differences according to carer relationship and age

	Total (N = 974)	Relationship to recipient[a]				Carer age[b]			
		Offspring %	Spouse %	Parent %	Other %	< 35 %	35–49 %	50–64 %	65+ %
<1 year	16	19	17	9	18	14	21	12	13
1–2 yrs	15	15	14	10	23	19	16	13	13
3–5 yrs	27	32	26	20	30	36	23	33	22
6–9 yrs	16	18	14	19	12	25	11	14	22
10+ yrs	16	25	21	43	18	7	28	28	30

Notes: a $x^2 = 62.45, p < .00001$
b $x^2 = 61.13, p < .00001$

Table 3.3 Changes in time spent caring

	No. of carers	%
Time increased		
Altered condition	177	30
No specific reason/other	166	28
Altered circumstances	27	5
Time decreased		
Altered circumstances	65	11
Altered condition	62	11
No specific reasons/other	58	10
Time varies/is ambiguous	33	6

Table 3.4 Changes in time spent caring according to relationship, carer sex, and living arrangements

	Increased %	Decreased %	No change %	x^2	$p =$
Relationship to care-recipient					
Adult offspring	47	16	37	86.81	.0000
Spouse	49	10	41		
Parent	21	40	39		
Other	37	15	49		
Carer sex					
Women	41	21	38	9.46	.008
Men	37	14	49		
Recipient lives					
With carer	41	17	42	46.21	.0000
Alone	45	10	45		
With partner/other	38	27	35		
In residential care	31	40	29		

Table 3.5 Percentage of care-recipients requiring a lot, some or no help in twelve ADLs

	N	A lot %	Some %	None %
Going out	910	49	30	21
Social services	905	56	17	27
Managing money	900	49	17	33
Medication/dressings	921	32	25	43
Bathing/showering	922	26	23	51
Dressing	926	18	27	56
Communicating	922	15	24	61
Bed–chair transfer	928	11	17	72
Moving about	926	9	16	75
Using toilet	928	11	11	78
Incontinence	925	10	11	79
Eating	929	0	15	80

Table 3.6 Differences in help needed with ADLs and IADLs according to relationship and carer age ($N = 900$–929)

	Relationship to recipient[a]				Carer age[b]			
	Offspring %	Spouse %	Parent %	Other %	< 35 %	35–49 %	5–64 %	65+ %
Needs help with ADL	ns	ns	ns	ns	1.44	1.37	1.42	1.55
Needs help with IADL	1.95	1.87	2.27	1.87	ns	ns	ns	ns

Notes: a $F = 14.47$, $p < .00001$
     b $F = 4.79$, $p < .01$

Table 3.7 Differences in help needed according to living arrangements and duration of care (N = 900–929)

	Needs help with ADLs			Needs help with IADLs		
	Mean	F	p <	Mean	F	p <
Recipient lives						
With carer	1.45	48.60	.0001	1.99	38.52	.0001
Alone	1.12			1.68		
With other	1.40			1.76		
In residential care	1.84			2.42		
Duration of care						
1 year or less	1.40	3.61	.01	ns		
13 months to 2 years	1.34					
3–5 years	1.40					
6–9 years	1.56					
10+ years	1.44					

Table 3.8 Percentage of carers providing all/most, some, or none of help required by recipient in twelve ADLs

	N	All/most	Some	None	No help required
		%	%	%	%
Going out	909	58	17	4	21
Social services	905	60	10	3	27
Managing money	900	53	8	5	33
Medications/dressings	921	37	10	10	43
Communicating	921	25	12	2	61
Bathing/showering	926	28	8	9	56
Dressing	921	25	8	16	52
Bed–chair transfer	928	17	8	3	75
Moving about	925	14	8	3	75
Eating	929	12	6	3	80
Using toilet	928	13	5	4	78
Incontinence	925	12	4	5	79

Table 3.9   Who helps when care-recipient needs help with personal care tasks?

	No. of care-recipients needing help	Carer	Residential care	CNS	SHH	F&F	No help from these sources
Help required with bathing/showering	446	304 68%	86 19%	92 21%	68 15%	116 26%	3 < 1%
Help required with dressing	409	328 80%	74 18%	74 18%	65 16%	101 25%	1 < 1%
Help required with medications/dressings	524	436 83%	90 17%	86 16%	66 13%	107 20%	2 < 1%

Note: Totals > 100% because care-recipients are often receiving help from several sources. CNS = community nursing service; SHH = specific home help service; F&F = family and friends.

Table 3.10   Differences in help given according to carer–recipient relationship and carer age (N = 900–929)

	Needs help with ADLs			Needs help with IADLs		
	Mean	F	$p <$	Mean	F	$p <$
Relationship						
Offspring	1.38	31.06	.0001	2.29	18.37	.0000
Spouse	1.85			2.41		
Parent	1.73			2.74		
Other	1.30			1.97		
Carer age						
< 35	1.67	6.67	.001		ns	
35–49	1.44					
50–64	1.51					
65+	1.7					

Table 3.11   Differences in help given according to living arrangements (means)

	Care-recipient lives					
	With carer	Alone	With other	Resid. care	F	$p <$
Gives help with ADLs	1.77	1.12	1.26	1.26	55.11	.0001
Gives help with IADLs	2.54	1.94	1.86	2.31	28.84	.0001

Table 3.12 **Recipient needs help with household tasks: percentage differences according to living arrangements**

	All (n = 363)	Alone %	With other %	Resid. care %	χ^2	p <
Preparing meals						
A lot	41	27	38	72	52.21	.0001
Some	19	23	24	5		
No help	41	50	38	24		
Washing/ironing						
A lot	41	28	41	66	37.36	.0001
Some	22	25	24	12		
No help	38	47	35	22		
General housework						
A lot	46	37	47	65	31.21	.0001
Some	31	42	30	8		
No help	23	21	23	27		
Home repairs						
A lot	68	67	68	68	23.54	.0001
Some	17	23	13	5		
No help	16	9	20	27		
Shopping						
A lot	61	ns	ns	ns		
Some	23					
No help	17					
Financial support						
A lot	11	3	15	20	24.52	.0001
Some	14	13	17	16		
No help	75	84	68	64		

Table 3.13   Carer provides help with household tasks: percentage
differences according to living arrangements

	All (n = 363)	Alone %	With other %	Resid. care %	χ^2	$p <$
Preparing meals						
A lot	17	20	14	15	77.38	.0001
Some	23	24	34	12		
None	19	7	14	49		
Not required	41	50	38	24		
Washing and ironing						
A lot	20	21	18	20	27.00	.0001
Some	18	15	26	19		
None	25	18	22	40		
Not required	38	47	35	22		
General housework						
A lot	16	20	13	10	42.81	.0001
Some	28	31	42	7		
None	33	28	22	57		
Not required	23	21	23	27		
Home repairs						
A lot	23	28	23	10	35.53	.0001
Some	19	23	21	5		
None	43	39	36	58		
Not required	16	9	20	27		
Shopping						
A lot	47	57	33	41	26.60	.001
Some	23	21	32	17		
None	13	8	13	24		
Not required	17	14	22	18		
Financial support						
A lot	12	7	11	23	24.97	.001
Some	7	6	10	8		
None	5	3	10	5		
Not required	75	84	68	64		

Table 3.14   Who helps when care-recipient needs help with household tasks?

	No. care-recipients need help	Carer	Resid. care	Meal service	GHH	HM	F&F	No help from these sources
Meal preparation	209	141	68	39	–	–	86	0
		68%	33%	19%			41%	
Washing/ironing	221	134	72	–	74	–	92	0
		61%	33%		35%		42%	
General housework	266	151	61	–	93	–	113	1
		57%	23%		35%		43%	
Shopping	291	245	74	–	89	–	118	0
		84%	25%		31%		41%	
Home repairs	287	141	58	–	89	26	98	0
		49%	20%		31%	9%	34%	

Note: Totals > 100% because care-recipients often receiving help from several sources.
GHH = general home help service; HM = home maintenance service; F&F = family and friends.

Table 3.15 Who has main responsibility for household tasks? percentage differences according to carer sex and relationship to recipient (N = 880–890)

	All carers %	Male %	Female %	χ²	p <	Offspring %	Spouse %	Parent %	Other %	χ²	p <
Cooking/meals											
Carer	80	92	40	290.18	.0001	76	87	84	74	20.41	.01
Other	12	3	45			16	8	7	17		
Shared	8	5	16			8	5	9	9		
Washing/ironing											
Carer	77	90	31	339.22	.0001	72	82	84	70	17.06	.01
Other	12	3	44			14	8	10	15		
Shared	12	7	26			14	10	6	15		
Light housework											
Carer	76	88	37	226.72	.0001	ns	ns	ns	ns		
Other	13	6	39								
Shared	11	7	25								
Heavy housework											
Carer	70	77	45	77.18	.0001	ns	ns	ns	ns		
Other	17	13	33								
Shared	13	10	23								
Repairs around home											
Carer	37	23	86	263.62	.0001	35	57	25	30	55.90	.0001
Other	51	63	10			52	33	64	59		
Shared	12	14	4			13	10	11	12		
Shopping											
Carer	77	85	49	125.00	.0001	74	85	76	72	22.90	.0008
Other	7	3	20			8	2	4	13		
Shared	17	13	31			18	13	20	16		

Table 3.15 Who has main responsibility for household tasks? percentage differences according to carer sex and relationship to recipient (N = 880–890) (continued)

	All carers	Male %	Female %	χ^2	p <	Offspring %	Spouse %	Parent %	Other %	χ^2	p <
Health/social services											
Carer	75	81	51	85.76	.0001	75	73	86	63	24.33	.001
Other	12	7	27			11	12	8	18		
Shared	14	12	22			15	15	7	20		
Managing finances											
Carer	60	ns	ns			56	74	63	48	32.49	.0001
Other	19					22	11	20	22		
Shared	21					23	15	17	30		
Driving people											
Carer	62	ns	ns			59	69	68	52	23.55	.001
Other	19					20	21	14	22		
Shared	19					22	10	18	26		

Table 3.16 Who has main responsibility for household tasks? percentage differences according to carer age and living arrangements (N = 880–890)

	All	Carer age				Care-recipient lives			
		< 35	35–49	50–64	65+	With carer	Alone	With other	Resid. care
Cooking/meals									
Carer	80	67	78	86	84				
Other	12	19	14	9	10	ns	ns	ns	ns
Shared	8	14	8	5	7				
Washing/ironing									
Carer	77								
Other	12	ns	ns	ns	ns	ns	ns	ns	ns
Shared	12								
Light housework									
Carer	76								
Other	13	ns	ns	ns	ns	ns	ns	ns	ns
Shared	11								
Heavy housework									
Carer	70	63	71	75	61				
Other	17	19	15	14	27	ns	ns	ns	ns
Shared	13	19	14	11	12				
Repairs around home									
Carer	37					42	26	32	34
Other	51	ns	ns	ns	ns	47	60	60	53
Shared	12					11	15	8	13
Shopping									
Carer	77								
Other	7	ns	ns	ns	ns	ns	ns	ns	ns
Shared	17								
Health/social services									
Carer	75	64	81	69	77				
Other	12	19	9	12	11	ns	ns	ns	ns
Shared	14	18	10	18	12				
Managing finances									
Carer	60	51	60	58	74	66	47	49	59
Other	19	31	18	20	9	17	25	19	19
Shared	21	19	23	22	17	18	28	32	22
Driving people									
Carer	62	60	66	59	61	67	50	60	55
Other	19	16	15	20	29	18	21	16	23
Shared	19	24	19	22	10	15	29	24	22

Table 3.17 Attitudes to caring role: extent of carer agreement and differences between relationship groups ($N = 970–975$)

	Carers				Carers strongly agree					
	Strongly agree %	Agree %	Strongly disagree %	Disagree %	Adult offspring %	Spouse %	Parent %	Other %	χ^2	$p =$
I would really feel at a loss if (name) wasn't around	50	32	14	2	42	62	66	30	68.24	.0000
I would feel very guilty if I did not care for (name)	40	42	14	2	41	45	44	29	12.47	.005
I get satisfaction from seeing (name) accomplish things	37	55	5	0	28	33	69	25	111.79	.0000
I feel reassured knowing that as long as I am helping (name) he/she is getting proper care	35	58	5	0	33	36	45	26	15.97	.001
I worry about what would happen to (name) if something happened to me	32	37	27	3	27	39	50	12	70.99	.0000
I grieve for the opportunities (name) doesn't have	22	40	32	4	16	26	38	9	56.88	.0000
I get a great deal of satisfaction from caring	21	63	12	2	ns	ns	ns	ns		ns
I care for (name) because no one else can	15	31	43	8	ns	ns	ns	ns		ns
Caring for (name) has made me more confident dealing with others	13	49	30	2	10	11	23	11	20.86	.0001
My friends don't visit as often because I am caring for (name)	7	20	58	13	14	7	5	0	15.24	.0016
I regret the opportunities I don't have	6	25	58	8	ns	ns	ns	ns		ns
I have lost control of my life since caring for (name)	6	17	58	18	ns	ns	ns	ns		ns
Nothing I can do seems to please (name)	5	13	57	23	ns	ns	ns	ns		ns
I am embarrassed over (name)'s behaviour	4	16	52	27	ns	ns	ns	ns		ns
I feel guilty about (name)	3	13	63	20	ns	ns	ns	ns		ns
I am angry when I am around (name)	2	12	60	22	ns	ns	ns	ns		ns
Caring for (name) takes up most of my time and I neglect the rest of the family	2	14	65	18	ns	ns	ns	ns		ns

Note: $N = 593$.

Table 3.18   Percentage of carers rating level of closeness and tension in their relationship with recipient according to relationship group

	Adult offspring	Spouse	Parent	Other	χ^2	$p <$	Women	Men	χ^2	$p <$
	n = 383	223	172	167						
	%	%	%	%						
Closeness										
Very close	62	65	76	55	21.90	.0012	ns	ns		
Close	32	28	22	41						
Not close	6			4						
Tension										
Low	47	43	36	67	49.79	.0000	45	56	9.4	.01
Moderate	41	43	38	25			39	34		
High	13	14	26	8			16	10		

Table 3.19   Percentage of carers finding difficulty coping according to relationship, care-recipient age and quality of relationship with recipient (*N* = 937)

	Difficulty coping %	χ^2	$p <$
Relationship to recipient			
Adult offspring	35	23.07	.0007
Spouse	39		
Parent	50		
Other	32		
Recipient age			
0–14	54	24.62[a]	.0000
15–29	47		
30–44	44		
45–59	43		
60–74	35		
75 and over	33		
Closeness of relationship			
Very close	34	31.37	.0000
Close	40		
Not close	73		
Level of tension			
Low	25	92.16	.0000
Moderate	44		
High	68		

Note: a   Significant Mantel-Haenszel chi squared indicates a linear association.

Table 3.20 Negative affect varying with most difficult aspect of recipient's disability

	n	Mean negative affect	F	p =
Emotions/personality/psychiatric problems/behaviour	200	0.25	9.66	.000
Co-operation/demands/dependence/time	183	0.23		
Carer's emotions/worries/fears/recipient's sickness/pain	158	0.20		
Physical inability/mobility	170	0.20		
Intellectual incapacity/communication	146	0.19		
None/no comment/unspecified	100	0.11		

Table 3.21 Changes in family environment since onset of caring and differences between relationship groups in reporting change in emotional attitudes

	All carers			Relationship groups reporting 'more'					
	More %	The same %	Less %	Offspring (n = 382) %	Spouse (n = 219) %	Parent (n = 198) %	Other (n = 163) %	χ^2	p =
Compassion	51	43	6	44	59	62	42	28.64	.0007
Tension	46	45	9	50	41	56	35	20.35	.0024
Closeness	39	45	16	33	46	49	34	27.72	.0001
Love	37	57	6	29	40	54	30	46.35	.0000
Conflict	25	62	13	28	16	35	17	30.10	.0000
Resentment	22	64	14	24	15	30	17	24.55	.0004

Table 3.22 Differences in reporting family disagreements according to carer sex, relationship and level of carer–recipient tension

	n	% Yes	χ^2	p <
Sex				
Women	754	30	10.66	.001
Men	213	19		
Relationship				
Adult offspring	384	33	30.06	.0000
Spouses	224	14		
Parents	199	33		
Other	168	25		
Tension				
Low	442	19	34.54	.0000
Moderate	355	32		
High	134	43		

Table 4.1   Country of birth NESB carer-dyads[a] (n = 223)

Western Northern Europe		Asia	
Netherlands	24	India	6
Germany	17	Sri Lanka	5
Austria	1	Bangladesh	1
Belgium	1	Vietnam	5
Sweden	2	China	3
Norway	2	Malaysia	3
Finland	2	E. Timor	1
	49 (22%)	Indonesia	1
		Cambodia	1
Southern Europe			26 (12%)
Italy	51		
Greece	18	Middle East/North Africa	
F.R. Yugoslavia	10	Turkey	4
Malta	10	Lebanon	2
Cyprus	1	Egypt	2
Albania	1	Iran	1
	91 (41%)	'Arabic'	2
			11 (5%)
Eastern Europe/USSR and Baltic States			
Poland	19	South/East Africa	
Hungary	4	Mauritius	4
USSR	4	Seychelles	1
Czech Republic	3	Uganda	1
Latvia	2		6 (3%)
Roumania	1		
	33 (15%)	South/Central America and Caribbean	
		Chile	3
Polynesia		Argentina	1
Samoa	1	El Salvador	1
	1 (4%)	Trinidad	1
			6 (3%)

Note: a   Carer's birthplace for 182 overseas-born NESB carers, and recipient's birthplace for remaining dyads. Data missing for 13 cases.

Table 4.2   Socio-demographic characteristics of NESB and Anglo carer–recipient dyads

	NESB (n = 198–236) %	Anglo (n = 773–775) %
Carer partnered	79	79
Relationship to recipient		
Adult offspring	45	38
Spouse	23	24
Parent	15	22
Other	18	17
Paid employment		
Full-time work	29	21
Part-time work	14	15
Not working	57	64
Has post-school qualifications	50	46
Household income		
< $15 000	35	34
$15 000–$35 000	25	24
$35 001–$55 000	24	28
> $55 001	16	14
House ownership		
Own outright	56	60
Mortgage	31	27
Rental/other	13	13
Care-recipient sex		
Female	61	57
Male	39	43
Care-recipient receives pension	82	89

Table 4.3   **Socio-demographic differences between non-Anglo and Anglo carers**

	Non-Anglo (n = 199–236) %	Anglo (n = 775) %	χ^2	p <
Carer sex				
Male	33	20	16.69	.0000
Female	67	80		
Carer age				
0–34	19	11	21.97	.0000
35–49	44	36		
50–64	23	33		
65+	14	20		
Care-recipient age				
0–20	10	16	14.19	.01
21–60	24	16		
61–80	40	35		
81+	26	33		
Living arrangements				
Co-resident	66	60	12.93	.01
Alone	13	20		
Other household	12	7		
Residential care	9	12		
Location (carer)				
Melbourne metropolitan	76	55	34.97	.0000
Country Victoria	24	45		
Carer on pension[a]	38	51	11.39	.001
Carer schooling level[a]				
Primary	9	3	29.99	.0000
Year 7–10	36	51		
Year 11–12	55	46		

Note: a   Extended interview only.

Table 4.4   Carers' feelings about the caregiving role

	NESB (n = 201) Agree/Strongly agree %	Anglo (n = 766) Agree/Strongly agree %
Positive feelings		
I feel assured knowing that as long as I am helping (recipient) is getting proper care	93	93
I get satisfaction from seeing (recipient) accomplish things	91	91
I get a great deal of satisfaction from caring	83	84
I would really feel at a loss if (recipient) was not around	80	82
Caring for (recipient) has made me more confident dealing with others	70	60
Negative feelings		
I would feel very guilty if I did not care for (recipient)	84	81
I grieve for the opportunities (recipient) doesn't have	64	61
I care for (recipient) because no-one else can	48	46
I regret the opportunities I don't have	39	29
Nothing I can do seems to please (recipient)	25	15
My friends don't visit as often because I am caring for (recipient)	24	28
I have lost control of my life since caring for (recipient)	23	22
I am embarrassed over (recipient's) behaviour	21	19
Caring for (recipient) takes up most of my time and I neglect the rest of the family	17	15

Table 4.5   Use of and need for community services and respite: percentage differences between non-Anglo and Anglo carers

	Use of community services				Need for community services			
	Non-Anglo (n = 218) %	Anglo (n = 686) %	χ^2	p <	Non-Anglo (n = 184) %	Anglo (n = 686) %	χ^2	p <
General home help	16	25	8.91	.01	20	12	8.77	.01
Personal care	7	15	9.37	.01	13	10	ns	
Transport	17	25	4.90	.05	17	11	4.90	.05
Community nursing	8	16	7.44	.01	8	5	ns	
Meals	1	9	13.34	.001	7	7	ns	
Maintenance	4	8	4.56	.05	19	17	ns	
	(n = 178)	(n = 674)			(n = 178)	(n = 674)		
Respite	6	13	6.71	.01	22	27	ns	

276

Table 4.6 **Source of service information: percentage differences between non-Anglo and Anglo carers**

	Non-Anglo (n = 199) %	Anglo (n = 771) %	χ^2	p <
None given	25	18	5.29	.05
Doctor	31	24	4.18	.05
Medical specialist	13	13	ns	
Health and welfare staff	15	23	6.65	.01
Support group	7	11	ns	
Government agency	15	22	4.54	.05
Media/pamphlets	6	9	ns	
Informal contacts	11	15	ns	

Table 5.1 **Factors predicting major health problems, medication use and health rating (N = 976)**

	Odds ratio	Wald	df	p =
Predicting major health problems (n = 976)				
Carer	1.43	12.35	1	.0004
Non-carer	0.70			
Working full-time	0.72	5.39	1	.0203
Working part-time	1.14	0.97	1	.3223
Not working	1.22	3.23	1	.0724
Predicting medication use (n = 976)				
Under 40 years	0.47	42.49	1	.0000
40–59 years	1.02	0.03	1	.8615
60 +	2.07	32.07	1	.0000
Carer	1.33	8.95	1	.0028
Non-carer	0.75			
Predicting poor health (n = 976)				
Carer	1.39	9.20	1	.0024
Non-carer	0.72			
Partnered	0.81	4.86	1	.0275
Single	1.24			

Table 5.2 Emotional well-being according to carer status, age and relationship status (means)

	Carer status				Age in years					Relationship status			
	Carer (n = 757)	Non-carer (n = 219)	F	p <	0–39 (n = 282)	40–59 (n = 475)	60+ (n = 219)	F	p <	Partner (n = 811)	No partner (n = 165)	F	p <
Life satisfaction	3.78	4.05	24.37	.000	3.86	3.81	3.87	ns	ns	3.87	3.67	7.79	.01
Positive effect	3.09	3.25	6.21	.05	3.18	3.16	2.96	4.91	.01	3.11	3.18	ns	ns
Negative effect	1.85	1.78	5.15	.05	1.96	1.84	1.67	11.24	.000	1.82	1.78	ns	ns
Social support	3.95	4.09	12.51	.000	3.96	3.98	3.99	ns	ns	4.01	3.85	9.31	.002
Overload	3.31	3.09	27.37	.000	3.55	3.24	2.95	33.00	.000	3.27	3.25	ns	ns

Table 6.1 Differences in recipient and carer characteristics according to
           carer group (means)

	Carer group			F	p =
	PD (n = 186)	**UML** (n = 182)	**DEM** (n = 117)		
Care-recipient severity of disability					
Physical	14.92	12.43	10.38	12.33	.0000
Mental	0.19	6.63	12.62	221.35	.0000
Care-recipient behaviour problems					
Aggressive	0.42	0.94	1.07	55.12	.0000
Depressive	0.97	1.46	1.61	38.06	.0000
Cognitive	0.79	1.91	2.53	235.39	.0000
Carer life satisfaction	3.96	3.65	3.67	15.44	.0000
Carer overload	2.94	3.24	3.22	4.27	.0054
Negative affect	1.53	1.85	1.81	11.87	.0000
ADL dependence	1.35	1.39	1.69	17.10	.0000
IADL dependence	1.58	2.07	2.53	128.04	.0000
IADL care provision	1.88	2.52	2.78	47.36	.0000
Carer resentment	2.32	2.69	2.51	11.53	.0000
Carer anger	1.89	2.39	2.36	27.33	.0000
Family conflict	2.08	2.19	2.26	5.90	.003
Social support	4.08	3.91	3.87	7.87	.0004

Table 6.2 Predicting carer burden and resentment in UML and DEM
           carers (n = 483)

	Beta	T	p =
Significant predictors of carer burden[a]			
Carer resentment	0.38	6.96	.0000
Family conflict	0.20	3.74	.0002
Depressive behaviour problems	0.15	2.83	.005
Close relationship	0.13	2.65	.0086
Carer anger	0.12	2.16	.03
Significant predictors of carer resentment[b]			
Social support (low)	0.29	5.48	.0000
Anger	0.24	4.64	.0000
Difficulty coping	0.22	4.00	.0001
UML	0.15	3.02	.0028

Notes: a Multiple $R = 0.60$, $R^2 = 0.36$, $F = 31.88$, $p = 0.0000$.
       b Multiple $R = 0.56$, $R^2 = 0.32$, $F = 32.13$, $p = 0.0000$.

Table 6.3 Differences in carer satisfaction and resentment, life satisfaction and positive affect according to living arrangements (means)

	Care-recipient lives				
	With carer (n = 238)	Alone or with another (n = 168)	In residential care (n = 77)	F	p =
Carer satisfaction	3.87	3.62	3.46	16.98	.0000
Carer resentment	2.68	2.30	2.39	15.22	.0000
Life satisfaction	3.69	3.88	3.80	4.93	.0076
Positive affect	3.01	3.21	3.10	3.19	.042

Table 7.1 Carer and care-recipient characteristics: differences according to carer sex and relationship to recipient

	Carer sex				Relationship to care-recipient				
	Female	Male	χ^2	$p <$	Parent	Offspring	Spouse	χ^2	$p <$
	(n = 630) %	(n = 177) %			(n = 199) %	(n = 385) %	(n = 223) %		
Relationship to recipient									
Offspring	47	50	27.9	.001	–	–	–		
Spouse	24	39			–	–	–		
Parent	28	11			–	–	–		
Carer female	–	–			90	77	69	27.9	.001
Carer aged									
0–44	ns	ns			62	34	10	316.7	.001
45–59					25	53	23		
60+					13	13	67		
Carer partnered	ns	ns			82	70	na	11.28	.001
Carer working	35	48	10.61	.001	34	53	15	86.20	.001
Female care-recipient	48	84	72.5	.001	36	80	31	177.9	.001
Recipient aged									
0–20	21	7	19.77	.001	71	0	0	744.63	.001
21–60	17	25			29	6	31		
61–80	36	42			0	45	57		
81+	27	25			0	49	12		
Recipient lives									
With carer	ns	ns			93	37	94	297.5	.001
Alone					2	34	0		
With partner/other					1	13	0		
In residential care					5	15	6		

Table 7.2 Differences in carer well-being and feelings according to sex, relationship to recipient, and age (means)

	Carer sex				Relationship to recipient					Carer age				
	F n = 630	M 177	F	p <	Parent 199	Offspring 384	Spouse 224	F	p <	0–44 278	45–59 305	60+ 223	F	p <
Carer well-being														
Life satisfaction	ns	ns			ns	ns	ns			3.78	3.69	3.86	6.11	.002
Positive affect	ns	ns			3.10	3.14	2.96	4.77	.009	3.19	3.10	2.91	4.79	.009
Negative affect	1.89	1.63	17.81	.00	ns	ns	ns			1.96	1.85	1.66	7.96	.000
Anxiety/depression	4.82	4.51	11.49	.001	ns	ns	ns			ns	ns	ns		
Overload	3.34	2.86	35.05	.000	3.48	3.25	3.00	8.94	.000	3.52	3.25	2.87	18.45	.000
Social support	ns	ns			ns	ns	ns			ns	ns	ns		
Family close	ns	ns			2.46	2.25	2.39	14.59	.000	ns	ns	ns		
Family conflict	2.24	2.11	8.93	.003	2.28	2.24	2.10	6.81	.001	ns	ns	ns		
Caring role														
Satisfaction	ns	ns			4.20	3.70	4.02	56.29	.000	4.04	3.77	3.94	6.97	.001
Resentment	ns	ns			ns	ns	ns			ns	ns	ns		
Anger	2.24	2.03	10.16	.001	ns	ns	ns			ns	ns	ns		

Table 7.3 **Differences in carers and recipients according to relationship groups in co-resident carers only (means)**

	Parent	Adult offspring	Spouse	F	p <
Carer well-being					
Life satisfaction	3.75	3.57	3.79	4.55	.01
Negative affect	1.93	1.86	1.71	4.35	.01
Overload	3.47	3.38	2.98	13.80	.000
Family closeness	2.48	2.40	2.25	8.39	.000
Family conflict	2.27	2.34	2.10	10.56	.000
Caring role					
Satisfaction	4.21	3.74	4.02	30.37	.000
Resentment	2.48	2.82	2.65	13.80	.000
Severity of disability					
Physical	7.72	9.67	9.24	20.50	.000
Mental	6.32	5.32	5.70	7.87	.000
Help provided[a]					
IADL	2.75	2.64	2.41	5.52	.000
Behaviour problems[b]					
Aggressive	1.23	0.82	0.70	32.15	.000
Depressive	1.16	1.48	1.39	7.89	.000
Cognitive	1.61	1.59	1.17	12.44	.000

Notes: a   ADL items were skipped for carers of recipients under 6 years old.
      b   Behaviour problem items were skipped for carers of recipients under 3 years old.

Table 7.4 Care-recipient disability, help provided, and behaviour problems: differences according to carer sex, relationship to recipient, and age (means)

	Carer sex				Relationship to recipient					Carer age				
	F	M	F	p<	Parent	Offspring	Spouse	F	p<	0–44	45–59	60+	F	p<
Severity of disability														
	n = 628	176			199	384	223			278	305	224		
Physical	ns	ns			7.72	9.21	9.34	20.60	.000	8.12	9.22	9.34	5.68	.004
Mental	ns	ns			6.42	5.42	5.90	11.25	.000	ns	ns	ns		
Help provided[a]														
	n = 588	173			155	383	223			233	305	223		
ADL	ns	ns			1.73	1.40	1.81	32.07	.000	ns	ns	ns		
IADL	2.47	2.19	12.14	.001	2.74	2.29	2.40	10.56	.000	ns	ns	ns		
Behaviour[b]														
	n = 614	173			182	382	223			260	304	224		
Aggressive	0.92	0.66	21.14	.000	1.24	0.76	0.71	36.78	.000	1.04	0.84	0.67	8.12	.000
Depressive	ns	ns			1.20	1.34	1.41	5.48	.004	ns	ns	ns		
Cognitive	1.57	1.22	17.55	.000	1.62	1.60	1.21	10.86	.000	ns	ns	ns		

Notes: a ADL items were skipped for carers of recipients under 6 years old.
b Behaviour problem items were skipped for carers of recipients under 3 years old.

Table 7.5   Effects of caring on work situation according to relationship and sex

	n	Traditional non-worker/retired %	Excluded worker %	Affected worker %	Unaffected worker %	χ^2	p =
Mother	179	31	38	26	6	76.32	.00000
Daughter	296	30	22	31	18		
Wife	145	54	35	10	2		
Father	20	35	10	45	6	38.06	.00000
Son	86	22	11	35	33		
Husband	66	52	26	20	3		

Table 7.6   Effects of caring on financial circumstances and difficulty in meeting living costs according to age and relationship

	n	No effect %	Effect, no difficulty %	Effect, difficulty %	χ^2	p =
Under 45 years					31.35	.0000
Parent	123	34	17	49		
Adult offspring	132	61	15	24		
Spouse	23	26	4	70		
45–59 years					68.70	.0000
Parent	50	34	22	44		
Adult offspring	204	72	13	15		
Spouse	51	14	37	49		
60 and over					25.79	.0000
Parent	26	69	8	23		
Adult offspring	47	79	13	9		
Spouse	150	43	39	19		

Table 8.1 Work status and caring impacts: percentage differences according to carer sex and relationship

	All carers %	Female %	Male %	χ²	p <	Offspring %	Spouse %	Parent %	Other %	χ²	p <
Employment status	(N = 976)	(n = 757)	(n = 219)	88.9	.0000	(n = 385)	(n = 223)	(n = 199)	(n = 169)	94.3	.0000
Full-time	24	17	46			35	10	16	25		
Part-time	14	16	4			18	5	18	18		
Not working	62	65	50			47	85	66	57		
Employment impacts: working carers	(n = 375)	(n = 267)	(n = 108)			(n = 202)	(n = 34)	(n = 67)	(n = 72)		
Work fewer hours	29	32	20	5.4	.05	27	39	51	10	30.7	.001
Take unpaid leave	22	26	12	8.7	.01	20	24	42	11	20.6	.001
Less responsible job	16	20	8	8.2	.01	11	24	37	6	33.1	.001
Refuse promotion	13	ns	ns			8	27	28	4	29.2	.001
Change jobs	11	13	6	4.5	.05	8	24	19	4	15.2	.01
Source of relief	58	67	35	30.9	.001	53	70	73	50	12.1	.01
Employment impacts: non-working, < 65	(n = 430)	(n = 374)	(n = 56)			(n = 169)	(n = 114)	(n = 76)			
Unable to take job	40	ns	ns			38	49	51	20	20.2	.001
Had to quit work	21	ns	ns			19	33	21	10	11.9	.01
Either exclusion	46	48	33	4.1	.05	42	58	58	23	27.4	.0000
Overall work impact	(N = 959)	(n = 744)	(n = 215)	20.9	.001	(n = 382)	(n = 212)	(n = 199)	(n = 166)	127.3	.0000
Unaffected worker	9	8	14			11	2	5	18		
Affected worker	30	28	37			42	14	29	26		
Excluded non-worker	24	26	14			19	32	35	11		
Traditional non-worker	37	38	35			28	53	31	46		

Table 8.2   Work status and caring impacts: percentage differences
according to disability type

	Minor %	Mental %	Physical %	Both %	χ^2	$p <$
Work status	(n = 154)	(n = 201)	(n = 220)	(n = 401)		
Full-time	23	28	29	18	14.8	.05
Part-time	19	12	15	15		
Not working	58	60	56	67		
Employment impacts:						
* working carers*	(n = 64)	(n = 80)	(n = 97)	(n = 134)		
Work fewer hours	11	21	20	48	12.1	.01
Less responsible job	8	23	15	54	12.8	.01
Interruptions	14	25	15	46	12.9	.01
Less energy	12	20	18	50	13.0	.01
Worry about recipient	14	20	22	44	16.8	.001
Source of relief	13	22	21	44	19.3	.001
Employment impacts:						
* non-working < 65*	(n = 67)	(n = 94)	(n = 86)	(n = 180)		
Unable to take job	22	47	28	51	24.9	.0001
Had to quit work	6	22	17	27	14.4	.01
Either exclusion	25	53	32	57	27.9	.00001
Overall work impact	(n = 152)	(n = 199)	(n = 217)	(n = 391)		
Unaffected worker	14	10	14	4	51.9	.00001
Affected worker	28	30	31	30		
Excluded non-worker	13	28	15	31		
Traditional non-worker	45	32	40	35		

Table 8.3   Carer well-being: differences according to work impact group
(means)

	Affected workers	Excluded non-workers	Unaffected workers	Traditional non-workers	F	$p <$
Positive affect	3.26	3.00	3.18	3.01	7.50	.001
Negative affect	1.93	1.89	1.45	1.70	12.7	.001
Overload	3.58	3.40	2.83	2.90	35.1	.001
Life satisfaction	3.76	3.64	4.11	3.88	13.3	.001
Social support	3.92	3.79	4.17	3.98	2.89	.001
Combined index	2.28	2.28	3.21	2.89	33.6	.001

Table 8.4 Preferences on participation in the workforce: differences according to carer characteristics (N = 274)

	n	Not work, no change %	Increase work %	Work, no change %	χ^2	p <
Total %		17	45	38		
Carer sex						
Female	223	18	50	31	20.36	.0001
Male	51	14	22	65		
Carer age						
< 35	33	9	51	39	18.82	.001
35–49	129	9	50	41		
50–64	112	30	37	33		
Schooling						
< Year 11	139	22	50	28	11.92	.01
Year 11+	135	13	40	47		
Further education						
None	132	22	47	31	8.72	.06
Trade/other	88	17	43	40		
Tertiary	54	7	43	50		
Household income ($)						
< 20 000	76	24	54	22	20.81	.05
20 000–30 000	60	17	53	30		
30 000–40 000	47	11	40	49		
40 000–50 000	37	16	38	46		
50 000–60 000	16	12	38	50		
60 000+	29	7	35	59		

Table 8.5 Preferences on participation in the workforce: differences according to care-recipient characteristics (N = 274)

	n	No work, no change %	Increase work %	Work, no change %	χ^2	p <
Total %		17	45	38		
Care-recipient sex						
Female	147	16	35	49	17.97	.001
Male	127	20	56	24		
Care-recipient age						
≤ 20	87	11	63	25	20.06	.01
21–60	56	16	39	45		
61–80	55	27	33	40		
81+	76	18	37	45		
Recipient lives						
With carer	202	18	51	31	15.06	.01
Alone	56	18	27	55		
With other	16	13	31	56		

Table 8.6 Preferences on participation in the workforce: differences according to characteristics of care situation (*N* = 274)

	n	Not work, no change %	Increase work %	Work, no change %	χ^2	*p* <
Total %		17	45	38		
Carer relationship to recipient						
Spouse	38	32	42	26	21.89	.01
Offspring	100	14	36	50		
Parent	114	15	57	28		
Other	11	23	27	50		
Hours of care						
< 10	84	18	30	52	27.30	.001
10–30	73	11	42	47		
31–100	63	17	60	22		
101+	54	26	54	20		

Table 8.7 Enabling factors for preferred employment while caring: carers desiring change in workforce participation and those already working full-time

	Carers desiring change in workforce participation (*n* = 78) %	Carers working full-time (*n* = 73) %
Flexible work conditions	82	51
Alternative care arrangements for care-recipient	54	30
Training and/or education	51	14
Financial assistance to cover alternative care costs	42	12

Table 8.8 Combined carer/partner income level: differences according to care-dyad characteristics (*N* = 911)

	n	0–$15 000 %	$15 001–$35 000 %	$35 001–$55 000 %	≥ $55 001 %	χ^2	*p* <
Total %		34	24	27	15		
Relationship							
Offspring	347	30	27	25	18	103.9	.00001
Spouse	214	67	16	12	5		
Parent	190	30	32	28	10		
Other	160	39	28	24	9		
Carer age							
< 35	119	31	39	23	7	154.9	.00001
35–49	350	21	28	31	20		
50–64	279	48	24	18	10		
65+	163	72	15	11	2		
Care-recipient age							
< 21	139	21	35	34	10	32.4	.0001
21–60	170	46	26	17	11		
61–80	331	43	23	21	13		
81+	271	42	24	21	13		
Living arrangements							
Co-resident	567	47	26	19	8	58.9	.00001
Alone	168	27	21	31	21		
Other household	73	21	37	30	12		
Residential care	103	36	25	21	18		
Carer status (< 60 yrs)							
Carer	594	30	29	26	15	35.9	.00001
Non-carer	193	15	22	32	31		

Table 8.9 Differences in carer well-being according to financial impacts of caregiving (means)

	Financial impacts				
	Nil/minor change	Effects, no difficulty	Difficult to meet costs	*F*	*p* <
All carers (*N* = 976)	(56%)	(19%)	(25%)		
Overload	3.03	3.24	3.61	29.6	.001
Negative affect	1.70	1.79	2.01	14.7	.001
Life satisfaction	3.93	3.74	3.55	27.9	.001
Social support	3.99	3.94	3.80	12.2	.001

Table 8.10   Financial impacts of caring: statistical differences by carer and recipient characteristics

	No effects (n = 550) %	Adverse effects, no difficulties (n = 185) %	Difficulty with living costs (n = 240) %	χ^2	p <
Work impact					
Unaffected worker	82	10	8	132.3	.00001
Affected worker	50	20	30		
Excluded non-worker	31	23	46		
Traditional non-worker	67	19	15		
Relationship					
Offspring	69	14	17	152.6	.00001
Spouse	34	35	31		
Parent	39	17	44		
Other	78	12	10		
Living arrangements					
Co-resident	45	23	32	99.7	.00001
Alone	82	10	8		
Other household	77	12	11		
Residential care	60	19	21		
Carer age					
< 35	51	15	34	124.1	.00001
35–49	54	15	31		
50–64	61	20	19		
65+	58	28	14		
Care-recipient age					
< 21	34	16	51	34.7	.00001
21–60	42	19	39		
61–80	59	23	18		
81+	73	15	12		

Table 9.1   Changes in caregiving status at 15 months (Time 2) and 30 months (Time 3)

	Times 1–2		Times 2–3		Times 1–3	
	N	%	N	%	N	%
Still caring	608	63	399	66	399	41
No longer caring	110	11	77	13	187	19
Still caring but < 4 hrs/week	(21)		(10)		(31)	
Recipient in residential care	(27)		(35)		(62)	
Recipient's condition improved	(25)		(7)		(32)	
Other primary carer	(23)		(15)		(38)	
Other	(5)		(10)		(24)	
Recipient died	101	10	38	6	139	14
Not interviewed	148	15	90	5	238	26
Total	967[a]	100	604[b]	100	963	

Notes: a   Nine cases were excluded due to misclassification in the Stage 2 interview.
     b   A further four cases were excluded as they were not followed up in the Stage 3 interview.

Table 9.2 Carer characteristics at Time 1 according to caregiving status at Times 2 and 3

	Time 2						Time 3					
	Total	Still caring	Recipient died	No longer caring	χ^2	$p <$	Total	Still caring	Recipient died	No longer caring	χ^2	$p <$
	(N = 819)	(n = 608) %	(n = 101) %	(n = 110) %			(N = 725) %	(n = 399) %	(n = 139) %	(n = 187) %		
Carer age												
< 35	99	77	2	21	27.36	.0001	81	62	6	32	39.52	.0000
35–49	313	77	9	15			286	58	12	30		
50–64	264	72	17	11			232	50	27	23		
65+	143	73	18	9			126	52	30	18		
Relationship to care-recipient												
Adult offspring	321	73	15	12	86.70	.0000	291	51	24	25	108.85	.0000
Spouse	184	74	18	8			155	53	30	17		
Parent	181	92	0	8			156	82	0	18		
Other	133	54	14	32			123	32	19	49		
Geographic location												
Metropolitan	476	70	14	16	9.02	.01	428	50	22	28	9.16	.01
Country	343	80	10	10			297	62	15	23		

Table 9.3 Care-recipient characteristics at Time 1 according to caregiving status at Times 2 and 3

	Time 2						Time 3				
	Total	Still caring	Recipient died	No longer caring	χ^2	$p <$	Total	Still caring	Recipient died	No longer caring	χ^2	$p <$
	(N = 819)	(n = 608) %	(n = 101) %	(n = 110) %			(N = 725) %	(n = 399) %	(n = 139) %	(n = 187) %		
Care-recipient age												
0–20	134	93	0	7	44.42	.0000	115	81	0	19	64.89	.0000
21–60	144	74	7	19			120	60	9	31		
61–80	278	70	15	15			248	49	24	27		
81+	263	70	18	12			242	47	28	25		
Recipient lives												
With carer	494	80	10	10	41.44	.0000	429	64	15	21	62.91	.0000
Alone	158	68	15	17			148	52	22	26		
With other	69	61	9	30			55	29	16	55		
In resid. care	98	62	24	14			93	33	37	30		

Table 9.4 Characteristics of caring situation at Time 1 according to caregiving status at Times 2 and 3

	Time 2						Time 3					
	Total	Still caring	Recipient died	No longer caring	χ^2	$p <$	Total	Still caring	Recipient died	No longer caring	χ^2	$p <$
	(N = 819)	(n = 608)	(n = 101)	(n = 110)			(N = 725)	(n = 399)	(n = 139)	(n = 187)		
	%	%	%	%			%	%	%	%		
Hours of care per week												
< 10	290	65	13	21	31.46	.0000	260	42	21	37	38.30	.0000
10–30	182	75	14	11			163	58	20	22		
31–100	126	86	6	8			108	64	11	25		
101+	214	79	13	8			188	65	19	15		
Years of care												
≤ 1	130	61	18	21	26.67	.0008	117	44	24	32	16.23	.05
13 months to 2 yrs	125	71	12	17			113	51	20	29		
3–5	212	73	11	16			185	53	18	29		
6–9	134	81	12	7			108	61	22	17		
10+	217	81	10	9			201	62	15	22		

Table 9.5 Differential change in well-being and health from Time 1 to Time 2 in carers and non-carers (means)

		Non-carer (n = 162)	Carer (n = 481)
Life satisfaction[a]	Time 1	4.07	3.77
	Time 2	3.98	3.67
Social support[b]	Time 1	4.11	3.96
	Time 2	4.22	4.03
Overload[c]	0–44	3.37	3.62
	45–59	2.73	3.30
	60+	2.70	3.06
Health rating[d]		3.18	2.88

Notes:
a Significant main effects for carer status, F = 18.58, $p < .001$, and time, F = 7.35, $p < .007$.
b Significant main effect for time, F = 7.84, $p < .005$.
c Significant main effects for carers' status, F = 12.39, $p < .001$, and age, F = 18.69, $p < .001$.
d Significant main effect for carers' status, F = 10.41, $p < .001$.

Table 10.1 Carers' perceptions about support from family and friends (N = 970–974)

	Strongly agree %	Agree %	Unsure or disagree %	Strongly disagree %
I know my family will always be there for me should I need them	44	46	8	2
When I want to go out and do things I know that many of my friends would enjoy doing these things with me	21	62	17	1
People who know me think I'm good at what I do	21	70	9	0
People in my family have confidence in me	28	67	4	1
My friends would take time to talk over my problems should I ever want to	28	61	10	1

	Strongly disagree %	Disagree %	Unsure or agree %	Strongly agree %
Sometimes I'm not sure if I can completely rely on my family	18	42	33	7
Even when I am with my friends I feel alone	15	60	22	3

Table 10.2 **Number of secondary carers and activities according to socio-demographic characteristics ($N = 974$) (means)**

	No. secondary carers			No. secondary activities		
		F	p		F	p
Carer sex						
Male	1.57	5.75	< .05	ns		
Female	1.79			ns		
Carer age						
< 35	ns			6.02	4.57	< .005
35–49	ns			4.93		
50–64	ns			4.43		
65+	ns			4.19		
Carer employment						
Full-time	1.82	3.54	< .05	5.04	3.39	< .05
Part-time	1.94			5.53		
None	1.66			4.50		
Relationship						
Spouse	1.60	2.79	< .05	3.91	4.29	< .005
Offspring	1.84			5.21		
Parent	1.83			5.15		
Other	1.60			4.52		
Recipient sex						
Male	1.64	5.06	< .05	ns		
Female	1.82			ns		
Recipient age						
< 21	1.92	3.11	< .05	5.60	3.51	< .05
21–60	1.54			4.01		
61–80	1.71			4.99		
81+	1.81			4.58		
Living arrangements						
With carer	ns			4.55	5.33	< .001
Alone	ns			5.53		
With other	ns			5.99		
Resid. care	ns			3.90		

Table 10.3 **Emotional well-being according to size of support network (means)**

	Number of helpers ($N = 974$)							
	0	1	2	3	4	5+	F	p =
Life satisfaction	3.54	3.73	3.76	3.78	3.79	3.89	3.94	.0015
Social support	3.75	3.86	4.00	4.05	4.06	4.07	9.36	.0000
Resentment	2.79	2.59	2.46	2.37	2.39	2.28	7.23	.0000
Anger	2.30	2.21	2.16	2.01	2.04	1.87	3.71	.0025

Table 10.4   Family relationship between primary and secondary carers

	(N = 1770)	%
Carer's offspring	448	26
Carer's sibling	323	19
Carer's spouse	311	18
Carer's parent	119	7
Other relative	245	14
Non-relative	254	15

Table 10.5   Distribution of secondary support: secondary carer relationship according to carer–recipient relationship

		Carer's relationship to care-recipient			
	n	Spouse %	Offspring %	Parent %	Other %
Carer's offspring	448	45	31	13	12
Carer's sibling	323	6	75	11	9
Spouse/partner	311	na	48	31	21
Carer's parent	119	9	16	53	22
Carer's parent-in-law	43	16	5	70	9
Carer's sibling-in-law	46	17	35	15	33
Other relative	156	23	42	8	27
Non-relative	254	31	29	25	15

Table 10.6   Type of secondary help according to relationship to carer

Helper's relationship	n	Nature of support provided		
		Emotional % helpers[a]	Indirect % helpers[b]	Direct % helpers[c]
Offspring	445	49	44	79
Siblings	311	39	48	87
Spouse	307	57	69	81
Parent	116	46	62	78
Other relative	243	37	47	81
Non-relative	251	47	32	78

Notes: a $\chi^2 = 32.5, p < .00001$.
    b $\chi^2 = 174.6, p < .00001$.
    c $\chi^2 = 50.1, p < .0001$.

Table 10.7   Carers' emotional well-being related to presence of emotional support and amount of direct help (means)

	Emotional support				Direct help				
	Yes	No	F	p <	Nil	1–2	2–5	F	p <
Life satisfaction		ns			3.67	3.79	3.88	10.6	.0001
Positive affect		ns			3.04	3.14	3.22	4.93	.01
Negative affect	1.83	1.73	7.29	.01	1.86	1.76	1.73	3.27	.05
Role resentment	2.48	2.39	6.70	.01	2.56	2.43	2.30	11.07	.0001

Table 10.8 Characteristics associated with desired additional informal support

	Desired spouse support (n = 523)				Desired family/friends support (N = 917)			
	Yes %	No %	χ^2	p <	Yes %	No %	χ^2	p <
No. secondary helpers								
0	41	59	19.53	< .0001	53	47	24.63	< .00001
1–2	18	82			31	69		
3–5	15	85			26	74		
Carer sex								
Male	4	96	16.54	< .0001	26	47	4.99	< .05
Female	22	78			34	66		
Carer age								
< 35	29	71	10.14	< .02	40	60	34.75	< .00001
35–49	21	79			39	61		
50–64	14	86			31	69		
65+	7	93			14	86		
Employment								
Full-time	13	87	10.57	< .01	ns			
Part-time	29	71			ns			
None	19	81			ns			
Relationship								
Spouse	na				20	80	24.52	< .00005
Offspring	15	85	18.57	< .001	38	62		
Parent	31	69			38	62		
Other	14	86			29	71		
Living arrangements								
With carer	25	75	14.61	< .005	ns			
Alone	10	90			ns			
With other	18	82			ns			
Resid. care	18	82			ns			

Table 10.9 Carer well-being and care-recipient disability factors associated with desired additional support (means)

	Desired spouse support (n = 523)				Desired family/friends support (N = 971)			
	Yes	No	F	p <	Yes	No	F	p <
Life satisfaction	3.45	3.87	45.33	.000	3.44	3.84	84.79	.000
Overload	3.92	3.21	44.31	.000	3.65	3.04	82.01	.000
Negative affect	2.11	1.72	25.53	.000	2.07	1.68	60.18	.000
Social support	3.72	4.01	38.31	.000	3.68	4.06	127.12	.000
Role satisfaction	3.95	3.79	4.92	.05	ns	ns	ns	ns
Role resentment	2.73	2.33	25.56	.000	2.85	2.23	85.66	.000
Role anger	2.46	2.07	21.56	.000	2.37	2.07	33.13	.000
Severity of disability	ns	ns	ns	ns	18.41	16.45	5.69	.02
IADL assistance needed	2.23	1.96	11.73	.001	2.08	1.94	8.89	.003
Aggressive behaviours	1.09	0.80	12.16	.001	1.05	0.75	40.78	.000
Cognitive behaviours	1.80	1.54	5.76	.02	1.72	1.41	20.38	.000
Depressive behaviours	ns	ns	ns	ns	1.57	1.20	48.14	.000

Table 10.10a Regular community care services: differences in relation to 'predisposing factors'

	Total	Carer's relationship to recipient						Care-recipient lives				
	(N = 862) %	Offspring %	Spouse %	Parent %	Other %	χ²	p <	With carer %	Alone %	With other %	χ²	p <
General home help												
Don't need	63	54	66	75	62	30.04	.0001	70	42	56	55.00	.0001
Met need	24	32	23	13	21			19	39	28		
Unmet need	13	14	10	12	17			11	19	16		
Personal home care												
Don't need	76	75	86	68	76	26.42	.001	ns	ns	ns		
Met need	13	13	7	22	11							
Unmet need	11	12	7	10	13							
Community nursing service												
Don't need	80	74	80	95	75	41.60	.0001	82	78	70	19.35	.01
Met need	14	18	17	3	19			13	18	15		
Unmet need	6	8	3	3	7			5	4	15		
Meal services												
Don't need	86	79	93	96	80	43.04	.0001	94	62	84	124.32	.0000
Met need	7	12	4	1	9			3	21	7		
Unmet need	7	9	3	4	10			3	17	9		
Home maintenance												
Don't need	76	72	69	89	77	30.92	.0001	80	63	79	25.28	.001
Met need	7	10	8	1	8			5	13	6		
Unmet need	17	18	23	10	15			15	24	15		
Transport services												
Don't need	64	ns						ns				
Met need	24											
Unmet need	12											

Table 10.10b   Regular community care services: differences in relation to 'predisposing factors' (continued)

	Care-recipient age						Care-recipient sex			
	< 21 %	21–60 %	61–80 %	81+ %	χ^2	p <	Female %	Male %	χ^2	p <
General home help										
Don't need	72	76	59	53	42.56	.0000	57	70	15.48	.001
Met need	15	9	30	32			28	19		
Unmet need	13	14	12	15			15	11		
Personal home care										
Don't need	63	87	77	75	34.52	.0001	ns	ns		
Met need	27	6	11	13						
Unmet need	11	7	12	12						
Community nursing service										
Don't need	97	86	76	71	45.93	.0000	ns	ns		
Met need	1	10	18	22						
Unmet need	2	4	7	7						
Meal services										
Don't need	99	93	85	77	44.64	.0000	83	91	13.92	.001
Met need	0	2	9	13			9	5		
Unmet need	1	5	7	11			9	4		
Home maintenance										
Don't need	89	83	70	71	34.85	.0000	ns	ns		
Met need	0	2	11	8						
Unmet need	11	15	18	20						
Transport services										
Don't need	74	67	64	58	17.04	.01	ns	ns		
Met need	13	23	23	31						
Unmet need	13	10	13	12						

Table 10.11   Regular community care services: differences in relation to 'need factors' (means)

	Don't need	Met need	Unmet need	F	p =
General home help					
Disability severity	14.92	17.77	18.53	8.28	.0003
ADL needs	1.34	1.40	1.47	3.67	.0259
IADL needs	1.85	1.91	2.05	4.38	.0259
BP aggression	0.80	0.76	1.01	5.26	.0054
BP depression	1.23	1.29	1.53	7.25	.0008
BP cognitive	ns	ns	ns	ns	ns
Carer overload	3.10	3.24	3.66	15.38	.0000
Personal home care					
Disability severity	15.04	18.66	20.29	13.02	.0000
ADL needs	1.31	1.64	1.51	26.86	.0000
IADL needs	1.82	2.11	2.13	16.28	.0000
BP aggression	0.76	0.99	1.07	12.95	.0000
BP depression	1.24	1.30	1.61	9.93	.0001
BP cognitive	1.33	1.58	1.79	10.39	.0000
Carer overload	3.10	3.44	3.69	18.28	.0000
Community nursing					
Disability severity	14.77	21.93	19.96	26.40	.0000
ADL needs	1.29	1.72	1.57	48.75	.0000
IADL needs	1.84	2.06	2.15	10.30	.0000
BP aggression	ns	ns	ns	ns	ns
BP depression	ns	ns	ns	ns	ns
BP cognitive	ns	ns	ns	ns	ns
Carer overload	3.17	3.24	3.78	8.66	.0002
Meals					
Disability severity	ns	ns	ns	ns	ns
ADL needs	ns	ns	ns	ns	ns
IADL needs	ns	ns	ns	ns	ns
BP aggression	ns	ns	ns	ns	ns
BP depression	1.28	1.10	1.54	5.05	.0066
BP cognitive	1.34	1.56	1.75	4.73	.0090
Carer overload	3.20	2.98	3.45	3.47	.0316
Home maintenance					
Disability severity	15.50	17.23	18.22	3.98	.0190
ADL needs	ns	ns	ns	ns	ns
IADL needs	ns	ns	ns	ns	ns
BP aggression	ns	ns	ns	ns	ns
BP depression	ns	ns	ns	ns	ns
BP cognitive	ns	ns	ns	ns	ns
Carer overload	3.16	3.18	3.43	4.35	.0132
Transport					
Disability severity	14.41	19.43	18.67	19.17	.0000
ADL needs	1.33	1.46	1.41	5.28	.0053
IADL needs	ns	ns	ns	ns	ns
BP aggression	0.79	0.81	1.00	4.12	.0166
BP depression	1.25	1.27	1.49	4.35	.0132
BP cognitive	ns	ns	ns	ns	ns
Carer overload	ns	ns	ns	ns	ns
Carer social support	3.96	3.95	3.74	8.34	.0003

Table 10.12   Regular community care service: reasons for unmet need

	GHH (n = 116) %	PHC (n = 93) %	CNS (n = 48) %	MEALS (n = 57) %	HM (n = 148) %	TRANS (n = 105) %
Don't know about it	17	27	17	7	39	31
Care-recipient not want	27	27	45	37	7	16
Considering enquiring	7	15	10	16	20	22
Not available in area	11	8	8	2	7	11
Can't afford it	8	4	4	2	5	4
Used before, dissatisfied	10	3	2	28	2	0
Ineligible	8	3	4	0	3	6
Have applied	5	8	2	5	3	10

Note: GHH: general home help; PHC: personal home care; CNS: community nursing service;
MEALS: meals on wheels; HM: home maintenance; TRANS: transport.

Table 10.13   Home modifications: differences in relation to 'need factors' (means)

	Had modifications	Not had modifications	F	$p <$
Severity	20.73	15.26	48.83	.0000
ADL needs	1.60	1.34	53.59	.0000
Depressive behaviours	1.38	1.27	4.50	.0341
Cognitive problems	1.37	1.56	7.20	.0074

Table 10.14   All services: user satisfaction[a]

	Number receiving	Satisfied %	Dissatisfied %
General home help	206	92	5
Personal home care	116	91	6
Community nursing	124	95	4
Meals	61	90	8
Home maintenance	60	93	1
Transport	203	89	6
Home modifications[b]	311	96	4

Notes: a   Measured on a five-point Likert scale, from Very dissatisfied to Very satisfied.
    b   Assessed *ever received* the service.

Table 10.15   Profile of carers: differences according to care-recipient age

| | Total (n = 862) % | Care recipient age | | χ² | p < |
		< 65 (n = 333) %	65+ (n = 529) %		
Female	78	80	77	ns	
Partnered	79	81	78	ns	
In paid employment	38	38	38	ns	
Co-resident	69	90	56	113.90	.0000
Carer age					
< 35	14	27	5	119.68	.0000
35–49	39	43	36		
50–64	30	22	35		
65+	17	7	24		
Caring for					
Partner	24	25	24	434.62	.0000
Parent	38	10	55		
Child	22	57	0		
Other	16	8	21		
Care-recipient sex					
Female	56	39	67	66.80	.0000
Male	44	61	33		
Hours of care/week					
< 10	32	19	40	42.61	.0000
10–30	22	24	21		
31–100	16	21	12		
101+	30	36	27		
Length of care					
< 2 years	32	28	35	18.45	.0001
3–9 years	43	40	46		
10+ years	25	32	19		

Table 10.16   Time since having a break from caring: differences according to care-recipient age

| | Total (n = 862) % | Care-recipient age | | χ² | p < |
		< 65 (n = 333) %	65+ (n = 529) %		
Time since break					
< 6 months	48	41	52	19.52	.0002
6–12 months	12	11	14		
1–2 years	7	6	7		
> 2 years	33	42	27		
Used respite in past 12 months	12	15	10	4.10	.0429
Would like (more) respite	26	25	27	ns	ns

Table 10.17 **Unmet and met need for respite care: differences according to care-recipient age**

	Total (n = 862) %	< 65 (n = 333) %	65+ (n = 529) %	χ^2	p <
			Care-recipient age		
No need	70	68	71	12.15	.0069
Met need	4	7	2		
Partly met need	8	8	8		
Unmet need	18	17	19		

Table 10.18 **Type of respite used and wanted: differences according to care-recipient age**

	Total (n = 862) %	< 65 (n = 333) %	65+ (n = 529) %	χ^2	p <
			Care recipient age		
Respite used (n = 101)					
In home, daytime	14	15	13	ns	ns
Away from home, daytime	3	6	0	ns	ns
In home, overnight/weekend	10	10	10	ns	ns
Away from home overnight/weekend	24	38	12	9.22	.0024
Longer respite	63	50	75	6.69	.0099
Respite wanted (n = 222)					
In home, daytime	22	17	25	ns	ns
Away from home, daytime	8	9	7	ns	ns
In home, overnight/weekend	25	34	20	5.12	.0236
Away from home overnight/weekend	27	38	20	8.02	.0046
Longer respite	44	32	51	7.43	.0064

Table 10.19 **Reasons for unmet need: differences according to care-recipient age**

	Total (n = 152) %	< 65 (n = 54) %	65+ (n = 98) %	χ^2	p <
			Care-recipient age		
Don't know about it	34	35	34	ns	
Care recipient would not like it	24	9	33	10.35	.0013
Need not great enough yet	14	7	18	ns	
Suitable service not available	11	22	4	12.16	.0005
Trying to arrange it	10	15	7	ns	
Support from family and friends	5	4	5	ns	
Can't afford it	4	4	4	ns	

Table 10.20 Emotional well-being according to need for respite and care-recipient age-group (means)

	Need respite				Care-recipient age			
	Yes (n = 222)	No (n = 640)	F	p <	< 65 (n = 333)	65+ (n = 529)	F	p <
Overload	3.55	3.09	35.74	.0001	3.35	3.11	11.26	.001
Negative affect	1.93	1.73	11.79	.001	1.94	1.69	22.99	.0001
Social support	3.81	3.99	20.11	.0001	3.86	3.99	13.67	.001
Life satisfaction	3.46	3.82	19.06	.0001	3.62	3.79	13.36	.001

Table 10.21 Counselling and training: percentage differences according to carer and care-recipient characteristics (N = 976)

	Counselling			Training		
	%	χ^2	p <	%	χ^2	p <
Total	17			11		
Relationship						
Offspring	11	84.28	.00001	ns		
Spouse	15					
Parent	39					
Other	10					
Care-recipient lives						
With carer	20	16.41	.001	ns		
Alone	8					
With other	12					
Residential care	20					
Carer age						
< 35 yrs	27	28.99	.001	17	18.33	.001
35–49	22			13		
50–64	11			9		
65+	10			3		
Care-recipient age						
< 21 yrs	44	107.17	.00001	ns		
21–60	23					
61–80	11					
80+	7					
Disability type						
Minor	9	27.6	.00001	ns		
Mental	28					
Physical	11					
Both high	18					

Table 10.22 Differences in carer well-being according to participation in counselling and training courses (means)

	Counselling				Training			
	Yes	No	F	p <	Yes	No	F	p <
Overload	3.44	3.16	10.84		ns			
Positive affect	ns				3.35	3.07	13.06	.001
Negative affect	2.05	1.74	24.24	.0001	ns			
Life satisfaction	3.48	3.78	28.93	.0001	ns			
Social support	3.80	3.96	13.52	.001	ns			

Table 10.23 Counselling and training: number and percentage of carers receiving and needing (N = 615)[a]

	Counselling		Training	
	n	%	n	%
Received in past year	74	12	33	5
Unmet need	63	10	78	13
Don't need	478	78	504	82

Note: a   Lower number due to change in carer status and attrition between Stages 1 and 2 of the survey.

Table 10.24 Need for counselling and training: statistically significant differences in percentage distribution in relation to care-dyad characteristics

	Need counselling (n = 534)				Need training (n = 574)			
	Yes %	No %	χ^2	p <	Yes %	No %	χ^2	p <
Total	10	90			13	87		
Relationship								
Spouse	9	91	8.50	.05	ns	ns		
Offspring	15	85						
Parent	13	87						
Other	3	97						
Carer sex								
Female	13	87	4.70	.05	ns	ns		
Male	11	94						
Carer age								
< 35 years	ns	ns			24	76	11.40	.01
35–49					15	85		
50–64					13	87		
65+					6	94		
Schooling								
< Year 9	ns	ns			6	94	8.40	.05
Years 9–10					12	88		
Year 11					14	86		
Year 12					19	81		
Ethnicity								
Australian-born	ns	ns			12	88	9.40	.01
Anglo country of birth					8	92		
NES country of birth					24	76		
Disability								
Minor	6	94	12.7	.01				
Mental	13	87			ns	ns		
Physical	5	95						
Both high	17	83						

Table 10.25   Need for counselling and training: differences in mean
scores for recipient behaviour problems and ADL
dependencies, and carer well-being

	Need counselling				Need training			
	Yes	No	F	p <	Yes	No	F	p <
Behaviour problems								
Aggression	2.14	1.79	14.9	.001	2.04	1.85	5.5	.05
Depression	2.74	2.15	38.3	.001	2.61	2.20	21.9	.001
Cognitive	2.96	2.45	15.4	.001	ns	ns		
Dependencies								
Needs IADL help	2.24	1.96	10.2	.001	ns	ns		
Gives IADL help	2.71	2.29	11.3	.001	ns	ns		
Carer well-being								
Overload	3.86	3.14	31.4	.001	3.74	3.19	21.3	.001
Negative affect	2.26	1.67	42.4	.001	2.18	1.75	23.8	.001
Social support	3.71	4.08	28.7	.001	3.81	4.04	11.4	.001
Life satisfaction	3.17	3.84	63.6	.001	3.43	3.74	13.5	.001

Table 10.26   Main reasons for not receiving desired counselling and
training

	Counselling (n = 63) %	Training (n = 78) %
Not yet enquired	43	33
Don't know about it	19	30
Time and other pressures	11	18
Not available in area	14	9
Has applied/waiting	0	4
Can't afford	0	3
Used, not satisfied	3	0
Service cuts	2	0
Other	8	4

Table 10.27   Support group membership at Stages 1 and 2 (n = 608)

	Stage 2 Current %	Past %	Never %
Total	18	19	63
Stage 1 member	35	8	3
Stage 1 non-member	62	92	97

Table 10.28 Current and past support group involvement: percentage differences according to care-dyad characteristics (n = 608)

	Current member %	Past contact %	None %	χ^2	p <
Carer relationship					
Spouse	18	16	66	94.1	.00001
Offspring	7	14	79		
Parent	35	30	35		
Other	8	18	74		
Care-recipient age					
< 21 yrs	32	30	38	70.9	.00001
21–60	28	21	51		
61–80	12	15	73		
80+	7	16	77		
Care-recipient sex					
Female	13	18	69	15.3	.001
Male	24	21	55		
Living arrangements					
With carer	22	18	60	25.7	.0005
Alone	6	18	76		
With others	10	17	74		
Residential care	11	30	59		
Disability					
Minor	11	14	75	35.1	.00001
Mental	25	28	48		
Physical	8	14	78		
Both high	21	20	59		
Hours of care provided					
< 10	11	22	67	23.4	.001
10–30	16	17	67		
31–100	19	22	59		
101+	31	14	56		

Table 10.29 Differences in care-recipient dependencies and carer well-being according to current and past support group membership (n = 608) (means)

	Current member	Past contact	None	F	p <
Behaviour problems					
Aggressive	2.08	1.98	1.81	7.7	.001
Cognitive	2.75	2.62	2.48	3.4	.05
Care-recipient dependencies					
ADL help needed	1.60	1.55	1.43	4.9	.01
IADL help needed	2.30	2.07	1.93	13.3	.001
ADL help provided	1.93	1.53	1.53	13.0	.001
IADL help provided	2.76	2.26	2.26	11.2	.001
Carer well-being					
Overload	3.49	3.28	3.28	5.1	.01
Life satisfaction	3.51	3.72	3.72	5.4	.005
Positive affect	3.25	3.12	3.12	3.1	.05

Table 10.30   Types of carer involvement with support groups or organisations

	% Carers (*n* = 232)
Newsletter	43
Support group	37
Social events	26
Education sessions	22
Telephone support	17
Volunteer work	12
Counselling	10
Information	7
Other	16

Table 10.31   Reasons for discontinued involvement with support groups or organisations

	% Carers (*n* = 114)
Limited usefulness	36
Carer's circumstances and commitments	22
Access and organisational factors	13
Loss of interest	13
Flexible contact	10
Recipient-related factors	6

Table 10.32   Main and preferred source of information about care-recipients' condition and services and organisations

	Information about condition		Information about services and organisations	
	Main source (*N* = 976) %	Preferred source (*n* = 399) %	Main source (*N* = 976) %	Preferred source (*n* = 399) %
General practitioner	56	51	25	25
Medical specialist	40	29	13	11
Allied health professional	15	15	21	16
Family and friends	11	9	14	13
Media or printed material	10	2	8	3
Society or support group	9	11	10	17
Care-recipient	9	5	3	1
Government agency	5	6	20	27
No information received	3	–	19	–

Note: Some carers nominated > 1 source, thus total > 100%.

Table 10.33 Differences between those nominating GP as preferred source for information about condition and those not (N = 399)

	Prefer GP %	Not prefer GP %	χ^2	$p <$
Total %	51	49		
Carer age				
< 35	32	68	32.35	.0001
35–49	37	63		
50–64	59	41		
65+	70	30		
Relationship to recipient				
Spouse	71	29	34.09	.0001
Offspring	57	43		
Parent	32	68		
Other	49	51		
Care recipient age				
< 21	25	75	32.16	.0001
21–60	51	49		
61–80	64	36		
81+	58	42		
Nature of disability				
Minor	58	42	12.61	.01
Physical	59	41		
Mental	34	66		
Both	53	47		

Table 10.34 Differences between those nominating medical specialist as preferred source for information about condition and those not (N = 399)

	Prefer specialist %	Not prefer specialist %	χ^2	$p <$
Total %	29	71		
Carer age				
< 35	44	56	9.49	.05
35–49	35	65		
50–64	23	77		
65+	23	77		
Relationship to recipient				
Spouse	33	67	29.00	.0001
Offspring	15	85		
Parent	44	56		
Other	23	77		
Care-recipient sex				
Male	35	65	5.36	.05
Female	24	76		
Care-recipient age				
< 21	52	48		
21–60	33	67	35.76	.0001
61–80	26	74		
81+	15	85		
Care-recipient lives				
With carer	35	65	14.97	.01
Alone	18	82		
With other	30	70		
Residential care	15	85		
Hours per week caring				
< 10	18	82	15.60	.01
10–30	35	65		
31–100	41	59		
101+	27	73		

Table 10.35 **Differences between those nominating government agency as preferred source for information about services and those not (N = 399)**

	Prefer govt agency %	Not prefer govt agency %	χ^2	p <
Total %	27	73		
Care-recipient lives				
With carer	24	76	7.64	.05
Alone	40	60		
With other	30	70		
Residential care	24	76		
Carer qualifications				
None	21	79	7.24	.05
Trade or other	33	67		
Tertiary	33	67		
Geographic location				
Metropolitan	32	68	7.50	.01
Rural	20	80		
Use community care services				
Yes	32	68	5.45	.05
No	22	78		

Table 10.36 **Preferred format for information about care-recipient condition and services and organisations (N = 399)**

	Information about condition %	Information about services and organisations %
Verbal/personal communication	81	77
Pamphlet	26	29
Television	5	3
Newspaper/magazine	4	4
Radio	1	2
Training program	1	1
Video	1	1

Note: Some carers nominated > 1 format, thus total > 100%.

Table 10.37 Differences between those nominating pamphlet as preferred format for information about condition and those not (*N* = 399)

	Prefer pamphlet	Not prefer pamphlet	χ^2	$p <$
Total %	26	74		
Carer age				
< 35	32	68	17.24	.001
35–49	36	64		
50–64	22	78		
65+	13	87		
Relationship				
Spouse	23	77	18.16	.001
Offspring	20	80		
Parent	39	61		
Other	13	87		
Care-recipient sex				
Male	32	68	5.41	.05
Female	21	79		
Care-recipient age				
< 21	43	57	29.13	.0001
21–60	36	64		
61–80	22	78		
81+	13	87		
Nature of disability				
Minor	29	71	8.24	.05
Physical	24	76		
Mental	38	62		
Both	21	79		

Table 10.38   Differences on the basis of type of information needed ($N = 399$)

| | Need information about | | | | | |
	Services %	Recipient condition %	Carer well-being %	None %	χ^2	$p <$
Total %	25	16	14	45		
Relationship						
Spouse	15	13	14	58	26.50	.001
Offspring	26	13	18	44		
Parent	31	25	12	32		
Other	24	3	9	64		
Care-recipient age						
< 21	29	32	14	25	26.72	.001
21–60	29	12	14	46		
61–80	21	11	16	52		
81+	24	11	12	53		
Level of schooling						
< Year 11	19	13	16	52	10.13	.05
Year 11+	31	18	12	39		
Qualification						
None	21	13	17	49	15.52	.05
Trade or other	21	21	10	48		
Tertiary	40	15	12	33		
Geographic location						
Metropolitan	33	15	15	37	15.02	.001
Rural	16	17	13	54		

Table 11.1 Using, considering or not considering residential care: percentage differences according to carer and recipient characteristics

	Using resid. care (n = 114) %	Considering resid. care (n = 213) %	Not considering resid. care (n = 629) %	χ^2	p <
Total %	12	22	66		
Relationship					
Offspring	15	30	55	79.83	.00001
Spouse	6	11	82		
Parent	5	15	80		
Other	20	28	53		
Carer age					
< 35	3	12	85	27.34	.001
35–49	11	23	65		
50–64	15	25	60		
65+	14	22	64		
Care-recipient age					
< 21	2	10	88	91.53	.00001
21–60	9	14	77		
60–80	10	22	68		
80+	21	32	47		
Care-recipient sex					
Female	15	27	58	34.91	.0001
Male	7	16	76		
Nature of disability					
Minor only	6	13	81	37.08	.00001
Physical	7	20	73		
Mental	10	26	64		
Both	17	25	58		
Hours spent caring					
< 10	22	24	54	68.27	.00001
10–30	13	23	64		
31–100	6	24	70		
101+	2	19	79		

Note: Twenty carers were using residential facilities < 5 days a week and are excluded from the analysis.

Table 11.2 Differences in care-recipient behaviour and dependencies and carer feelings according to using, considering or not considering residential care (means)

	Using resid. care (n = 114)	Considering resid. care (n = 213)	Not considering resid. care (n = 629)	F	p <
Behaviour problems					
Aggressive	0.91	0.94	0.78	5.09	.01
Depressive	1.43	1.43	1.24	6.63	.01
Cognitive	2.04	1.72	1.31	35.70	.0001
Amount of help needed					
ADLs	1.84	1.47	1.34	43.16	.0001
IADLs	2.42	2.08	1.83	48.88	.0001
Amount of help provided					
ADLs	1.26	1.59	1.58	8.94	.001
IADLs	2.31	2.52	2.27	5.93	.01
Caregiving role					
Anger	2.18	2.34	2.10	8.08	.001
Resentment	2.50	2.69	2.48	6.17	.01
Satisfaction	3.60	3.70	3.96	27.68	.001

Note: Twenty carers were using residential facilities < 5 days a week and are excluded from the analysis.

Table 11.3 Reasons for not using residential care

	Carers (n = 219) %
Care-recipient wouldn't like it	46
Not currently necessary	36
Carer wouldn't like it	10
On waiting list	10
None available	5
Family opposed to it	5
Can't afford it	3

Note: Total > 100% because more than one reason given.

Table 11.4   Movement into residential care over a 15-month period: percentage differences according to carer and care-recipient characteristics

	Moved into resid. care %	Still in community %	χ^2	$p <$
Total %	8	92		
Relationship				
Offspring	13	87	17.12	.001
Spouse	7	93		
Parent	1	99		
Other	10	90		
Care-recipient age				
< 21 years	1	99	16.50	.001
21–60	4	96		
61–80	10	90		
80+	12	88		
Care-recipient resides				
With carer	6	94	7.23	.05
Alone	12	88		
With other	13	87		
Nature of disability				
Minor only	2	98	13.77	.01
Physical	2	98		
Mental	9	91		
Both	12	88		
Duration of care				
< 1 year	13	87	9.30	.06
1–2 years	9	91		
3–5 years	9	91		
6–9 years	2	98		
10+ years	6	946		
Considered resid. care				
Yes	19	81	33.99	.00001
No	4	96		

Table 11.5 Movement into residential care: differences according to care-recipient dependencies and carer feelings (means)

	Moved into resid. care	Still in community	F	$p <$
Behaviour problems				
Depressive	1.65	1.23	13.05	.001
Cognitive	2.04	1.47	13.82	.001
Amount of help needed				
ADLs	1.52	1.38	3.66	.05
IADLs	2.22	1.91	9.21	.01
Caregiving role				
Anger	2.35	2.17	ns	
Resentment	2.69	2.54	ns	
Satisfaction	3.52	3.96	21.31	.0001

Table 11.6 Use of services at Stage 1: percentage differences according to movement into residential care over a 15-month period

	Moved into resid. care ($n = 44$) %	Still in community ($n = 519$) %	χ^2	$p <$
Total %	8	92		
General home help				
Don't need	38	65	15.21	.001
Need, don't get	14	13		
Getting	48	22		
Specific home help				
Don't need	55	77	10.95	.01
Need, don't get	18	10		
Getting	27	13		
Community nursing				
Don't need	55	85	27.61	.00001
Need, don't get	11	5		
Getting	34	10		
Meal service				
Don't need	71	87	11.35	.01
Need, don't get	18	6		
Getting	11	7		
Transport				
Don't need	50	67	11.22	.01
Need, don't get	7	12		
Getting	43	21		
Use respite care				
Yes	27	12	8.94	.01
No	73	88		
Like more respite				
Yes	52	26	13.69	.001
No	48	74		

Table 12.1   Ratings of usefulness for each component of the Carer Support Kit for those who read or used it (n = 24)

	Number who read/used	Very useful	Moderately useful	Not useful
Stories tape	14	10	4	0
Home safety booklet	23	10	12	1
Emergency plan	20	10	7	2
Relaxation tape	14	5	7	2
Services directory	18	6	9	3
Pathway	20	5	8	5
Fact sheets				
Self-care	21	9	11	1
Respite	22	8	10	4
Medicines	20	7	10	3
Finances	22	6	7	8
Legal issues	20	6	9	5
Dementia	3	2	1	0
Stroke	2	2	1	0

Note: Disability fact sheets requested by only one carer are not shown in table.

Table 12.2   Main supports to be organised by aged care assessment team

	% care-dyads (*n* = 67)
Respite care	31
Aids	31
Paramedical services, esp. physio. and occup. therapy	31
Home modifications	23
Financial assistance (e.g. Parental Allowance for Disabled)	15
Day centre and day hospital	15
Transport	12
Volunteer services	12
Specific home help	11
General home help	9
Community nursing	9
Recreation services	9

SURVEY METHODS

SURVEY INSTRUMENT

Information gathered in the Stage 1 structured interview included the following:

A. In relation to the carer, socio-demographic data (age, sex, marital status, education level, employment status, relationship to care-recipient, relationship to carer), and various measures of physical and emotional well-being and mediating factors. *Physical health* was assessed by a four-point rating scale, which has been found to be a good predictor of survival,[1] having a major illness in the past year and use of medication. *Life satisfaction* was assessed on a six-item scale covering health, personal, emotional life, independence, financial situation, respect and recognition (based on Headey & Wearing 1981). *Psychological well-being* was measured by Watson's twenty-item Positive and Negative Affect mood scales. Substantial positive correlations have been reported between the Negative Affect scale and the Hopkins Symptom Checklist, Beck Depression Inventory and STAI State Anxiety Scale (Watson et al. 1988). For social support, a seven-item modified version of the Provision of Social Relations Scale was used (Turner et al. 1983). *Overload* in the carer was assessed by three items from the four-item scale developed by Pearlin and colleagues (1990). The extent to which there was more or less conflict or closeness in the family environment since the onset of caregiving was assessed using two three-item scales (family *closeness* and family *conflict*).

B. In relation to the caregiving role, in addition to factual information such as hours spent caring, there were three attitudinal scales including:

- carer *'satisfaction'* containing seven items assessing a positive emotional response to the care-recipient and the caregiving role
- carer *'resentment'* with five items focusing on the negative effects of caregiving on the carer's life, time, opportunities and social relationships
- carer *'anger'* containing four items assessing negative emotional responses to the care-recipient such as anger, embarrassment and guilt.

Information about assistance needed and provided with twelve activities of daily living formed two broad functional dependence or 'help needed' measures respectively covering ADLs and IADLs; and two 'help provided' measures covering the same domains.

C. In relation to the care-recipient, in addition to age and sex, three disability measures were computed using carer responses to seven broad classifications of disability. Taking into consideration the number of impairments plus the severity of each (severe = 3, moderate = 2, minor = 1, none = 0) a *physical disability* measure was computed by summing the number of reported physical impairments (physical/mobility, coordination, sensory and long-term health problems); a *mental disability* measure by summing the number of mental impairments (intellectual, communication and psychiatric/emotional problems); and a *total severity of disability* measure by summing all impairments. In addition, three scales were used to assess frequency of behaviour problems:

- a four-item scale characterised as *depressive* behaviours (comprising items such as gets depressed, listless, fearful, withdrawn)
- a nine-item scale designated *aggressive* behaviours (comprising items such as becomes aggressive, uncooperative, violent, cranky, hyperactive)
- a three-item scale named *cognitive behaviour problems* (comprising items such as forgetful, confused, wanders, repeats questions).

Reliable scales measuring various aspects of emotional well-being, attitudes to caregiving, family environment, care-recipient dependency and behaviour problems were constructed on the basis of factor analyses undertaken using Stage 1 data. Psychometric properties of these scales, together with other findings in relation to scale construction, are presented in Schofield, Murphy et al. (1997).

VALIDATION OF CARER REPORTS

Constructed from the carer interview data, scales for level of care-recipient disability, amount of help needed and amount of help provided by the carer were validated against ACAT assessments.

A sub-sample of 67 carers participated with the care-recipient in an in-home clinician assessment in conjunction with local ACATs. ACAT visits are conducted primarily to identify and meet service needs, but provided the additional opportunity for a clinician to assess the care-recipient's disabilities and dependencies. Thus carers' reports (from the interview) were correlated with clinicians' ratings (made during ACAT visits) for three areas:

- level of disability
- level of help needed with ADLs
- level of help provided with ADLs.

The sub-sample of 67 carer/care-recipient pairs or 'care-dyads' were from the Northern and Eastern Metropolitan and the South Western Rural regions of Victoria. In keeping with the inclusion requirements of the ACATs, this group was restricted to care-recipients over 25. They therefore tended to be older than the full sample: 36% were 60–79, and 46% were 80 or older. Just over half were cared for by adult offspring, while a third were cared for by their spouse. Most were co-resident (72%). Again a range of illnesses and disabilities was present. According to ACAT ratings, 45% had two or more moderate or severe impairments across six functional areas:

- long-term health (61%)
- sensory functioning (28%)
- mobility (27%)
- psychological functioning (20%)
- communication (15%)
- intellectual functioning (12%).

Carer reports were recorded using global scores derived from three of the scales described earlier: a score of care-recipient's disabilities derived by adding carer ratings across the seven functional areas (sensory, intellectual, psychiatric, communication, coordination, mobility, and long-term health), a score of the amount of help needed derived by adding carer ratings across the seven ADLs (incontinence, toileting, dressing, bathing, moving about, bed–chair transfer, and eating), and a score of the amount of help provided by the carer derived by adding carer ratings across each of the seven ADLs.

In-home clinician assessment The ACAT routinely collects information about client health, current treatment and level of independence using various validated measures.[2] ACAT team members were trained in either occupational therapy, nursing, social work, geriatric medicine, physiotherapy, or psychiatric care. The ACAT member was accompanied by a member of our research team, which consisted of a general practitioner, a social worker, a psychologist and an occupational therapist.

The clinician, without knowing carer ratings, conducted the assessment according to the usual ACAT protocol, with additional ratings for the purpose of this study made during or after the visit. Because several disability measures were used, an additional rating of 'level of disability' in each of the seven disability areas was made by the clinician, informed by ratings on the validated disability measures. The mean of the summed ratings provided a global score for 'level of disability'. Because none of the validated measures directly assessed the amount of help provided by the carer, an additional rating of 'help provided' with each of the seven ADLs was made by the clinician, informed by scores on the Barthel index. The mean of the summed ratings provided a score of 'amount of help provided'. It was not necessary to make an additional rating for 'help needed': the total score on the Barthel index of ADLs, which assesses level of dependency in sixteen ADLs, provided a score of 'amount of help needed'. Use of the latter in correlations with carer ratings constituted concurrent validation.

RESULTS

Table A.1 shows Pearson correlations between clinician ratings and carer reports for level of disability, help needed, and help provided. There were substantial and significant correlations between carer reports and clinician ratings in all three areas. In particular, the high correlation of 0.76 between the carer-rated 'help needed' scale and the validated Barthel index indicates good concurrent validity for this carer-rated scale.

Scales developed from carers' reports of the severity of their relative's disability, the amount of help needed, and the amount of help they provided correlated highly with clinician ratings. These findings thus support the validity of carer reports. More specifically, the three carer-rated scales for measuring disability, ADL help needed, and ADL help provided, have been externally validated.

Table A.1   Correlations between carer ratings and clinician ratings

Scale	n	Pearson	$p <$
Disability	51[a]	.6366	.0001
ADL help needed	67	.7602	.0001
ADL help provided	67	.6680	.0001

Note: a   Sixteen care-recipients were unable to complete the depression questionnaire required for establishing a rating of psychological problems.

ANALYSIS OF DATA

Throughout the chi-squared statistic was used, on all categorical variables, to assess differences between groups: for example men and women; relationship groups; age-groups; carers and non-carers. Standardised residuals < 1.96 were used in the interpretation of analyses.

One-way, two-way or three-way analyses of variance (ANOVAs) were used to assess differences between groups on all continuous variables. *Post hoc* Scheffe tests or the Newman Kuels procedure were applied in the interpretation of analyses using factors with more than two levels.

Details of other analyses and specific statistical information are pre in appended tables and endnotes.

BIBLIOGRAPHY

Abramowitz, I. and R. Coursey (1989) 'Impact of an educational support group on family participants who take care of their schizophrenic relatives', *Journal of Consulting and Clinical Psychology* 57(2):232–6

ABS (1990) *Carers Of The Handicapped At Home, Australia 1988* (Catalogue 4122.0), Canberra: AGPS

—— (1991) *The Labor Force, Australia* (Catalogue No. 62020), Canberra: AGPS

—— (1992) *1989–90 National Health Survey Consultations with Professionals*, Canberra: AGPS

—— (1993) *Disability, Ageing and Carers—Australia 1993: Summary of Findings* (Catalogue No. 4430.0), Canberra: AGPS

—— (1995) *Focus On Families: Caring in Families—Support for Persons Who are Older or Have Disabilities* (Catalogue No. 4423.0), Canberra: AGPS

Action (1988) HACC and Children with Disabilities: A Home and Community Care Demonstration Project. Melbourne: Action Group for Disabled Children

Ade-Ridder, L. and L. Kaplan (1993) 'Marriage, spousal caregiving and a husband's move to a nursing home: a changing role for the wife', *Journal of Gerontological Nursing* 19(10):13–23

Adler, G., L. Ott, M. Jelinski, J. Mortimer and R. Christensen (1993) 'Institutional respite care for dementia patients and caregivers', *International*

National Non-English Speaking Background Women's 'S

ing and Coping with Schizophrenia: 14 Principles for ne: Wilkinson Books

and B.S. Willer (1994) 'Family burden following *ation Psychology* 39:29–48

tewart-Wynne (1995) 'A population-based assess- of caregiving for long-term stroke survivors', *Stroke*

(1983) 'Societal and individual determinants of Jnited States', *Millbank Quarterly* 51:95–124

324

Ashby, J. and A. Moo (1993) Time out for carers: respite carer provision in the Melbourne Municipality. Paper prepared for the City of Melbourne

Atkin, K. (1992) 'Similarities and differences between informal carers', in J. Twigg (ed.), *Carers: Research and Practice*, London: Her Majesty's Stationery Office

Baldock, J. and C. Ungerson (1991) '"What d'ya want if you don' want money?": a feminist critique of "paid volunteering"', in M. Maclean and D. Groves (eds), *Women's Issues in Social Policy*, London: Routledge

Barnett, K. and M. Cricelli (1990) 'Caring for caregivers: the Multicultural Respite Care Project', *Australian Journal of Social Work* 43(3):39–43

Barrowclough, C., N. Tarrier, S. Watts, C. Vaughan, J. Bamrah and H. Freeman (1987) 'Assessing the functional value of relatives' knowledge about schizophrenia: a preliminary report', *British Journal of Psychiatry* 151:1–8

Barusch, A.S. (1989) 'Problems and coping strategies of elderly spouse caregivers', *The Gerontologist* 28:677–85

Barusch, A. and W. Spaid (1989) 'Gender differences in caregiving: why do wives report greater burden?', *The Gerontologist* 29:667–76

Bass, D.M., K. Bowman and L.S. Noelker (1991) 'The influence of caregiving and bereavement support on adjusting to an older relative's death', *The Gerontologist* 31:32–42

Bass, D., W. Looman and P. Ehrlich (1992) 'Predicting the volume of health and social services. Integrating cognitive impairment into the modified Andersen Framework', *The Gerontologist* 32:33–43

Baum, S. and S. Gallagher (1985) 'Case studies of psychotherapy with depressed caregivers', *Clinical Gerontologist* 4:19–29

Baume, P., B. Isaacson and J. Hunt (1993) 'Perceptions of unmet need in four community services for elderly people', *Australian Journal of Public Health* 17:267–8

Baumgarten, M., R.N. Battista, C. Infante-Rivard, J.A. Hanley, R. Becker and S. Gauthier (1992) 'The psychological and physical health of family members caring for an elderly person with dementia', *Journal of Clinical Epidemiology* 45:61–70

—— (1994) 'Health of family members caring for elderly persons with dementia—a longitudinal study', *Annals of Internal Medicine* 120(2):126–32

Beckman, P.J. (1991) 'Comparison of mothers' and fathers' perceptions of the effect of young children with and without disabilities', *American Journal on Mental Retardation* 95:585–95

Bentley, K.J. (1990) 'An evaluation of family-based intervention with schizophrenia using single-system research', *British Journal of Social Work* 29:101–16

Beresford, B. (1994) 'Resources and strategies: how parents cope with the care of a disabled child', *Journal of Child Psychology and Psychiatry* 35(1):171–209

Bernardi, E. (1993) *A Multicultural Perspective in National Family Summit Report: November 1992 Parliament House Canberra*, Sydney: Capricorn

Biegel, D., D. Bass, R. Schulz and R. Morycz (1993) 'Predictors of in-home and out-of-home service use by family caregivers of Alzheimer's Disease patients', *Journal of Aging and Health* 5(4):419–38

Birkel, R.C. (1987) 'Toward a social ecology of the home-care household', *Psychology and Aging* 2:294–310

Bland, R. (1994) 'Supportive approaches to families in Australia: drawing conclusions from practice', *New Directions for Mental Health Services* 62:61–9

Bloch, S., G. Szmukler, H. Herrman, A. Benson and S. Colussa (1995) 'Counselling caregivers of relatives with schizophrenia: themes, interventions and caveats', *Family Process* 34:413–25

Bodnar, J.C. and J.K. Kiecolt-Glaser (1994) 'Caregiver depression after bereavement— chronic stress isn't over when it's over', *Psychology and Aging* 9:372–80

Bowman, D. (1994) *Listen to the Carers! The Many Voices of Care*, Canberra: CAV

Bozic, S., H. Herrman and H. Schofield (1993a) 'A profile of carers in Victoria: analysis of the ABS survey of disabled and aged persons 1988: co-resident carers of severely handicapped persons', Department of Psychiatry, University of Melbourne

—— (1993b) 'Government policy and unpaid family: an overview of Federal and Victorian government policy in relation to unpaid family caregivers', Department of Psychiatry, University of Melbourne

Braithwaite, V. (1990) *Bound to Care*, Sydney: Allen & Unwin

Braun, H. and M. Nichaus (1990) 'Caring for disabled family members', in L. Montada and H.W. Bierhoff (eds), *Altruism in Social Systems*, Toronto: Hogrefe & Huber

Breslau, N. and G.C. Davis (1986) 'Chronic stress and major depression', *Archives of General Psychiatry* 43:309–14

Brodaty, H. and M. Gresham (1989) 'Effects of a training programme to reduce stress in carers of patients with dementia', *British Medical Journal* 299:1375–9

Brodaty, H. and D. Hadzi-Pavlovic (1990) 'Psychosocial effects on carers of living with persons with dementia', *Australian and New Zealand Journal of Psychiatry* 24:351–61

Brodaty, H., G. Howarth, A. Mant, S. Kurrie (1994) 'General practice and dementia: a national survey of Australian general practitioners', *Medical Journal of Australia* 160:10–14

Brodaty, H. and K. Peters (1991) 'Cost effectiveness of a training program for dementia carers', *International Psychogeriatrics* 3(1):11–22

Brodaty, H., K. Roberts and K. Peters (1994) 'Quasi experimental evaluation of an educational model for dementia caregivers', *International Journal of Geriatric Psychiatry* 9:195–204

Brody, E.M. (1990) *Women in the Middle: Their Parent-Care Years*, New York: Springer

Brody, E.M. and C.B. Schoonover (1986) 'Patterns of parent care when adult daughters work and when they do not', *The Gerontologist* 264:372–81

Brody, E.M., M.H. Kleban, P.T. Johnsen, C. Hoffman and C.B. Schoonover (1987) 'Work status and parent care: a comparison of four groups of women', *The Gerontologist* 27(2):201–8

Brody, E.M., S.J. Litvin, S.M. Albert and C.J. Hoffman (1994) 'Marital status of daughters and patterns of parent care', *Journal of Gerontology* 49:95–103

Brown, L., J. Potter and B. Foster (1990) 'Caregiver burden should be evaluated during geriatric assessment', *Journal of the American Geriatrics Society* 38:455–60

Bruce, E. and C. Schultz (1992) 'Complicated loss: considerations in counselling the parents of a child with an intellectual disability', *Australian Counselling Psychologist* 8(2):8–20

Burdz, M., W. Eaton and J. Bond (1988) 'Effect of respite care on dementia and nondementia patients and their caregivers', *Psychology and Aging* 3(1):38–42

BIPR (1994) *Statistical Focus: Birthplace and Related Data from the 1991 Census Expanded Community Profiles*, Canberra: BIPR Publications

Cantor, M.H. (1983) 'Strain among caregivers: a study of experience in the United States', *The Gerontologist* 23(6):597–604

Carpenter, G. and G. Demopoulos (1990) 'Screening the elderly in the community:

controlled trial of dependency surveillance using a questionnaire administered by volunteers', *British Medical Journal* 300:1253–6

Carrafa, G., C. Schultz and K. Smyrnios (1997) 'Differences between Anglo-Celtic and Italian caregivers of dependent elderly persons: a pilot study', *Ageing and Society* 17: 699–713

Cattanach, L. and J.K. Tebes (1991) 'The nature of elder impairment and its impact on family caregivers' health and psychosocial functioning', *The Gerontologist* 31:246–55

CAV (1995) Annual Report 1994–95, Melbourne

Chappell, N. (1985) 'Social support and the receipt of Home Care services', *The Gerontologist* 25(1):47–54

—— (1991) 'Living arrangement and services of caregiving', *Journal of Gerontology: Social Sciences* 46:S51–8

Chappell, N. and R. Littenhaus (1995a) *Informal Caregivers to Adults in British Columbia*. Joint Report of the Centre on Aging, University of Victoria, and the Caregivers Association of British Columbia

—— (1995b) *Informal Caregivers to Children with Disabilities in British Columbia*. Joint Report of the Centre on Aging, University of Victoria, the Caregivers Association of British Columbia, and the Respite Advisory Committee, BC Ministry of Health

Chiverton, P. and E. Caine (1989) 'Education to assist spouses in coping with Alzheimer's disease: a controlled trial', *Journal of the American Geriatrics Society* 37:593–8

Clarke, R.M. and P. Finucane (1995) 'Care-receivers' and care-givers' experience and perceptions of respite care: implications for service provision', *Australian Journal on Ageing* 13(4):183–7

Clipp, E. and L. George (1989) 'Caregiver needs and patterns of social support', *Journal of Gerontology* 45(3):S102–11

Cohen, C.A., D.P. Gold, K.I. Shulman, J.T. Wortley, G. McDonald and M. Wargon (1993) 'Factors determining the decision to institutionalize dementing individuals: a prospective study', *The Gerontologist* 33(6):714–20

Cohen, C., J. Teresi and C. Blum (1994) 'The role of caregiver social networks in Alzheimer's disease', *Social Science and Medicine* 38:1483–90

Colerick, E.J. and L.K. George (1986) 'Predictors of institutionalization among caregivers of patients with Alzheimer's Disease', *Journal of the American Geriatrics Society* 34:493–8

Cooper, B., H. Bickel and M. Schaufele (1992) 'Dementia and cognitive impairment among elderly patients in general practice: findings of a survey', *Nervenarzt* 63:551–60

Cullinan, K. (1993) *Respite Care Plan: Shires of Kyneton, Newham and Woodend and Romsey*, Daylesford, Vic.: Jim Crow Press

Dalley, G. (1988) *Ideologies of Caring*, UK: Macmillan Education

Davis, C., A. Wilson and S. McCarthy (1996) 'Ethnicity and aged care assessment teams in Queensland', *Australian and New Zealand Journal of Public Health* 20(1):33–40

de Vaus, D. (1994) *Letting Go: Relationships Between Adults and Their Parents*, Melbourne: Oxford University Press

Deimling, G. and S. Poulshock (1985) 'The transition from family in-home care to institutional care: focus on health and attitudinal issues as predisposing factors', *Research on Aging* 7:563–76

Doress-Worters, P. (1994) 'Adding elder care to women's multiple roles: a critical review of the caregiver stress and multiple roles literature', *Sex Roles* 31(9/10):597–616

Draper, B.M., C.J. Poulos, A.M.D. Cole, G.G. Poulos and F. Ehrlich (1992) 'A comparison of caregivers for elderly stroke and dementia victims', *Journal of the American Geriatrics Society* 40:896–901

Dwyer, J.W. and R.T. Coward (1992) *Gender, Families, and Elder Care*, Newbury Park, Calif.: Sage

Dyson, L.L. (1993) 'Response to the presence of a child with disabilities: parental stress and family functioning over time', *American Journal of Mental Retardation* 98:207–18

Edelman, P. and S. Hughes (1990) 'The impact of community care on provision of informal care to homebound elderly persons', *Journal of Gerontology: Social Sciences* 45(2):S74–84

Elton, B. and Associates (1995) *Review of the Aged Care Assessment Program—Victoria, Final Report*, Melbourne: Brian Elton & Associates, Human Services and Health (Vic.)

Enright, R.B. (1991) 'Time spent caregiving and help received by spouses and adult children of brain-impaired adults', *The Gerontologist* 31:375–83

Fabacher, D., K. Josephson, F. Pietruszka, K. Linderborn, J. Morley and L. Rubenstein (1994) 'An in-home preventative assessment program for independent older adults: a randomised controlled trial', *Journal of the American Geriatrics Society* 42:630–8

Fenig, S., I. Levav, R. Kohn and N. Yelin (1993) 'Telephone vs face-to-face interviewing in a community psychiatric survey', *American Journal of Public Health* 83(6):896–8

Fine, M., and C. Thomson (1993) 'A partnership in care? The use of formal services and informal support in the home by home and community care clients', in P. Saunders and S. Shaver, *Theory and Practice in Australian Social Policy: Rethinking the Fundamentals*, Sydney: Social Policy Research Centre, University of NSW

Finley, N.J. (1989) 'Theories of family labor as it applied to gender differences in caregiving for elderly parents', *Journal of Marriage and the Family* 51:79–86

Fischer, D. (1995) 'Care issues for people from a non-English speaking background', in *Towards a National Agenda for Carers: a Workshop on Carer Issues*, Canberra: Dept of Human Services and Health

Fitch, S., E. Papanicolaou and G. Maligeorgos (1992) *Developing Accessible Services For People with a Disability and of Non-English Speaking Background: Report 1*, Melbourne: Action on Disability in Ethnic Communities Ltd

Fitting, M., P. Rabins, M.J. Lucas and J. Eastham (1986) 'Caregivers for dementia patients: a comparison of husbands and wives', *The Gerontologist* 26:248–52

Flemming, A. (1994) 'After placement care experiences: differences between spouse and child carers', in Conference Proceedings of the Alzheimer's Association Australia, Fourth National Conference, Sydney, pp. 193–5

Fortinsky, R.H., C.V. Granger and G.B. Seltzer (1981) 'The use of functional assessment in understanding home care needs', *Medical Care* 19(5):489–97

Franklin, S., B. Ames and S. King (1994) 'Acquiring the family eldercare role', *Research On Aging* 16(1):27–42

Frey, J.F. (1983) *Survey Research by Telephone*, London: Sage

Furlong, M., J. Young, A. Perlesz, D. McLachlan and C. Riess (1991) 'Schizophrenia—some views and experiences', *Dulwich Centre Newsletter* 4:58–68

Gallagher, D., S. Lovett and A. Zeiss (1989) 'Interventions with caregivers of frail elderly persons', in M. Ory and K. Bond (eds), *Aging and Health Care: Social Science and Policy Perspectives*, New York: Routledge

Gallagher-Thompson, D. and A.M. Steffen (1994) 'Comparative effects of cognitive-behavioural and brief psychodynamic psychotherapies for depressed family caregivers', *Journal of Consulting and Clinical Psychology* 62:543–9

Geiser, R., L. Hoche and J. King (1988) 'Respite care for mentally ill patients and their families', *Hospital and Community Psychiatry* 39(3):291–5

George, L.K. and L.P. Gwyther (1986) 'Caregiver well-being: a multidimensional examination of family caregivers of demented adults', *The Gerontologist* 26:253–9

Gerstel, N. and S. Gallagher (1993) 'Kinkeeping and distress: gender, recipients of care, and work–family conflict', *Journal of Marriage and the Family* 55:598–607

Gilhooly, M. (1987) 'Senile dementia and the family', in J. Orford (ed.), *Coping With Disorder in the Family*, London: Croom Helm

Gilleard, C.J. (1984) *Living with Dementia: Community Care of the Elderly Mental Infirm*, London and Philadelphia: Croom Helm and The Charles Press

Gold, D., M. Reis, D. Markiewicz and D. Andres (1995) 'When home caregiving ends: a longitudinal study of outcomes for caregivers of relatives with dementia', *Journal of American Geriatrics Society* 43(1):10–16

Goldstein, K.J. and D.J. Miklowitz (1994) 'Family intervention for persons with bipolar disorder', *New Directions for Mental Health Services* 62:23–35

Gonyea, J. and N. Silverstein (1991) 'The role of Alzheimer's disease support groups in families' utilization of community services', *Journal of Gerontological Social Work* 16:43–55

Goodman, C. and J. Pynoos (1990) 'A model telephone information and support program for caregivers with Alzheimer's Disease', *Gerontological Society of America* 30(3):399–404

Grafstrom, M., L. Fratiglioni, P.O. Sandman and B. Winblad (1992) 'Health and social consequences for relatives of demented and non-demented elderly. A population based study', *Journal of Clinical Epidemiology* 45:861–70

Graham, H. (1991) 'The concept of caring in feminist research: the case of domestic service', *Sociology* 25:61–78

Graham, S. (1987) *The Extra Costs Borne by Families Who Have a Child with a Disability*, Social Welfare Research Centre, Reports and Proceedings No. 68, University of NSW

Green, H. (1988) *Informal Carers: General Household Survey 1985*, Office of Population Censuses and Surveys, Social Services Division, Series GH5 No. 15 Supplement 15, London: Her Majesty's Stationery Office

Greene, V.L. and D.J. Monahan (1989) 'The effect of a support and education program on stress and burden among family caregivers to frail elderly persons', *The Gerontologist* 27:716–21

Groves, R.M. (1990) 'Theories and methods of telephone surveys', *Annual Review of Sociology* 16:221–40

HACC (1989) National Guidelines, Canberra: AGPS

—— (1991) 'Getting it Right', National Service Standards, Canberra: AGPS

H&CS (1993) The Victorian Home And Community Care Program Ethnic Policy Statement, Melbourne: H&CS

Hagemann-White, C. (1984) 'The societal context of women's role in family relationships and responsibilities', in V. Garms-Homolova, E.M. Hoerning and D. Schaeffer (eds), *Intergenerational Relationship*, Toronto: Hogrefe Inc.

Haley, W. (1989) 'Group intervention for dementia family caregivers: a longitudinal perspective', *The Gerontologist* 29(40):478–80

Haley, W.E., E.G. Levine, S.L. Brown and A.A. Bartolucci (1987) 'Stress, appraisal, coping and social support as predictors of adaptational outcome among dementia carers', *Psychology and Aging* 2:323–30

329

Harper, S. and D. Lund (1990) 'Wives, husbands and daughters caring for institution-alized and noninstitutionalized dementia patients: towards a model of caregivers burden', *International Journal of Aging and Human Development*, 30(4):241–62

Harrison, S., E. Martin, S. Rous and S. Wilson (1985) 'Assessing the needs of the elderly using unsolicited visits by health visitors', *Journal of the Royal Society of Medicine* 78:557–61

Hartley, R. (1995) 'Families, values and change: setting the scene', in R. Hartley (ed.), *Families and Cultural Diversity in Australia*, Sydney: Allen & Unwin

Headey, B. and A.J. Wearing (1981) *Australians' Priorities, Satisfactions and Wellbeing.* Monograph in Public Policy Studies No. 4, Department of Community Welfare Service, University of Melbourne

Hebert, R., D. Girouard, G. Leclerc, G. Bravo and R. Lefrançois (1995) 'The impact of a support group programme for care-givers on the institutionalisation of demented patients', *Archives of Gerontology and Geriatrics* 20:129–34

Hendrickson, C., E. Lund and E. Stromgard (1984) 'Consequences of assessment and intervention among elderly people: a three year randomised controlled trial', *British Medical Journal* 389:1522–4

Herrman, H., H. Schofield, B. Murphy and B. Singh (1994) 'The experiences and quality of life of informal caregivers', in J. Orley and W. Kuyken (eds), *Quality of Life Assessment: International Perspectives*, New York: Springer

Herrman, H., B. Singh, H. Schofield, R. Eastwood, P. Burgess, V. Lewis and R. Scotton (1993) 'The health and wellbeing of informal caregivers: a review and study program', *Australian Journal of Public Health* 17:261–6

Hicks, C. (1988) *Who Cares: Looking After People at Home*, London: Virago

Hinrichsen, G.A. (1991) 'Adjustment of caregivers to depressed older adults', *Psychology and Aging* 6:631–9

Hoenig, J. (1968) 'The de-segregation of the psychiatric patient', *Proceedings of the Royal Society of Medicine* 61:115–20

Hoenig, J. and M.W. Hamilton (1966) 'The schizophrenia patient in the community and his effect on the household', *International Journal of Social Psychiatry* 12:165–76

Hollingsworth, J. (1990) *Service Needs of Children with Disabilities and their Families: A Study.* Final Report, Melbourne: Action

Horowitz, A. (1985) 'Sons and daughters as caregivers to older parents: differences in role performance and consequences', *The Gerontologist* 25:612–17

Horton, R.L. and D.J. Duncan (1978) 'A new look at telephone interviewing method-ology', *Pacific Sociological Review* 21:259–73

House of Representatives Standing Committee on Community Affairs (1994) 'Home but not alone'. Report on the HACC Program, the Parliament of the Common-wealth of Australia

Howe, A., H. Schofield and H. Herrman (1997) 'Caregiving: a common or uncommon experience?', *Social Science and Medicine* 45(7):1017–29

Idler, E.L., S.V. Kasl and J. Lemke (1990) 'Self-rated health: a predictor of mortality among the elderly in New Haven, Connecticut and Iowa and Washington counties, Iowa', *American Journal of Epidemiology* 131:91–131

Jakubowicz, A. (1989) 'Community Care and the Needs of the Ethnic Aged', *Advances in Behavioural Medicine* 6:435–59

James, R. (1992) 'Telephone follow-up in program evaluation', *Health Promotion Journal of Australia* 2:45–8

Jette, A.M., S. Tennstedt and S. Crawford (1995) 'How does formal and informal community care affect nursing home use?', *Journal of Gerontology: Social Sciences* 50B(1):S4–12

Johnson, C.L. and D.J. Catalano (1983) 'A longitudinal study of family supports to the impaired elderly', *The Gerontologist* 23:612–18

Johnson, M. and M. Maguire (1989) 'Give me a break: benefits of a caregiver support service', *Journal of Gerontological Nursing* 15(11):22–6

Jorm, A.F. and A.S. Henderson (1993) *The problem of dementia in Australia*, 3rd edn, Canberra: AGPS

Jorm, A., S. Henderson, A. Mackinnon, A. Korten and H. Christensen (1994) 'Do mental health surveys disturb? Further evidence', *Psychological Medicine* 24:233–7

Jutras, S. and F. Veilleux (1991a) 'Gender roles and caregiving to the elderly: an empirical study', *Sex Roles* 25:1–18

—— (1991b) 'Informal caregiving: correlates of perceived burden', *Canadian Journal on Aging* 10:40–55

Kahan, J., B. Kemp, F.R. Staples, K. Brummel-Smith (1985) 'Decreasing the burden in families caring for a relative with a dementing illness. A controlled study', *Journal of the American Geriatrics Society* 33:664–70

Kasper, J.D. and A.D. Shore (1994) 'Cognitive impairment and problem behaviours as risk factors for institutionalization', *Journal of Applied Gerontology* 13(4):371–85

Kaye, L.W. and J.S. Applegate (1990) 'Men as elder caregivers: a response to changing families', *American Journal of Orthopsychiatry* 60:86–95

Kazak, A.E. (1987) 'Families with disabled children: stress and social networks in three samples', *Journal of Abnormal Child Psychology* 15:137–46

Kendig, H. (1983) 'Blood ties and gender roles: adult children who care for aged parents', in *Support Networks* vol. 5, Melbourne: Institute of Family Studies

—— (1988) 'Aging, intergenerational support, and social change in Australia', in M. Bergener, M. Ermini and H.B. Stahelin (eds), *Crossroads in Aging*, London: Academic Press

Kendig, H. and J. McCallum (1986) *Greying Australia: Future Impacts of Population Ageing*, Canberra: AGPS

Kendig, H., A. Hashimoto and L.C. Coppard (eds) (1992) *Family Support for the Elderly: The International Experience*, New York: Oxford University Press

Kiecolt-Glaser, J.K., R. Glaser, E.C. Shuttleworth, C.S. Dyer, B.S. Ogrocki and C.E. Speicher (1987) 'Chronic stress and immunity in family caregivers of Alzheimer's Disease victims', *Psychosomatic Medicine* 49:523–35

Kingson, E. and R. O'Grady-LeShane (1993) 'The effects of caregiving on women's social security benefits', *The Gerontologist* 33(2):230–9

Kinnear, D. and A. Graycar (1984) 'Ageing and family dependency', *Australian Journal of Social Issues* 191:13–27

Kirkham, M. and R. Schilling (1989) 'Life skills training with mothers of handicapped children', *Journal of Social Services Research*, Special Issue: Advances in Group Work Research, 13:67–87

Kirwin, P. and L. Kay (1991) 'Service consumption patterns over time among adult day care program participants', *Home Health Care Services Quarterly* 12(4):45–58

Kosloski, K. and R.J. Montgomery (1994) 'Investigating patterns of service use by families providing care for dependent elders', *Journal of Aging and Health* 6:17–37

Kuipers, L., B. MacCarthy, J. Hurry and R. Harper (1989) 'Counselling the relatives of the long-term mentally ill: a low-cost supportive model', *British Journal of Psychiatry*, 154:775–82

Ladanyi, T. (1996) Strength in numbers: best practice in carer support groups. An Issues Paper, Melbourne: CAV

Lawton, M.P. and E.M. Brody (1969) 'Assessment of older people: self-maintaining and instrumental activities of daily living', *The Gerontologist* 9:179–86

Lawton, M.P., E.M. Brody and A.R. Saperstein (1989) 'A controlled study of respite service for caregivers of Alzheimer's patients', *The Gerontologist* 29(1):8–16

Lawton, M.P., M.H. Kleban, M. Moss, M. Rovine and A. Glicksman (1989) 'Measuring caregiving appraisal', *Journal of Gerontology* 44:61–7

Lechner, V. (1991) 'Predicting future commitment to care for frail parents among employed caregivers', *Journal of Gerontological Social Work* 18:69–84

—— (1993) 'Support systems and stress reduction among workers caring for dependent parents', *Social Work* 38(4):461–9

Legge, V. and M. Westbrook (1991) 'The frail aged living in the community and their carers: a survey of Chinese, Greek and Anglo Australians', *Australian Journal on Ageing* 10(3):3–10

Leibrich, J. (1992) 'Against the odds: community based care and psychiatric disabilities in Britain and New Zealand', in P. Close (ed.), *The State and Caring*, London: Macmillan

Levin, E., I. Sinclair and P. Gorbach (1989) *Families, Services and Confusion in Old Age*, Aldershot, England: Avebury

Lewis, J. and B. Meredith (1988) *Daughters Who Care*, London: Routledge

Lieberman, M.A. and J.H. Kramer (1991) 'Factors affecting decisions to institutionalize demented elderly', *The Gerontologist* 31(3):371–4

Lippmann, S., W. James and R. Frierson (1993) 'AIDS and the family: implications for counselling', *AIDS CARE* 5(1):71–8

Livingston, G., M. Manela and C. Katona (1996) 'Depression and other psychiatric morbidity in carers of elderly people living at home', *British Medical Journal* 312:153–6

Lund, D.A., M.A. Pett and M.S. Caserta (1987) 'Institutionalizing dementia victims: some caregiver considerations', *Journal of Gerontological Social Work* 11:119–35

MacCarthy, B., A. LeSage, C.R. Brewin, T.S. Brugha, S. Mangin and J.K. Wing (1989) 'Counselling the relatives of the long-term mentally ill adult: evaluation of the impact on relatives and patients', *British Journal of Psychiatry* 154:768–75

MacFarlane, W.R. (1994) 'Multiple-family groups and psychoeducation in the treatment of schizophrenia', *New Directions for Mental Health Services* 62:13–22

McCallum, J. and D. Gelfand (1990) *Ethnic Women in the Middle: A Focus Group Study of Daughters Caring for Older Migrants in Australia*. Report to the National Centre for Epidemiology and Population Health, Canberra: Australian National University, pp. 1–47

McCallum, J., B. Shadbolt, Dong Wang (1991) 'Self-rated health and survival. A y-year follow-up study of Australian elderly', *American Journal of Public Health* 84:1100–5

McVicar and Reynolds Pty Ltd (1993) *Commonwealth Respite for Carers Planning Project*. Prepared for Bundoora Extended Care Centre and Department of Health, Housing, Local Government and Community Services, Canberra: AGPS

Magidson, J. (1993) SPSS for Windows CHAID Release 6.0, Chicago: SPSS Inc.

MaloneBeach, E., S. Zarit and D. Spore (1992) 'Caregivers' perceptions of case management and community-based services: barriers to service use', *Journal of Applied Gerontology* 11(2):146–59

Matthews, S.H., J.E. Werkner and P.J. Delaney (1989) 'Relative contributions of help by employed and nonemployed sisters to their elderly parents', *Journal of Gerontology: Social Sciences* 44:S536–44

Miller, B. and L. Cafasso (1992) 'Gender differences in caregiving: fact or artifact?', *The Gerontologist* 32(4):498–507

Miller, B. and S. Furner (1994) 'Change in the Number of Informal Helpers of Frail Older People', *Public Health Reports* 109(4):583–6

Miller, B., S. McFall and A. Montgomery (1991) 'The impact of elder health, caregiver involvement and global stress on two dimensions of caregiver burden', *Journal of Gerontology: Social Sciences* 46(1):S9–19

Mittelman, M., S. Ferris, G. Steinberg, E. Shulman, J. Mackell, A. Ambinder and J. Cohen (1993) 'An intervention that delays institutionalisation of Alzheimer's Disease patients: treatment of spouse carers', *The Gerontologist* 33:730–40

—— (1995) 'A comprehensive support program: effect on depression in spouse-caregivers of AD patients', *The Gerontologist* 35(6):792–802

Moen, P., J. Robison and V. Fields (1994) 'Women's work and caregiving roles: a life course approach', *Journal of Gerontology: Social Sciences* 49(4):S176–86

Mohide, E., D. Pringle, D. Streiner, J. Gilbert, G. Muir and M. Tew (1990) 'A randomized trial of family caregiver support in the home management of dementia', *Journal of the American Geriatrics Society* 38:446–54

Montgomery, R. and E. Borgatta (1989) 'The effect of alternative support strategies on family caregiving', *The Gerontologist* 29(4):457–64

Montgomery, R.J.V., J.G. Gonyea and N.R. Hooyman (1985) 'Caregiving and the experience of subjective and objective burden', *Family Relations* 34:19–26

Morris, R., L. Morris and P. Britton (1988) 'Factors affecting the emotional wellbeing of the caregivers of dementia sufferers', *British Journal of Psychiatry* 153:147–56

Moseley, P., W. Preston, H. Davies and J.M. Priddy (1988) 'Support groups for male caregivers of Alzheimer's patients: a followup', *Clinical Gerontologist* 7:127–36

Mossey, J.A. and E. Shapira (1982) 'Self-rated health: a predictor of mortality among the elderly', *American Journal of Public Health* 72:800–8

Mui, A.C. (1992) 'Caregiver strain among black and white daughter caregivers: a role theory perspective', *The Gerontologist* 32:203–12

Murphy, B., J. Nankervis, H. Schofield, H. Herrman, S. Bloch and B. Singh (1997) 'The role of general practitioners and pharmacists in information exchange with family carers', *Australian and New Zealand Journal of Public Health* 21(3):317–22

Murphy, B., H. Schofield and H. Herrman (1995) 'Information for family carers: does it help?', *Australian Journal of Public Health* 19(2):192–7

Murphy, B., H. Schofield, J. Nankervis, S. Bloch, H. Herrman and B. Singh (1997) 'Women with multiple roles: the emotional impact of caring for ageing parents', *Ageing and Society* 17:277–91

Nankervis, J., H. Schofield, H. Herrman and S. Bloch (1997) 'Home-based assessment for family carers: a preventative strategy to identify and meet service needs', *International Journal of Geriatric Psychiatry* 12:193–201

Ngo, B. (1994) Social and Psychological Well-being of the Vietnamese elderly in Australia (Victoria). PhD, Dept Intercultural and Language Studies, Royal Melbourne Institute of Technology, Melbourne

Noelker, L. and D. Bass (1989) 'Home care for elder persons: linkages between formal and informal caregivers', *Journal of Gerontology* 44:S63–72

NSW Women's Health (1993) *Who Cares? The Health and Wellbeing of Women Who Are Carers*, Sydney: Women's Advisory Council

O'Connor, D.W., P.A. Politt, M. Roth and C.P. Brook (1990) 'Problems reported by relatives in a community sample of dementia', British Journal of Psychiatry 156:835–41

Opie, A., L. Fulcher, G. Hawke and N. Allen (1992) There's Nobody There: Community Care of Confused Older People, Auckland: Oxford University Press

Orbell, S. and B. Gillies (1993a) 'Factors associated with informal carers' preference not to be involved in caring', Irish Journal of Psychology 14(1):99–109

——(1993b) 'What's stressful about caring', Journal of Applied Social Psychology 23:272–90

Ozanne, E. (1990) 'Development of Australian Health and Social Policy in relation to the aged and the emergence of home care services', in A. Howe, E. Ozanne and C. Selby Smith (eds), Community Care Policy and Practice: New Directions in Australia, Melbourne: Monash University

Pahl, J. and L. Quine (1987) 'Families with mentally handicapped children', in J. Orford (ed.), Treating the Disorder, Treating the Family, Baltimore: Johns Hopkins University Press

Pakenham, K. and M. Dadds (1987) 'Family care and schizophrenia: the effects of a supportive educational program on relatives' personal and social adjustment', Australian and New Zealand Journal of Psychiatry 21:580–90

Pearlin, L.M., J.T. Mullan, S.J. Semple and M.M. Skaff (1990) 'Caregiving and the stress process: an overview of concepts and their measures', The Gerontologist 30:583–93

Penning, M. (1995) 'Cognitive impairment, caregiver burden, and the utilization of home health services', Journal of Aging and Health 7(2):233–53

Perlesz, A., M. Furlong and D. McLachlan (1992) 'Family work and acquired brain damage', Family Therapy 13:145–53

Pfeiffer, E. (1995) 'Institutional placement for patients with Alzheimer's Disease: how to help families with a difficult decision', Postgraduate Medicine 97(1):25–131

Piktialis, D. (1990) 'Employers and elder care: a model corporate program', Pride Institute Journal of Long Term Health Care 9:26–31

Pinkston, E.M. and N.L. Linsk (1984) 'Behavioural family intervention with the impaired elderly', The Gerontologist 24:576–83

Plunkett, A. and S. Quine (1996) 'Difficulties experienced by carers from non-English-speaking backgrounds in using health and other support services', Australian and New Zealand Journal of Public Health 20(1):27–32

Power, P.W. (1988) 'An assessment approach to family intervention', in P.W. Power, A.E. Dell and M.B. Gibbons (eds), Family Intervention Throughout Chronic Illness and Disability, New York: Springer

Pruchno, R.A. and S.L. Potashnik (1989) 'Caregiving spouses: physical and mental health in perspective', The Gerontologist 37:697–705

Pruchno, R.A. and N. Resch (1989) 'Husbands and wives as caregivers: antecedents of depression and burden', The Gerontologist 29:159–65

Pruchno, R.A., K.H. Kleban, J.E. Michaels and N.P. Dempsey (1990) 'Mental and physical health of caregiving spouses: development of a causal model', Journal of Gerontology 45(5):P192–9

Rabins, P.V. (1985) 'Dementia and the family', Danish Medical Bulletin 32(1):81–3

Rabins, P.V., M.D. Fitting and J. Eastham (1990) 'The emotional impact of caring for the chronically ill', Psychosomatics 31:331–6

Ramsdell, J., J. Swart, J. Jackson and M. Renvell (1989) 'The yield of a home visit in the assessment of geriatric patients', Journal of the American Geriatrics Society 37:17–24

Reynolds, A., H. Kendig, G. McVicar, L. Rijneveld and A. O'Brien (1993) *Community Care for People with Dementia: An Evaluation*, Melbourne: Dept of Health, Housing, Local Government and Community Services

Richardson, C.A., C.J. Gilleard, S. Lieberman and R. Peeler (1994) 'Working with older adults and their families—a review', *Journal of Family Therapy* 16:225–40

Roberts, M. (1986) 'Three Mothers: Life Span Experiences', in R.R. Fewell and P.F. Vadassy (eds), *Families of Handicapped Children*, USA: Pro-ed

Romans-Clarkson, S.E., J.E. Clarkson, I.D. Dittmer, R. Flett, C. Linsell, P.E. Mullen and B. Mullin (1986) 'Impact of a handicapped child on mental health of parents', *British Medical Journal* 293:1395–7

Rose, J. and S. Del Maestro (1990) 'Separation-individuation conflict as a model for understanding distressed caregivers: psychodynamic and cognitive case studies', *The Gerontologist* 30:693–7

Rosenman, L. (1991) Community care: social or economic policy? SPRC National Social Policy Conference, University of NSW

Rosenman, L. and R. LeBroque (1996) 'The Price of Care', in *Towards a National Agenda for Carers: Workshop Papers*. Department of Health and Human Services, Aged and Community Care Division, No. 22, Canberra: AGPS

Rosenman, L., C. Tilse and R. LeBrocque (1992) Economic, social and emotional costs of the care of dementia to families and the community. University of Queensland, Dept of Social Work and Social Policy

Rowland, D. (1986) 'Family structure, ageing and families: a social network perspective', in H. Kendig, *Ageing and Families Support Network*, Sydney: Allen & Unwin

—— (1991) *Pioneers Again: Immigrants and Ageing in Australia*, Bureau of Immigration Research, Canberra: AGPS

Sanborn, B. and S. Bould (1991) 'Intergenerational caregivers of the oldest old', *Marriage and Family Review* 16:125–42

Sanson-Fisher, R. and J. Cockburn (1993) 'The use of behavioural change principles to promote rational prescribing: a review of commonly used interventions', *Australian Prescriber* 16(1):82–6

Sarason, B.R., G.R. Pierce, E.N. Shearin, I.G. Sarason, I.A. Waltz and L. Poppe (1991) 'Perceived social support and working models of self and actual others', *Journal of Personality and Social Psychology* 60:273–87

Scharlach, A.E. (1994) 'Caregiving and employment: competing or complementary roles', *The Gerontologist* 343:378–85

Scharlach, A. and S. Boyd (1989) 'Caregiving and employment: results of an employee survey', *The Gerontologist* 29:382–7

Scharlach, A.E., E.L. Sobel and R.E.L. Roberts (1991) 'Employment and caregiver strain: an integrative model', *The Gerontologist* 316:778–87

Scharlach, A.E., M.C. Runkle, L.T. Midanik and K. Soghikian (1994) 'Health conditions and service utilisation of adults with elder care responsibilities', *Aging and Health Care* 6(3):336–52

Schofield, H. and H. Herrman (1993) 'Characteristics of carers in Victoria', *Family Matters* 34:21–9

Schofield, H., S. Bozic, H. Herrman and B. Singh (1996) 'Family carers: some impediments to effective policy and service development', *Australian Journal of Social Issues* 31:157–72

Schofield, H., H. Herrman, S. Bloch, A. Howe and B. Singh (1997) 'A profile of

Australian family caregivers: diversity of roles and circumstances', *Australian and New Zealand Journal of Public Health* 21(1):59–66

Schofield, H., B. Murphy, H. Herrman, S. Bloch and B. Singh (1997) 'Family caregiving: measurement of emotional wellbeing and various aspects of the caregiving role', *Psychological Medicine* 27:647–57

Schofield, H., B. Murphy, J. Nankervis, B. Singh, H. Herrman and S. Bloch (1997) 'Family carers: women and men, adult offspring, partners and parents', *Journal of Family Studies* 3:149–68

Schofield, T. (1995) 'The health of Australians of non-English-speaking background: key concerns', *Australian Journal of Public Health* 19(2):117–19

Schultz, C.L. and N.C. Schultz (1991) 'Caring for family caregivers', *Australian Journal of Marriage and the Family* 11:84–93

Schultz, C., K. Smyrnios, C. Grbich and N. Schultz (1993) 'Caring for family caregivers in Australia: a model of psychoeducational support', *Ageing and Society* 13(1):1–25

Schultz, C.L., N.C. Schultz, J. Bruce, K.X. Smyrnios, L.B. Carey and C.L. Carey (1993) 'Psychoeducational support for parents of children with intellectual disability: an outcome study', *International Journal of Disability, Development and Education* 40:205–16

Schulz, R., C.A. Tompkins and M.T. Rau (1988) 'A longitudinal study of the psychosocial impact of stroke on primary support persons', *Psychology and Aging* 3:131–41

Schulz, R., P. Visintainer and G. Williamson (1990) 'Psychiatric and physical morbidity effects of caregiving', *Journal of Gerontology* 45(5):181–91

Schulz, R., A.T. O'Brien, J. Bookwala and K. Fleissner (1995) 'Psychiatric and physical morbidity effects of dementia caregiving: prevalence, correlates, and causes', *The Gerontologist* 35:771–91

Seltzer, G., A. Begun, M. Seltzer and M. Krauss (1991) 'Adults with mental retardation and their aging mothers: impacts of siblings', *Family Relations* 40:310–17

Silliman, R. (1993) 'Predictors of family caregivers' physical and psychological health following hospitalisation of their elders', *Journal of the American Geriatrics Society* 41(10):1039–46

Silliman, R., S. McGarvey, P. Raymond and M. Fretwell (1990) 'The Senior Care Study: does inpatient interdisciplinary geriatric assessment help the family caregivers of acutely ill older patients?', *Journal of the American Geriatrics Society* 38(4):461–6

Singer, G.H.S. (1993) 'When it's not so easy to change your mind: some reflections on cognitive interventions for parents of children with disabilities', in A.P. Turnbull, J.M. Patterson, S.K. Behr, D.L. Murphy, J.G. Marquis and M.J. Blue-Banning (eds), *Cognitive Coping, Families, and Disability*, Baltimore: Brookes

Skipwith, D. (1994) 'Telephone counselling interventions with caregivers of elders', *Journal of Psychosocial Nursing* 32:7–12

Smith, J. and M. Birchwood (1987) 'Specific and non-specific effects of educational intervention with families living with a schizophrenic relative', *British Journal of Psychiatry* 150:645–52

Smith, G., M. Smith and R. Toseland (1991) 'Problems identified by family caregivers in counselling', *The Gerontologist* 31(1):15–22

Solomon, P. and E. Evans (1992) 'Service needs of youth released from a state psychiatry facility as perceived by service providers and families', *Community Mental Health Journal* 28:305–15

Spencer, M.P. and M.F. Folstein (1986) 'The Mini-Mental State Examination', in A. Keller (ed.), *Innovations in Clinical Practice: A Source Book*, Sarasota, Fl.: Professional Resources Exchange

Stoller, E. and K. Pugliesi (1989) 'Other roles of caregivers: competing responsibilities or supportive resources', *Journal of Gerontology: Social Sciences* 44:S231–8

Stommel, M., C. Collins and B. Given (1994) 'The cost of family contributions to the care of persons with dementia', *The Gerontologist* 34(2):199–205

Stone, R. and P. Short (1990) 'The competing demands of employment and informal caregiving to disabled elders', *Medical Care* 28(6):513–26

Stone, R., G. Cafferata and J. Sangl (1987) 'Caregivers of the frail elderly: a national profile', *The Gerontologist* 27(5):616–26

—— (1987) 'Caregivers of the frail elderly: a national profile', *The Gerontologist* 27:616–26

Stull, D.E., K. Bowman and V. Smerglia (1994) 'Women in the middle: a myth in the making', *Family Relations* 43:319–24

Sutcliffe, C. and S. Larner (1988) 'Counselling carers of the elderly at home: a preliminary study', *British Journal of Clinical Psychology* 27:177–8

Szwarc, B. (1988) *A Stitch In Time: A Study Into the Respite Needs of Families of Disabled Children in Victoria*, Melbourne: The Children's Bureau of Australia

Taylor, R., G. Ford and M. Dunbar (1995) 'The effects of caring on health: a community based longitudinal study', *Social Science and Medicine* 40(10):1407–15

Tennstedt, S., G. Cafferata and L. Sullivan (1992) 'Depression among caregivers of impaired elders', *Journal of Aging and Health* 4:58–76

Tennstedt, S., L.M. Sullivan, J.B. McKinley and R.B. D'Agostino (1990) 'How important is functional status as a predictor of service use by older people?', *Journal of Aging and Health* 2:439–61

Thomas, T. and M. Balnaves (1993) *New Land, Last Home: The Vietnamese Elderly and the Family Migration Program*, BIPR, Canberra: AGPS

Thornicroft, G. and P. Bebbington (1989) 'Deinstitutionalisation: from hospital closure to service development', *British Journal of Psychiatry* 155:739–53

Tilse, C. (1994) 'Long term marriages and the transition to residential care', in Conference Proceedings of the Alzheimer's Association Australia, Fourth National Conference, Sydney, pp. 213–15

Toseland, R. and C. Rossiter (1989) 'Group interventions to support family caregivers: a review and analysis', *The Gerontologist* 29:438–48

Toseland, R. and G. Smith (1990) 'Effectiveness of individual counseling by professional and peer helpers for family caregivers of the elderly', *Psychology and Aging* 5(2):256–63

Toseland, R., C. Rossiter and M. Lebrecque (1989) 'The effectiveness of Peer-led and Professionally-led groups to support family caregivers', *The Gerontologist* 29(4):465–71

Toseland, W.R., C.G. Blanchard and P. McCallion (1995) 'A problem solving intervention for caregivers of cancer patients', *Journal of Social Science and Medicine* 40:517–28

Tsuji, I., S. Whalen and T.E. Finucane (1995) 'Predictors of nursing home placement in community-based long-term care', *Journal of the American Geriatrics Society* 43:761–6

Turner, J. R., B.G. Frankel and D.M. Levin (1983) 'Social support: conceptualization, measurement and implications for mental health', *Research in Community and Mental Health* 3:67–111

Twigg, J., K. Atkin and C. Perring (1990) *Carers and Services: A Review of Research, Social Policy Research Unit*, London: Her Majesty's Stationery Office

VCP (1996) Care-recipient dependencies, carer benefits and work. Research Reports on Carers No. 3, VCP, for Dept Health and Family Services

Vetter, N., D. Jones and C. Victor (1984) 'Effect of health visitors working with elderly patients in general practice: a randomised controlled trial', *British Medical Journal* 288(4):369–72

Waerness, K. (1984) 'Caring as women's work in the welfare state', in H. Holter (ed.), *Patriarchy in a Welfare Society*, Oslo: Universitetsforlaget

Wagner, D. and M. Neal (1994) 'Caregiving and work: consequences, correlates and workplace responses', *Educational Gerontology* 20(7):645–63

Watson, D., L.A. Clark and A. Tellegen (1988) 'Development and validation of brief measures of positive and negative affect: the PANAS scales', *Journal of Personality and Social Psychology* 54:1063–70

Wells, Y., A. Jorm, F. Jordan and R. Lefroy (1990) 'Effects on care-givers of special daycare programs for dementia sufferers', *Australian and New Zealand Journal of Psychiatry* 24:82–90

Westbrook, M. and V. Legge (1991) 'Pathways to a mainstream nursing home: a survey of Chinese, Greek and Anglo Australians', *Australian Journal on Ageing* 10(4):3–10

Whelan, A. (1986) 'The Ethnic Elderly in Wollongong: Ageing in a Steel City', Department of Health, Wollongong, NSW

Whitlatch, C., S. Zarit and A. von Eye (1991) 'Efficacy of interventions with caregivers: a reanalysis', *The Gerontologist* 31:9–14

Whittick, J.E. (1988) 'Dementia and mental handicap: emotional distress in carers', *British Journal of Clinical Psychology* 27:167–72

Wilson, P., S. Moore, D. Rubin and P. Bartels (1990) 'Informal caregivers of the chronically ill and their social support system: a pilot study', *Journal of Gerontological Social Work* 15(1–2):155–70

Wolcott, I. (1997) 'Work and family', in D. de Vaus and I. Wolcott (eds), *Australian Family Profiles: Social and Demographic Patterns*, Canberra: AIFS

Wolcott, I. and H. Glezer (1995) 'Impact of the work environment on workers with family responsibilities', *Family Matters* 41:15–19

Wolinky, F. and R. Johnson (1991) 'The use of health services by older adults', *Journal of Gerontology* 46:S345–57

Wolstenholme, R. (1994) 'I want to be sure they know what Jack likes on his toast': an investigation into consumer perspectives of service performance and quality assurance for people residing in the Riverina-Murray area who have disabilities requiring high support needs. The Rural Development Centre, University of New England, Armidale, NSW

Yeatman, R., K. Bennets, N. Allen, D. Ames, L. Flicker and W. Waltrowaicz (1993) 'Is caring for elderly relatives with depression as stressful as caring for those with dementia? A pilot study in Melbourne', *International Journal of Geriatric Psychiatry* 8:339–42

Zarit, S. (1990) 'Interventions with frail elders and their families: are they effective and why?', in M. Stephens, J. Crowther, S. Hobfell and D. Tennenbaum (eds), *Stress and Coping in Later Life Families*, New York: Hemisphere, pp. 241–65

Zarit, S. and C. Whitlatch (1993) 'The effects of placement in nursing homes on family caregivers: short and long term consequences', *Irish Journal of Psychology* 14(1):25–37

Zarit, S.H. and J.M. Zarit (1982) 'Families under stress; interventions for caregivers of senile dementia patients', *Psychotherapy: Theory, Research and Practice* 19:461–71

Zarit, S., C. Anthony and M. Boutselis (1987) 'Interventions with caregivers of dementia patients: a comparison of two approaches', *Psychology and Aging* 2:225–32

Zarit, S., P. Todd and J. Zarit (1986) 'Subjective burden of husbands and wives as caregivers: a longitudinal study', *Gerontology* 26:260–6

INDEX